THE GARLIC PEANUT Story

Deer Leah,

Spread the Love,

♡

JONATHAN RACHMAN

J Ra

8·18·22

Saritaksu

The Garlic Peanut Story
© Jonathan Rachman
Cover Design: Jeffrey Fulgencio
Book design and layout by Saritaksu Editions
First published 2020
Published by Saritaksu Editions, Bali

Author's note: The events described in this story are real.
Other than the family members, the characters have
fictitious names.

First Printed in the USA by crashPAPER

ISBN: 978-979-1173-37-7

SARITAKSU Editions
Jl. Padanggalak 101
Denpasar, Bali 80237 Indonesia.
email: saritaksu.editions@gmail.com

THE GARLIC PEANUT
Story

~ Letters to my sister's children ~

For my sister Wewe, and her two children, Grace and Zef

"….and now these three remain: faith, hope and love.
But the greatest of these is LOVE."

Contents:

X

Prologue

I have a confession to make: my greatest fear is of going blind. Perhaps because of that I have developed the gift of memorizing my surroundings, the people who inhabit them, their expressions, and the colors that emanate from them, right down to the tiniest detail.

When my sister came through the doors of the Dharmawangsa in Kebayoran Baru, South Jakarta, on that last day, it was as if this was another version of my beautiful childhood protector, the one who had always taken the pain out of my world and rekindled the love in my heart. Now she was almost ephemeral, like an angel, about to fly away at any moment. Her eyes shone, but her body had shrunk, and her colors had almost run dry. This was a sepia-tinted version of my bright and vivacious sister Wewe, the angel of my life, and she was now moving in a damaged body, every step filled with pain.

This time, it was my time to support her frail body, the way she did mine when I was just a child, resting fully on hers, arms intertwined. As we turned the corner of the lobby, the air was heavily scented with *melati* flowers, the jasmine of Java that grew in our childhood garden. We both looked at each other, far beyond the iris of our eyes, deep into each other's souls. No words were necessary—our hearts were so heavy, yet filled with love. That scent always took us back to our past, memories of our grandma's chignon and her pillow filled with jasmine petals and buds as fat as the gecko eggs we used to play with.

Tonight, as candles and chandelier reflections collided, shimmering dimly as if they understood the pain in our hearts, a path opened towards the restaurant's majestic doors. Kind strangers and hotel staff lined the hallway on both sides, their smiling eyes upon us, offering understanding and support as they showed us the way. They seemed to be holding their breath and giving us their energy, hands gesturing as if they would carry us through the door. Silently they witnessed our passing as we took one unbearable step after another, struggling to reach the doors. Little did my sister know, her loved ones awaited on the other side of those doors for her arrival, just as the eager spirits of our dearly departed aunts, uncles, cousins and ancestors awaited her on the other side. They all waited to greet my angel, my dear sister Wewe. It was then that I finally knew... I no longer had a grip on time, nor could I hold her much longer in my arms.

Author's note: Although my sister's name is spelt Wewe, it is actually pronounced Wéwék, or if we spell it phonetically, /weɪ/ /weɪ/ with just a hint of the consonant k at the end.

~ *satu* ~

"When I am blind…"

Dear Grace and Zefanya,

I am your uncle. I know you may not remember me…and that's not a problem. I was not able to be a part of your life as you grew up. But I think of you all of the time and wonder how life is treating you in this world without your mother.

I have a confession to make—it's about my greatest fear—the fear of going blind. You see, all my life I have been afraid of turning diabetic, as it runs in my genes and that troublesome gene is generally passed on from generation to generation. Everyone from my mother's side, (your adoptive grandma's family), has become diabetic at some point of their lives. All my life I have been warned to be careful, as chances are I too will 'turn' diabetic. That might sound to you like I will turn into a zombie. To me, it would be equally as bad as that, because I don't think I could live without sight. Did you know that one of the worst consequences of having diabetes is blindness? For an awfully long time I was obsessed with the thought that I might turn blind. I knew that when that day came color, flowers, fabrics, sunsets, all those things that I loved, things that had helped me heal in my saddest times, would be gone.

When I—we—lost your mother, my sister, one of the first things I thought I should do was to write to you both. At least I wanted to, and the thought stayed with me, although it has taken me a long time to do it. Now, after all this time, here is the story I so wanted to tell you.

It goes without saying, when I am blind I won't be able to write this. The only way I will be able to send you this story is if I write this down now, just in case... I hope it never happens, but just in case.

I am not sure why I could not start writing you letters about your Mom. She was my big sister, and like a mother to me too. All I know is that I want to tell you her stories, our stories... there were so many times I wanted to start, but I always felt paralyzed, maybe not physically, but mentally and emotionally, so the desire remained just a thought, and was never translated into action.

I didn't know where or how to begin. Even now I am not sure why I want to write letters to you about her in the first place, then or now, I just know I need to share my memories of her. I feel afraid that writing about her will make me sad. And I also worry that I won't do a good enough job in capturing the essence of her being—of explaining who she truly was.

My doubts go on for ever: What if I feel bad, if in writing about her life from my point of view, because I cannot do justice to her and all her special qualities? I am doubtful of my ability to describe them in all of their nuanced detail. I am also concerned that by writing about her I will create even more sadness and unrequited longings in both your lives and mine.

At times I think I am being selfish in wanting to reminisce upon the short life of my late sister because of the self-serving nature of my wish to write about her and my time spent with her, to heal my own wounds and sadness. This is the other side of the coin, when I am feeling the burden of not sharing, when I know what an amazing human being she was.

Perhaps I also feel guilty for having abandoned her. I was not able to spend enough quality time with her; I left her alone while she was well, for all those years when I was away overseas, fighting my own battles, studying, trying to find some meaning in my own world. I wasn't able to make myself a real part of her life as much as I should have, while she was still on this earth.

I am scared as I write about my sister—your Mom—scared that I will not express myself well enough to truly portray her personality, and all those things that remain with me of her brief time in this world—her gestures, expressions, her wit, her generosity, her love and her patience. I want to share with you her sense of humor, her cuteness and more importantly her selflessness. Then there's her confidence, her talents, her lightheartedness and her laughter. I also want to share with the world her sadness, her pain, tears and sorrow, as it was all a part of her life, along with her remarkable energy, spirit and tenderness, her work and creations.

I don't want to forget anything! I need to tell you about her simplicity, her beauty, her thoughts and feelings, her presence, her strength and her greatness—if I could I would tell you her entire story and include every detail in her life. But I am worried I would not describe each of them well enough for the world to know her. Of course, I'd also love to share her most joyous moments in life: giving birth and raising you both, the apples of her eye, but I was not with her during those times.

I regard your Mom as a perfect creature. To me she was an angel on earth then and she is an angel now. I am reminded of my own imperfections in trying to share her perfections. And although I was not with you and your Mom while you were little, I know this much: she would have been the perfect mother to you both, the way she was with me when I was a child, as in many ways she was my mother too.

Perhaps you already know that I was not the most present brother to her? As I grew up I spent long periods of time away from her, and I wonder if I write these letters to you, can I make up for some of my time lost with her? A time now lost to us both in two different worlds, hers and mine, here and there, then and now.

I wonder—am I trying to find a way to ask for forgiveness and show my tardy gratitude toward her? I feel scared—what if… what if when I write about her, I catch myself trying to make myself feel better, instead of doing this out of pure care and love for her and for both of you?

I do know, however, why I want to tell you these stories. They are stories of love and forgiveness.

There are lots of reasons why I want to keep her memories alive. First and foremost I believe she deserves to know how much she was loved, more than anyone in the world. I tried my best to tell her. She deserves to be celebrated—with all of the memories, the honor and respect, the attention and the love I can give her, and now she's gone I still feel this, so please let me share with you.

Second, I want both of you to know your Mom the way I knew her. As you grow older, your memories of her may fade. When that happens, don't feel bad or sad—it is normal—and you are not guilty of forgetting her. To the contrary, you were blessed to have had her as your mother, regardless of the short time she was with you. I want to share all my experiences I had with her, so when you grow up and grow older, you will have more insights toward understanding the special woman in our life: your mother—the woman who gave birth to you and the woman who gave me and taught me unconditional love.

Third, and this weighs heavily upon me, I promised her to keep an eye on you. She asked me to take care of you and to be part of your life. As you know, your father does not agree with this. Because we remain separated by such vast physical distance, I feel I can do my best to fulfill my promise in part by writing my memories of her to share with you, and sharing with you the difficult and joyful times that have shaped my life, so you may come to know me better. Keeping my promise to my sister is important to me. Having you, her children, in my life is a precious, living gift from your Mom that I treasure.

I want the whole world to know that your mother was, still is, and will always be the most prominent figure in my life. I want to tell the whole world who this amazing woman was. There is so much to learn from how she lived her life, and the world needs to hear about her, her life and love, as the world was, is and will always be better because of her. Her legacy will live on.

I do not know if I will ever send these words to you or if I will ever finish writing them, for every time I think of your mother, more memories, thoughts and feelings rush into my head and heart and I feel overwhelmed. The tough thing is, every time my mind is inundated by those memories, I have the most challenging time in putting my thoughts into words. It is a vicious circle I know I must overcome.

I think of how she overcame the most difficult obstacles in her life, with determination and grit and it gives me the impetus I need to carry on. Some days I wish there was a miracle invention that would simply allow me to push a button whenever those memories are in my mind, and letters would turn into words and phrases, then sentences, chapters and stories would appear like magic upon a piece of paper. I wish this was a lot easier, but I also know it is only fair that it should take a lot of work and dedication for me to complete this story for you, for her; and I know that much—that is the least she deserves from me.

I just finished asking your uncle Stephen, my husband, for advice. I have been bombarding him with questions such as "How the heck am I going to start writing stories about my sister?" and "Do you think I will ever finish it and give it to her children?"

I surely would like to. Then there is the language barrier

which itself is a huge obstacle for me to overcome in telling your Mom's stories. One of these days, I will tell you a story of one of my gifts to her: a secret language I only spoke to her and she to me. Did she ever teach you our secret language?

I have told Stephen that my memories about my sister are all fragmented, and begged him for advice so many times.

"How can I even begin to tell these stories?" I ask him.

He suggests that I simply write the fragments as they come to me. Maybe he is wise in suggesting that, because after all, these fragments are the truth, my life and your mother's life have been broken into pieces by events, space and time.

As I am writing this, I am also reading *Books: A Memoir* by Larry McMurtry. In it, he says that due to human tendency, we look farther back as we get older. Well, as I am getting older, I wish I could squint my eyes as hard as possible so I may retrieve just a glimpse of my earliest memories, enough to bring back all of my recollections of my sister!

Grace and Zef, you may wonder why I cry so endlessly for your mother—for me—for us. You may find it hard to understand, but there are so many different reasons I cannot possibly describe them all. I shed so many tears every time I remember and feel her presence. I am not sure myself, to be honest, why I cry every time I think of her. Is it because I miss her so much? Is it because I cry for lost time, the time that I did not spend with her? Perhaps I am full of regrets? Or is it the thought of all the pain she went through in her last days, such agony that I could barely stand to imagine and witness?

And compounding this is the bitter realization that none of us will ever see her again in our lifetime.

At times the simple thought that I can't ever hug or be hugged by her again breaks my heart. I can't bear this although I must accept it, and the knowledge is made worse by the realization that you, too, may experience a similar sorrow.

I feel responsible for not making her have her breast examined by the doctor. If we had known earlier we could have done something. I now know that breast cancer is one of the easiest of the many different kinds of cancer to heal, as long as it is treated in the early stages.

I miss her terribly. I never did miss her this much until I saw her the last time—exactly a month before she died. But a couple of years before that I remember calling her one night after I saw her childhood picture and I had been thinking about what she must be going through after the test. I wept, then I called her, and when I said hello, separated by thousands of miles, all she could do was cry. Her sobs were so loud, deep and painful, and she repeated, over and over again: "*I am scared, I am scared, I am really scared...*"

Knowing her so well I could picture her clenching her phone tightly as she spoke, her knuckles white with tension, and I just wished it was me she could hold tight and hang on to.

That was the most haunting secret she had ever told me. At that moment, I felt so very close to her—and yet for selfish reasons I wanted to believe that she trusted me more than anyone. As she wailed, sobbed and wept, all I could do was to grip my own phone tightly, wishing it were her hand I was holding. I wanted to comfort her the way she used to do when she held me during all those times when I had been scared, or beaten by the evil 'monsters' of my childhood.

Back then when I was small she would cradle me on her lap, and protect me from my beater, and from all the evils and monsters of the world. That was when I knew she was truly my angel. In my mind I saw her portrayed in the same way as the reliefs and paintings in churches, the ones I saw when I was a kid. I saw myself as the helpless, limpid body being cradled by a beautiful angel with wings.

I knew she would protect me and she would take the beatings, the bruises and the pains I would have otherwise had to endure—she took my pain away, physically, mentally and emotionally—something I could never say I could do for her. I only wish I could have done the same for her when her time came, but I could not protect her from the illness, the pain and all the fears she had to endure. These thoughts haunt me endlessly.

Lately I dream about her at least once, sometimes more, each passing week. She has brought me many memories from our past, and at times she delivers messages about death; it is almost as if she is calling me.

Last night I dreamed of being in a huge ferry just like the one we used to take to go back home to Sumatra from Java, except in my dream the ferry was a lot nicer. It was more like a yacht, with a shiny hardwood floor. It was completely different to the ferries we used to take when I was a child. They were filled with the stench of human urine, cigarette smoke and filthy cushions. In my dream, it was she and I and all my junior high school friends together on the sea, but the ferry was on top of a huge ship, sort of like a Titanic, and our ferry was being lowered to the pitching waters of a dark ocean, like a lifeboat. I know what my husband the psychologist would say if I asked him what the dream means. "Well, what do you think?" he would reply.

Rather than think about what it might mean, I focus more on the memories it had triggered. I supposed this dream relates back to a real trip I took with your Mom, crossing in the ferry from Jakarta to Sumatra. I was about eight or nine years old at the time, and she must have been nearly nineteen as we were ten years and seven months apart. We were coming home from an end-of-school-year vacation I had spent with your Mom in Jakarta. At the time my parents still lived in Sumatra and they allowed me to spend a few weeks with your mother. Those were the best weeks of my childhood—weeks of freedom, and fun, my tummy filled with ice creams and street-food, completely free from any threat of beatings and the yelling and screaming wars at home.

At the end of my vacation we had to go back to Sumatra—just the two of us. We took a five-hour, (or was it six?) bus ride in a dingy old bus, the kind mostly taken by poor folks at that time in Indonesia. I don't think anyone else in our family had ever taken such a humble form of transportation. I am not sure why we did not fly, as our family usually did. Had we flown, the trip would have only lasted for an hour or two. Instead, with six hours in the bus from Jakarta to the ferry terminal, another four to five hours in the ferry, plus another five-hour bus trip from the ferry terminal to our home, it must have taken us the whole day to reach home.

I would like to believe that it was her way of extending our vacation, stretching out our 'private' time together, adding to our precious memories that we would always have, memories of her lifetime and mine. Or maybe it was her way of introducing me to the real world, a world that I could previously only imagine. This world was one I would later come to know so well, the world she lived in. But this time, it felt like our world: hers and mine, shared as one.

The other possible reason for this trip was one I would rather not think about, as it would break my heart. Maybe she felt that she had no right to ask for a large budget for a luxurious means of transportation, to travel in comfort to our family home, because she knew she was an adopted child. Being the considerate soul and adopted daughter that she was, she might not feel she had the right to ask for the same method of transportation or amount of budget as the other children in the family. This thought always makes me sad. I could not comprehend the possibility that she felt of less value than we were. In my mind, heart and soul, I knew she was such a superior human, the best kind of daughter, sister and family member anyone could have, in every possible way. Her self-consciousness as an adopted child always broke my heart. Her selflessness was beyond admirable, and she was always so thoughtful towards everyone else, except for herself.

Your mother was like that—she always seemed simply content just to be part of our family, without any of the luxury the rest of us demanded. Whatever the reason was, I surely was glad that I had the chance to travel the way we did and experience the world that I had previously been insulated from. It was such a special adventure to travel with her: I found it elating and invigorating—I remember sitting in the hot, crowded and stinky, shabby bus and thinking how brave and tough she was. She knew every alley, every turn and every street we had to take from our aunt's house to the bus station. It was as though she already knew the world, although she had never traveled as much as the rest of us. She haggled with the '*becak*' driver on his three-wheeled pedal-powered bike to get us to the bus station and she bought us street food on the way: curried chicken wrapped in banana leaves, savory snacks and sweet cakes we called '*jajanan*'. As she climbed onto the bus while instructing the coolies to handle our bags to be stored and tied down with the rest of the passengers' luggage on top of the dilapidated bus, balancing her backpack, purse and our lunch, never once letting go of my hand, all eyes were on us. As I am typing the words to this story my eyes fill with tears...somewhere in the distance, I still see her, holding the hand of a little boy. That little fellow was myself. I can still feel the grip of her hand on mine.

I don't believe, in the history of Jakarta's public

transportation at that time, they had ever witnessed passengers of the ethnic Chinese minority group climbing on their bus before—to me it could have been, in retrospect, a kind of reversed version of Rosa Parks getting on a white bus in the deep South of the United States. Half-amazed, half-proud, I saw everybody staring at me as I walked behind her and she ushered me to our seats right in the middle of the bus, while she smiled and greeted other passengers. I still remember her crisp, melodic laugh—not only was it aimed at us, at that moment, in cheerful self-deprecation, somehow it resulted in us being surrounded with smiling, nodding faces, as we celebrated that special time, enjoying our happy time together.

She wore her usual 'uniform': comfortable attire that consisted of jeans, t-shirt and a pair of shoes she had owned for years. Perfect for the occasion, her simple and practical outfit exuded a "don't mess with me" sort of attitude way ahead of her time, as if she were already a feminist, a strong woman and marcher for women's rights, without any of the fancy labels. Not only was I in awe of her bravery, leadership, her independence and her knowledge of the system, I also admired her ability to speak to all kinds of people.

Jakarta was and still is a diverse big city with multiple layers of different socio-economic groups, and she seemed to move effortlessly among all levels. I paid attention to the way she spoke and the slang she used. Her style of communication varied, according to whom she was talking. She adapted her tone and accent, depending on the person she was talking to.

I had never seen her in these roles before and I was amazed. Like a little actress she transformed herself at every moment to fit in with those she was relating to, as well as adjusting her decorum. She even got the mannerisms and body language right. This was a great lesson in flexibility and style of communication that would inspire me in everything I did, well into my future.

Not a second during that trip did I feel afraid; to the contrary, I felt so safe, safer than in my own home. Here was a slender young student nurse, of minority Chinese-Indonesian ethnicity, with her beloved little brother in a tough, rough and dirty bus full of stinky, dirt-poor and often misunderstood people. She managed not only to deliver me back to our parents safely, but she left a mark in my heart and an experience of a lifetime I would never forget…another precious gift she never knew she gave me.

*   *   *

Earlier today, as I was writing this letter, I looked out of the window. It was warmer than the last few days; a winter Sunday in the middle of February. It's been raining off and on for the last five days and finally the sun came out. I looked out and I saw thick clouds moving across a blue sky—the color suddenly reminded me of my hometown. While the climate and the weather of these far distant places are hugely different, certain visuals always bring me back to my childhood, which ultimately brings thoughts of your Mom back to me.

For a split second I had the feeling that my sister was about to come home from school in her school uniform. All of the other children in my family wore dark brown shorts or a skirt, with a white short-sleeved shirt. She, on the other hand, wore a gray skirt, a mark of the public school she attended, quite different to the uniform at our private Catholic school, the one that was considered the best school in town. Even when I was still young, this thought made me upset and angry. Out of any of us, she was the one who deserved the best of the best, I knew. But instead she was made to feel less than we were, sent to a government school, while I and my parents' other biological children went to the more exclusive private school. Once again, my emotion runs high, as it always does when I look back upon my memories of our different upbringings, in our extended family.

* * *

There is one story I must tell the whole world, yes, even people in the most remote parts of Africa, of every continent should know about it, even people I never meet or will never encounter—it is the soon-to-be-famous story of your mother, garlic-flavored '*Kacang Atom*' peanuts, and me.

Every day after school, when I was about four or five years old, I would change into my 'monkey' clothes—practically just a pair of old underwear, full of holes. This was my preferred outfit as that's what she and my parents liked to call me, '*the monkey*'. I would patiently wait for your mother to come home, sitting on my own, playing, drawing or scratching pictures with a stick in the dirt and singing or humming out of tune to myself while the rest of the family was busy doing their chores.

At the sight of my sister arriving home I would drop whatever it was I was doing, run as fast as I could towards her, and she would drop her school bag and books, pick me up with both of her arms and give me the biggest hug, showering me with kisses and laughter, asking me what I was doing and then kissing me some more. Then she would reach into her pocket and pull out a tiny pack of '*Kacang Atom*' garlic peanuts she had purchased from the street-vendor next to her school and give it to me. Still in her arms, I would devour the peanuts with her helping to open it without spilling the contents of the tiny thin plastic bag they came in, not such an easy thing to do, as the plastic had been sealed by running a candle flame along the end of the bag. Even if hell had frozen over, I knew she would not let me go until I had enjoyed every single peanut in that package, every crumb at the bottom of the tiny plastic square.

Later I learned that every day our mother would give her pocket money, enough for her to buy candy or a pack of chips or a homemade lollypop, but instead she spent every penny on me, buying me my favorite package of peanuts. To this day, whenever I visit Indonesia, every time I see the same brand of small garlic-flavored peanut packages in a market or on the side of the street, sold by the meek street vendors who wheel their trolleys up and down, I buy as many as they have. My eyes will well up with tears—tears of love for my sister, as the memories I have of her come rushing back, always touching my soul to the core.

I hope you will help me tell my 'garlic peanuts' story—a story of unconditional love from a sister to her brother; the most generous gift she gave me every day, of everything she had to give, in the most selfless gesture one could ever imagine.

Every day, for the longest part of my childhood, as long as I can remember, she spent her allowance on me, using up every single ration she had. I sincerely believe if she were still alive she would still do the same. She would give me every drop of her blood, sweat and tears: her hard work and her love not only to me, but to you both and for her loved ones as well as for strangers. That love, dear Grace and Zef, was the essence of your Mother.

Needless to say, today when I looked out the window, and for a split second I thought I saw a blurred figure that looked just like my sister, your Mom, coming home from school, I was very happy, feeling excited and ready to run as fast as I could, just as I always did back then. It was a kind of 'déjà vu' from my early childhood, the kind that triggers all of my happy memories. I felt again that anticipation and joy of greeting her every day when she came home, feeling so happy to be picked up, lifted, embraced and held by her.

But, if there was another word that I could use to describe the sadness, pain and sorrow I felt as soon as I came back to reality, I needed to find it then. I am lost for words to describe my misery at having to accept that it was already the year 2007, I was in California, the United States of America, and my sister had passed away almost ten months earlier, in West Java, Indonesia, more than ten thousand miles away.

Now I am learning to be happy for the memories she bestowed upon me. I feel so happy to have been cradled in her arms. Even now, I can still feel her embrace, although tears are streaming down my face and dripping onto the page of this letter for you, my dear niece and nephew.

- *dua* -

"Let's play dolls..."

I was watching one of my favorite movies today, *Billy Elliot*—
the story about the son of an Irish coal miner who became a
principal dancer in the English Royal Ballet[1]. One of these
days, I would love to watch this movie with you both, as
I think it is one of the greatest coming-of-age movies ever
made, and it truly resonates with me. Half way through
the movie I was drowning in my tears, thinking about the
sacrifice of a father who has to do whatever it takes to support
his son and to accept his son for who he is—a dancer, a
sissy. It made me think of my own family and friends where I
grew up but mostly, it reminded me of my sister, Wewe, who
always believed in me.

In the early 1970's, Teluk Betung was a very small
town. It was so small that nobody had any secrets. I was
pretty sure that if I picked my nose, the whole town would
find out. As it was, our mother and my sister Wewe always
reminded me that if I had to do that I should do it in
my own privacy and I should always wash my hands! The
thought of this has always made me chuckle. Being the son
of a preacher, from one of the most prosperous and well-

1. ***Billy Elliot*** (2000) is a British dance-drama film directed by Stephen
Daldry and written by Lee Hall. Set in Country Durham, England
during the 1984-85 miners' strike, the film is about a working-class boy
who discovers his passion for ballet, despite his father's objection and the
negative stereotype associated with being a male ballet dancer.

known families in town, I was well aware that everyone knew me, or at the least, knew of me. It was no secret in the neighborhood, at church, at school, and at parties that your uncle was a sissy boy. In fact people had no qualms about saying it out loud and publicly. Lampung people aren't famous for their tactfulness, and they would even talk about it in front of me, as if I wasn't even present.

I was so much of a sissy that my own father hated me for crying. He often warned me not to cry or he'd have to give me something to cry about. I was so sissy that my PE coach had to assign me to a team because none of my classmates would ever pick me as a teammate. When I was finally allocated to a team, everyone in that team sighed with disappointment for having to endure having such a sissy on their team. I was so sissy that for an elective final exam in my arts and crafts class, I chose to make a silk flower when I could have done carpentry, which other boys would have chosen as was expected of them; mind you, it did earn me an 'A' for the project. I was so sissy that I failed carpentry and any other masculine activities that boys were required to participate in by the curriculum.

I was considered to be very sissy. I used to beg my mother to let me go with her to the salon for all of her beauty appointments. As part of my sissy-ness, I loved playing with my Mom's lipsticks and nail polishes, although my Mom rarely wore them. Did I mention how much I adored my sister Edna's hair rollers and various kinds of hair brushes? I would sit in front of a vanity mirror with my Mom's beauty case and primp myself endlessly. Of course, I did it in my own privacy. I made sure the door was locked or I went to one of the empty guest rooms to indulge myself in the luxurious talcum powder and its fluffy feather brush before I started to apply my lipstick or the rouge which my Mom hardly ever used except for rare occasions such as a big wedding party or particular days when we had family photograph sessions. When busted, I would play coy and pretend that I had done nothing wrong—well, I hadn't, as far as I was concerned.

Each person who was unkind enough to shame me would make fun of me, call me names, and do their best to make me feel so ashamed. This was a torture I put up with for most of my childhood, and I can't begin to count how many names they called me. From polite, relatively cute name-calling to extremely vulgar, rude and abusive names, I heard them all. I can still remember a few words in Indonesian. In particular the words "*Kayak anak perempuan*" have stuck with me. It means "Like a girl" and this was perhaps the most common comment I overheard as a child, because I have two deep dimples and of course in their eyes I looked and behaved more like a girl.

'Homo' was a name meant to shame me, but it was not until later that I understood the meaning of this word. Two other strange words, '*Banci*' (pronounced ban-chee) and *Bencong* (ben-chong), which essentially mean "transvestite" and "transgender", were also used against me, which I found very ignorant.

Till this day, I still cringe and my blood boils when I

hear these expressions being used in a derogatory manner, even when they are not directed at me. They also called me slut, whore and cocksucker and accompanied these labels with obscene gestures. Imagine, a child my age being called all those cruel, unnecessarily abusive and vulgar names, at times by perfect strangers. Even my own brother, your other uncle, shamed me in front of my friends, laughing so cruelly. It became a permissible reaction for my own friends to copy his behavior from that moment forward. At the time I did not have the ability to identify or to measure how I felt, but now I think I can categorize it as a life-scarring event.

Well, I think you probably get the point of how sissy your uncle was and still is. Uncle David, who I considered to be the devil reincarnated, never ceased to do his best to make me feel lower than dirt. Beyond calling me names and laughing at me, he was also very good at teasing me. He would keep it up until I cried, which then annoyed him so he would slap me or hit me, throw me to the ground or slam my head against the wall. He liked to display me in front of his friends as the 'sissy boy' as if it would enhance his own image as the righteous, manly boy, the masculine child, and a kind of role model of just how society expected boys to act and behave.

Thank God for your Mom, my lovely, kind hearted, sweet and accepting sister. She made me feel loved for who I was, by joining me on my escapades in my 'dressing room'. There, she transformed herself into my stylist. She played with my hair, added hairpins, brushed my hair and helped me clean the smudges of lipstick that went over my lip lines, gingerly and light heartedly. We would laugh and laugh until it hurt our tummies. At times, we did not even bother to talk, we just enjoyed each other's company as we played in silence.

I never felt the need to say anything to your mother and I knew she understood me. Never did she ever make fun of me, make me feel of less value than any other child or person, nor shame me for being me. To the contrary, she would join me in my fantasy, smiling or kissing my rouged cheeks and laughing a good laugh, a laugh that gave me a sense of confidence. Hers was a laugh of approval, a laugh of acceptance. It was a laugh that told me that I was all right and it left its mark, a beautiful mark in my heart for the rest of my life. It is that mark, imprinted so hard in my heart and soul, which gives me a sense of peace to be me, to be who I am, to be the kind of person that feels complete and happy within myself.

Your mother left a mark on me that is so precious and valuable that I always touch my chest and I know I could locate that mark, that love that she planted right there, in my heart. There were some terrible days throughout my childhood and growing up to become an adult when I felt of less value then other children and human beings as a result of the cruelty inflicted upon me. On those days when I felt so alone I would touch my chest, rubbing the same spot where she used to rub it, and I knew that I would feel as if it were her palm rubbing and soothing my beating heart and I would feel better.

While other boys my age were busy playing with toy cars, or pretending to be Cowboys and Indians, or swinging homemade swords and pistols or slings, I was busy playing with my girlfriends, or my sister Edna's dolls. Did I forget to mention that almost all my friends in the neighborhood or school were girls? I found boys repulsive, rude, mean, dirty and smelly. They were my cruel and unkind enemies. They called me names, they pushed me and they mugged me.

I think I was around five years old when I first bribed a boy in a sandbox not to bully me by telling him that I would bring him more chocolates and candies tomorrow. Your grandma always took me to the most fancy candy stores and I could have whatever I wanted, so it seemed the best way out of a sticky situation. While it might stop him for a day or two, the bullying usually continued when the bribe ran out and I learned not to do that again and simply let him and the rest of the bullies do whatever it was they would do to me, feeling helpless to stem the flood.

Girls, on the other hand, were so sweet to me. They lent me their dolls, their cooking toys, and we played nicely with each other. This was before we learned cattiness. They were clean, polite and dainty and generally speaking they did not smell bad—well, at least the non-tomboy ones. Your Mom always welcomed these girls and she would join us in our play. We would pretend we were in the classroom, play housewives, farmers, stewardesses, beauty salons or cooking, and my favorite game was to play dolls.

My big sister was so creative, she made us dolls out of

newspapers or fabric scraps. She sewed the dolls' dresses and we gave them all names and roles. There was a mother doll, daughter doll, teacher doll and even a hairdresser doll. We spent hours making all these dolls while the rest of the family's anxiety grew. Ominously, they warned your Mom that I would grow up to become a fag and never stop being a sissy! Well, they were right, and now I am glad.

Your Mom would respond with her killer smiles. Smiles that said "It doesn't matter, leave him alone," and those extra specially loving smiles which meant she loved me anyway. Not only did I fully understand her smile and appreciate the meaning of each smile I also felt her emotions and her love for me.

As and adult, looking back, in my interpretation her smiles also said: "Stay the fuck out of his way!" No, she never actually told them that, but she led by example, stroking my hair and showering me with kisses and love.

There were times when, unbeknownst to anyone, I would eavesdrop on adult conversations and I heard them talking about me behind my back. They were so worried how girly I was. They were worried about me trying on my Mom's high-heeled shoes that were in style at that time, or my sisters' dresses. Edna's dress would drag along behind me like a train as she was taller. Your Mom's dress would just touch the floor or it would be like a long dress. And the maids' pyramid bras were so hard and pointy they made me laugh.

They were worried about my future. What would they do if indeed I turned out to be a transvestite? The only point of reference they had for gay men at that time in our backward little town was a group of transvestites next to the Buddhist temple who came out only after dark. Every time we had a night out with our family or friends we would pass a group of them huddled in an alley there. We never saw their faces during broad daylight. We only saw their silhouettes in the dark, heard their hisses and deep voices, and glimpsed their big hair and their tight dresses that looked like ball gowns.

I was guilty of mocking them too; a behavior I copied from my peers and the adults I suppose. We always yelled from our cars or *becak* trishaws and called them not nice names; ironically these were the same kind of names the bullies called me. Then we would run away. Every time we caught a ride on the Pedi cab past that dark alley we always giggled and talked about them, the poor souls. As an adult, I feel awfully guilty for what I did and wish I could apologize to them, but there is no way to know who they were as I had never seen their faces.

Even the hairdressers at the salon were given a tongue-lashing. Our neighbor was a super-gay hairdresser, most men who worked in hair salons were. They were never openly discussed, their 'wrongness' never confirmed, just assumed, and they seemed to put up with this. They were simply used to being made fun of and degraded. If you were a hairdresser you were considered to be gay, a homosexual or transvestite. I couldn't really understand why I saw the hairdressers being treated in the same way they behaved around me, but not the barbers. Stereotypes were so set in place that barbers were considered manly, but hairdressers or stylists were considered '*banci*' or transsexual.

Later in life, during my early relationship with my partner, who is now my husband, we went out to an Indonesian restaurant one night in San Francisco. It must have been around 1994. We were excited to try some Indonesian food, as Stephen had not yet been to Indonesia. As we entered the restaurant, an Indonesian woman, presumably the owner, had the audacity to ask me—before she could even sit us at a table—"Do you work in a hair salon?"

The hair on the back of my neck instantly stood on end, and my first reaction was to be angry as her careless question instantly brought back bad memories. I was immediately defensive. Her presumptuousness indicated that she assumed I was a gay man based on either I was a sissy or my demeanor was effeminate or I was with another man. While by this time I was out and proud to be a homosexual, I found her attitude, body language and speech condescending. My instinct told me to walk away, but my heart held me there.

What would Wewe say or do in this situation? I asked myself. Stephen didn't react, but he has always been a calm and kind-hearted person. Something clicked in me and I decided I would not perpetuate the hatred and anger. However, I decided to give her a chance to learn and be a kinder person. I made a decision to let her know how she hurt me by assuming I was a hairdresser, so I took my time and explained, "Yes, I am gay, but neither everyone who is gay works in a hair salon nor is everyone who works in a hair salon gay."

She was so shocked that I would even try to engage and explain my thoughts and emotions to her and I told her a quick story about my childhood. She said how sorry she was, because in Indonesia, that was simply what people assumed—it was considered to be the norm. I informed her that besides it being rude, one should never assume someone's sexuality simply because of how they walk or talk or act. Masculinity or femininity has nothing to do with sexuality—besides, what does sexuality matter anyway, we are all different. She thanked us for talking to her and I told her I certainly hoped that she would share the lesson she learned that day with other people.

Dolls seemed to be considered a barometer for 'girlishness' when I was young, but as a child I always had a good time with all kinds of stuff perceived girly such as cooking or sewing or fashion oriented activities. Your Mom and I, we made prayer rugs, decorative soap with ribbons, and created stories of our own. Life was simple and fun with my sister. I felt safe, entertained, listened to and acknowledged, and most of all, I felt loved. In those days, TV didn't start until 5 pm, and there was only one channel, the Indonesian government channel. All day long, after school and lunch, my big sister and I would entertain ourselves with all kinds of activities—drawing, playing with dolls or make up, even playing with airplanes occasionally and we always kept each other company.

Airplanes were my only so-called 'boyish' toys…of course I preferred the big commercial passengers airplanes vs. the fighter kinds, I still do. My favorite was my 'giant' Boeing 747. My parents bought me a model that took eight D-cell batteries and even with all those batteries it wouldn't last too long. I only played with it on special occasions with my sister, as I didn't want it to break. I wished I could ride it and I dreamed of flying in it. My sister would patiently sit with me on the floor playing airports and airplanes "…flying to London, Paris and San Francisco." There is not one flight that I have taken as an adult when I have not thought of her, and I have now most probably collected millions and millions of miles and been around the globe many times. Every time I fly she is always with me in my heart.

Airplanes were my obsession from an early age, and when I was being a brat and refused to eat for whatever reasons, your Mom was the only one who could 'bribe' me. She lured me to eat by playing "airplane". My food was the plane, and I was the hangar, as she followed me everywhere I went in the house, around the front yard, the badminton court and the garage. It was her job to try to catch me and feed me with a spoon. She would not give up until I had finished a bowl of steamed white rice and fried Chinese spam, the essential food of my childhood. She would feed me the mush we called 'maling' on a spoon that became an airplane, making appropriate noises. At some point when I was exhausted or feeling hungry, I'd finally relinquish and open my mouth to let the 'plane' land in it. This could go on for hours before I finished my meal. Her persistence, patience and love were always without limit for me.

She once reminded me about it as an adult and told Stephen and everyone else at our family gathering how I had used to run around naked or in my monkey outfit.

"He would run to catch a plane that was flying over our house or out on the street and made a funny sound like the *kapal terbang*," the words for airplane in Indonesian, which literally mean 'flying ship'. I was so young I could barely say it and the word sounded more like 'puckbung', followed by the sound of the engines 'ndookndook'. Everyone laughed and I still wonder what the last word meant.

How I would do anything if only I could now, for one more time play 'airplane' and be chased and fed by my dear sister, how I miss her whenever I am at any airport, no matter where it is on this earth and I watch the planes take off and land. She used to come with me to our local airport to greet visitors, or sometimes, I would just ask our driver to drive us to the airport to watch the planes taking off and landing for hours on end, and my sister always managed to be there with me.

I also recall her teaching me how to make decorative soap to keep the air filled with the fragrance of the soaps. This was before fancy aromatherapy diffusers or room sprays ever existed. We each picked up soaps of various shapes and scents and then she instructed us—the maids, a few friends and I—to start with pins in the inner circumference of the soaps then later she delicately went over it with ribbons of all colors essentially wrapping the soaps with them in a pattern, woven skillfully in colorful ways and finishing off by tying them up with little ribbon flowers. The end results made the soaps look like flower baskets, very cute and pretty. We left them in our parents' display cabinets.

Two years ago when I visited the house, I saw some of them still there. Although the ribbons and flowers were sun-bleached, they still held their shape and when I opened the glass cabinet, I could detect a whiff of scent, faint but unmistakably the same old perfumed soaps we used. Involuntarily, my eyes welled up and tears made wet lines down my face as I stood in our old family room just a few feet away from where she had taught us in the carpeted room.

Another lesson she gave us was how to make a shaggy floor mat. One school vacation she came home and brought a kit from Jakarta. There was a roll of plastic mesh we could cut to custom size, and some were already precut and printed with various patterns. She also brought yarns of wool in various colors and tools with a wooden handle and metal hook with which to insert pieces of cut yarn through the mesh and pull them through one at a time to be knotted at the bottom, both sides forming a sort of wooly rug. Later as an interior designer, I learned that this would be called a 'cut-pile' rug; as both sides look like a perfectly mown lawn. We followed the printed patterns provided: there were flowers, rainbows and animals, or sometimes we created our own designs. We had so much fun and it was addicting to do and I enjoyed the final results: plush floor mats for your feet or comfy to sit on the floor.

Today, my father still sits on the mat she made him to do his daily meditation and prayers next to his bed facing his old aviary. It has a green background and a big yellow flower that your Mom made to match the color tones of our parents' geometric window. The last time I visited my parents' room, I rubbed my hands over the mat and I couldn't help but cry.

It didn't matter that I was the only boy in her 'class'— she diligently and lovingly guided my little hands to learn each step of the process. Whatever it was that she was teaching us, we always had fun and our times were filled with jokes and laughter. Sometimes we would take a nap, or have afternoon snacks around the dining table. There would be boiled peanuts, *jambu* rose apples dipped in salt and chili, plantains cooked in coconut milk with palm sugar and *kolang kaling* palm fruits also known as 'roof fruit', fried cassava, *lemper* or other *jajanan* snacks.

Our Mom or sister Edna purchased some of these treats. Others they made at home, or were conjured up by the cooks. Any children who were playing with us would join in. We would all gather around the big table, or in the family room along with my parents and siblings to share stories, reminiscing of the old times and share anecdotes of family history.

Wewe usually wore a hand-me-down sundress from Mom or shorts and a T-shirt, always looking comfortable and casual. She never wore lipstick or make up as long as I can remember, except for going to wedding parties or at her own wedding, which I missed because I was overseas. I only saw it from pictures, regretfully.

Wewe also taught me how to play cards in various game styles, particularly Rummy which was fairly complex for a child but she did such a good job at it to a point that I got fairly addicted, always wanting to play the game with my friends, the maids or anyone who would. Our Dad did not approve of card games, citing them as unchristian as he thought that they could be an entry-portal to gambling for children. It was probably because David and I ended up fighting whenever we played cards. I remember when my father burned all our card decks after I cried and cried— I don't remember the reason for our argument but I am sure David was picking on me or hitting me behind the sofa, our favorite place to play whenever no one was looking.

One of my fondest memories of playing cards with your Mom was when we still lived in the rental house, so at this time I would imagine I was still around four or five years old. Wewe, being the biological daughter of the driver, slept in the room with the maids and cooks in her early years of coming to our house. She shared a bed with Puji, the senior cook, who also doubled as a maid and nanny, in a big room shared with other staff.

In the middle of that room there was a large table where they would gather to enjoy their snacks or write letters. Your Mom used it as her study desk. It was there that I would join her and the rest of the staff every night just to hang out, watching your Mom, I simply just wanted to be near her. We were inseparable, like conjoined twins, attached at the hip. As power outages were very common there were always a few half-burned candles with their copious wax drips left over on the old wooden table, marked with its aging patina of burn-marks.

Wewe would study and do her homework on that table night after night before or after dinner and I would continue to lean against her or play with her hair. I loved to nap or cuddle with her on her bed as she sat on the mattress working on her school homework. The cozy and safe feelings I had spending time with her and other female members of the family in this room where I spent a lot of my childhood remain a treasure of fond, warm and fuzzy memories. It was here that she taught me how to play cards for the first time and it was here that I first slept in the same bed with her, sharing the bed with Puji, the three of us all squeezed in together.

Later, that table Wewe had used as a desk became a lunch table for the male staff in our new home, the giant new estate. I wish I knew what happened to it, as it holds so many memories for me; I would have kept it for the rest of my life. I have a feeling that it is these memories, and the nostalgia and melancholy that come with them, that influenced me to become a collector of antiques and vintage objects. I am an emotional buyer, shopper and collector of certain objects and artifacts that bring back childhood and youth memories of years gone by, things like telephones, old books, furniture, architectural artifacts and dolls trigger my memories and emotions.

I don't remember exactly what happened next, but my memories tell me that the next thing I knew, Wewe and I were moved to the guest room next to the kitchen. That's where we spent many nights together, years upon years, and later we moved together into the giant room next to my parents room which my sister Edna, David, Wewe and I all shared, a room with multiple beds and bunks. But I always shared a bed with her. We were inseparable until she went to Jakarta to study.

Even though I liked to tag along with my Mom and the cook to the wet market early mornings before my father or anyone else was up in the house, it was Wewe that would get me up and ready to go, dressing me as I was still half asleep and washing my face. I refused an early morning bath or shower—the market was not the cleanest place anyway, and we all would shower afterwards.

She handed me over to my Mom if she wasn't coming. On the days we didn't go to the market we would squat together in the garage or on the badminton court while our Mom or the cooks bargained with the neighborhood vendors who came in with their carts of meat and vegetables. They all had distinctive voices. The butcher with the high pitched voiced would call out, announcing his arrival: "Abang daging!"—"Your big brother with the meat". His voice would come chiming in over the calls of the softer-spoken "Abang sayur!"—"Your big brother with the vegetables!" and the strident tones of Suseno from our famous local bakery,

"Abang roti!"—"Your big brother selling bread!" as they all competed for our attention.

While I would relish the opportunity to grab more treats, Mom always had to coax Wewe to choose sweet bread filled with cheese or chocolate, or local custards and other snacks.

We Indonesians generally love to eat and snack, but our family takes this to the extreme. My husband used to be told by his parents to finish what was on his plate during meals. As is common in America, he was told: "There are children going hungry in Africa and Indonesia!" Jokingly Stephen told me that he believed that until he met my family. Clearly no one had gone hungry in our family ever. As he started to visit Indonesia he was forever amazed when he saw how frequently and how much my family eats. He says there is only one meal in our family, and it lasts from the moment we wake up (we are probably not even out of bed yet) until the moment we sleep. We snack before breakfast, between breakfast and lunch or if we go out, we would eat an extra lunch in the car before we even get to the restaurant. Essentially Stephen says we eat before we eat and after we eat, and he is not exaggerating.

Mealtime is an important part of our family ritual; we always eat together as a family. When I was young there were usually two or three siblings at home unless it was a holiday. My parents always waited until everyone was home to have lunch or dinner together, and this included our cousin Ci Tian who lived with us but worked in a local hospital as an ER doctor. We started by saying grace as a family, taking turns, and everyone would volunteer. Sometimes Mom or Dad asked one of us to pray, or they would. We were supposed to close our eyes, but I would be naughty and open mine to see if anyone else would peek like me. I discovered I was the only one.

We also had our own ritual with favored seating places around the table. Our Mom and Dad always sat next to each other, facing the entrance to the dining room; Dad on the far right, then Mom. Next to Mom was the place David insisted on having. He claimed he was their favorite. (I am rolling my eyes now). Across from Mom usually was me and I was flanked by my sisters or cousin Ci Tian and a sister. When there were a guest or two, we children would give up our seats and move to the end of the table, filling the 'leftover' seats. Whatever the arrangement was, I insisted on sitting next to Wewe, my dearest sister.

The same would happen when we went out to restaurants or the night market or hawker centers. Your Mom would be the first to offer her seat for any visitors, gracious lady that she was. She always had such a selfless nature and she always seemed to know 'her place' and put herself at the end of the queue—this was a constant sad reminder to me as I knew she deserved better than any of us.

Of course, after dinner, one of our favorite pastimes was hanging out and snacking. In our house anything from ten to twenty glass jars of tempting snacks were permanently displayed between the dining room and family rooms. These were filled with peanuts, chips, dried fruits and candies, and all kinds of local savory and sweet delicacies.

When we got bored with these our other option was to supplement them by calling the street vendors into our property. In this way we could order freshly grilled chicken satay served with rice cakes wrapped and steamed in banana leaves, like little logs, known as *lontong*. The sticks of satay would be cooked to order, topped with savory peanut sauce and *kecap manis*—our favorite sweet soy sauce that we liberally splashed on everything—served in a banana leaf shaped like a half upside down pyramid and liberally sprinkled with crispy fried shallots. I salivate as I am writing this, I can still smell the aroma and taste the perfectly grilled little sticks of satay and slices of pressed rice-cake which had the most perfect texture and was infused with the color and aroma of the banana leaf they were cooked in.

I could finish from twenty to thirty satay sticks, even after dinner. Oh yes, your uncle was a li'l piggy, although you couldn't tell from my appearance as I was always on the scrawny side. Another thing we loved to order was *Mie tek-tek*, a local fried-noodle dish with a savory sauce. The name *tek-tek* comes from the sound the Abang mie (Big brother noodle-seller) made as he carried his stove and supplies on his shoulder in a T-shaped carrier. It looked as if he was carrying two giant water jugs but actually they were all his ingredients to make the wok-fried noodles, including the wok and some kind of cooking apparatus. The satay was grilled on charcoal in earthenware, as was the *Mie tek-tek*. He would hit his cleaned wok with his giant bamboo chopsticks or ladle as he

walked, to create the '*tek-tek*' noise, all the time shouting out
to announce his presence. Another favorite of my family is
Bakso noodles, a noodle soup with beef balls in clear broth,
but we always added lots of *sambal* chili sauce. I would squat
next to my sister watching whichever 'Big-brother *Abang*' was
summoned, and impatiently wait for our snacks to be served.

While Indonesia is under the equator and always hot
and humid, the breeze or rainy seasons make it relatively cool,
especially in the evenings. If it felt chilly while we waited for
our snacks Wewe would hug me, or I would snuggle up to
her or hide behind her skirt. Kas—our dog and best friend—
would tag along. The family, the staff and guests would join
us too, and my parents always loved to treat everyone.

As if the delicious choices offered by the street vendors
were not enough, often we would go to the outdoor night
market. Every night in our town several blocks of streets
would be closed and vendors would come out at dusk to
set up their stalls and start selling food. The street was
transformed into a local hawker center with bright lights and
the constant roar of gas stoves and steel woks bursting with
aromatic food. Our night market food vendors were mostly
mixed *Peranakan* and local ethnic Chinese. We had relatives
who had their own stall, we called them Ko Wie and Cie
Lien. I still have no idea how we are related but we came from
a very big family, your grandma had eight siblings. Their stall
was famous, all the locals knew them and their specialty *Nasi
Uduk* was the local favorite, savory coconut rice served with
turmeric-fried chicken, *tofu* bean curd and fermented *tempeh*

soya cake, with some mean but delicious spicy *sambal.*

My stomach would literally bulge as I would demand anything from three to four helpings at a sitting, and I would be so uncomfortable after I stuffed myself with their food I would beg your Mom or our Mom to rub Vicks all over my tummy to make it feel better. They obliged while laughing and showing everyone my fat li'l piggy tummy. Our family's favorite stall was the one selling Chinese porridge served with savory fried Chinese bread (double carbohydrates).

To top this off there were all kinds of sweet iced drinks with local fruits and jello, condensed milk and syrup called Ice Shanghai or *Es teler*, with avocado added to the mixture of papaya and other tropical fruits, grass jelly and syrup. There was also a range of the famous Javanese *Cendol* drinks, which I still prefer to the 'Pearl boba' drink that's become famous in the U.S. Our choice of foods was more Indonesian than Chinese, with sweet *Martabak* omelets, as big as a car-tire, filled with cheese and condensed milk, nuts and chocolate jimmies, and of course there was a range of the various fish cakes known from Palembang called *Empek-empek*, not to be confused with the word *Empek* I call your grandpa, which means uncle.

On these outings with our family, Wewe and I always remained tightly hand-in-hand. We would sit next to each other or she would carry me. She was my security blanket in a crowded market. As long as I had her next to me, I knew I was not only safe but I could enjoy my time in the middle of all the commotion and crowd.

She would take every opportunity to educate me about our surroundings and bearings, telling me where home was in relation to where we were. In some ways at that time it was assuring for me to know that we were not too far from home, as I had no sense of distance as a child and even now I am terrible at following directions. I would panic if I could not see her or she wasn't next to me. Thinking about it now, I think it was subconscious of her in realizing my dependency, a kind of mother's instinct to always let me know where home was, metaphorically for her as well as for me. Now, I can better understand that I always felt where she was, was home for me.

While dolls were her one non-verbal way of telling me that she loved me no matter what other people said about me or thought of me, Wewe's actions and daily dedication to me were her constant way of showing me her love without ever saying the word. From everything I have told you and will tell you in this book, you will understand how much she loved. But Wewe was also very comfortable in using the words "sayang" or "cinta" to address me. She would call me "Yoyo, sayang"— "Yoyo, my dear". And she would write me letters that started off with "Yoyo yang tercinta"—"My dearest Yoyo". As I am writing this, I can still hear her voice and see her handwriting on the lined paper she tore out of her notebook to write to me on; I still keep some of her letters.

I think perhaps the strongest memory I have of her was her touch—a touch like no others. From holding my hands to carrying me, to kissing me on my cheeks or forehead as well as her signature hugs, a hug and a squeeze so hard I would squeeze my own face or I would break out in laughter, or her way of rubbing my chest to calm me down and to let me know everything would be fine, as she was next to me. There are days where I still close my eyes to remember how she would hug me and laugh to herself out loud, making me laugh. It still makes me smile and laugh and cry, all at the same time. What would I have done if I had not had laughter, hugs and kisses back then in my life?

- *tiga* -

"The top of the stairway..."

It just takes one particular scene to trigger another memory that makes me miss your Mom. Today I watched a movie about a woman who betrayed her sister's boyfriend in her past, which affected her sister and him in a terrible way. She never had a chance to apologize or to make up for it until it was too late. Guess what she did? She wrote a book at the end of her life as an act of atonement, and in it she was able to give them the happiness they deserved.

I may never be able to do the same for my sister, but I know I can tell you stories about your mother so you may know her better, so let me tell you a very special story about the special trips I shared with my sister in a certain phase of our lives.

In the house in which I was born, where I first lived with your Mom, my parents hosted our church Sunday school at home. Sunday school was not my favorite thing to do—I found it more of an obligation than anything. I could not wait until each Sunday school session ended, when our older sister Edna or our Mom handed out treats to all the children: there were sweet Chinese plum coin candies we called 'Sancha', SunMaid raisins, sweet 'wafers'—a kind of éclair filled with chocolate or vanilla cream, Mochi squares in pink and white and other sweets. After each Sunday school, when my parents came back from their church, we would sit together to watch Little House on the Prairie on TV. If the weather was nice, we would go to the beach and then take a nap, or visit relatives for hours.

On some Sundays, Wewe would ask permission from our Mom to visit her biological mother. At the time she still called my Mom 'Tante' the ubiquitous French word Indonesians all use for Auntie. I was already like a parasite, always glued to my sister, and I would beg to go with her.

Strangely my Mom would discourage me from going with my sister. Who knows what her reasons were, maybe she felt that Wewe needed privacy, maybe the fact that it was a Sunday, so there was no driver working and we had to travel by *oplet*, the local covered jeeps that provided public transportation. Perhaps she worried if it would be a safe way for me to travel. After all, we were thought of as a member of the upper class, and if I went through some of the poorer neighborhoods it could be dangerous. I don't know what her reasons were, and I didn't really care. I insisted on tagging along.

Once I knew Wewe had plans I quickly got my bag packed, and refused to let my favorite sister out of my sight. I would resist any threat of being left behind, by throwing a tantrum and crying endlessly. Your Mom needed no convincing, she was always happy to have me with her, anywhere, at any time. This was in total contrast to my older brother David, who could not stand me and refused to allow me to tag along, always too embarrassed to take his sissy younger brother anywhere.

After much nagging on my behalf, off we would go. We

started by walking to the end of our block, along the semi-paved asphalt road, a concoction of half rock and mud, half asphalt. We passed our regular spot where she and I would often get grilled corn at dusk, during the week. It was sold by one of our neighbors, who grilled it over an earthenware pot filled with glowing charcoal, brushed with spicy condiments and salt—I salivate whenever I think about it, even today.

At the end of the block we would hire a local three-wheeled trishaw, the one that we call a *becak*, if there was one available. Our favorite *becak* was the one pedaled by an *Abang*, or 'older brother' who had a limp. I still remember his real name. It was Abang Jafar but most Indonesians can't pronounce the 'f' and it became 'Japar'. He was a tall, funny guy, super sweet and warm, with irrepressible laughter and bad teeth with which he gripped his *kretek*, the ever-present clove cigarette. Because of the odd shape of one of his feet he could not wear sandals or shoes, so he always walked and pedaled with his bare feet. He was so sweaty, I was always amazed to see him dripping in the heat of the day, but he performed his strenuous job without an iota of self-pity, in a completely unapologetic, strong and confident way.

If no *becak* was to be found, we continued to make a right at the end of the block and walked for another long block, but this part of the road was paved better. This was also the block where our other sister Edna's future in-laws lived. She always pointed it out to me saying that is where our future brother-in-law lives. I had a crush on him, his name was Ko Ise, and he was the sweet, handsome boyfriend of our elder sister. Once past his place we then made another left and walked the longest distance of all, before we could find a place to wait for the next motorized *oplet*.

The afternoon was always scorching hot and I complained a lot so Wewe would pick me up and carry me along with everything she and I had: bags, water canteen and little sacks carrying treats for us and for her family. Now in retrospect I realize what a whiner I was. My sister always held my hand as long as I would walk, and then she would carry me when I got too lazy. She never scolded me, nor did she ever ask me to walk longer then I wanted to.

Once the *oplet* arrived, if we were lucky, we would sit next to each other. If it looked like we would have to be separated, she would instead put me on her lap, hugging me tight. She never missed an opportunity to educate me about what we saw as we travelled along, commenting on animals people brought along as pets, or for food, different types of fabrics people wore and scenery along the way. I saw monuments to the Krakatoa island volcanic eruption, learned the locations in relation to our house, her school and mine, and she taught me the names of the streets we passed.

The ride that I now know as a short distance felt like it took hours in my childish mind. The heat, the smell of the passengers, the pollution of car exhaust fumes, clove cigarettes, the chickens and fish around us and the loud blasting music over the loud speaker was more that I wanted to endure. In spite of this it was always very special to me, as I was with my sister and it was our own private time together for the afternoon.

We got off at the base of a steep stairway and started our way up. For little me then, those were the most challenging steps I had ever had to climb. From the sidewalk at the bottom it looked as if it would take us an entire day to climb to the top, plus I was so scared of the height and gradient of the steps. The way I remember it, it felt as if my sister and I would tip over backwards, and fall head over heels. I dreaded this moment, on every single trip. But I also knew once we got there we would have so much fun.

From the look on my face, my sister probably knew how scared I was, as she usually scooped me off my feet and carried me. She was not much taller than me, plus she had our bags to carry as well. Once we reached the top of the stairs, there was a long road awaiting us. Rain or shine, that road was always muddy and rocky, and full of nasty sharp stones too. The sun would be blazing, and sweat rolled down our cheeks making our t-shirts soaking wet. Wewe would make sure that we stopped midway for a break, and she would pull out a canteen for us to drink from or we would stop at a roadside *warung* to get homemade snacks sold by her neighbors in the hills. They were always happy to see us and always said how cute her 'little brother' was and this always made me so proud, to be referred as her brother. The way to her parents' house was still far, and uphill all the way. Finally we would reach a bend and we could see their house perched in the distance, on a tiny cliff. It was such a big relief and joy to be there, we would run the rest of the way, all the way to the back door of her family house. I remember it was the one with the Dutch-style door, the top one, that was always ajar.

I didn't know her Mom's name, I still don't; I just called her Auntie, or Mami Wewe—Auntie Wewe's Mother. It wasn't her name but that's what I called her, I guess it was the adults' way, to simplify her relationship to my sister, but I was still confused at times. Was this really her Mom? Was it her Aunt? It was not until later, as I grew older, that I learned the real relationship of Wewe to our parents and her biological parents.

Auntie Mami Wewe would get up quickly from her kitchen floor where she had been working, which was literally plain earth, covered with a *tikar* mat—a handmade rug woven out of dried leaves. Always busy preparing some food or her famous 'Es Mambo' popsicles; she would wipe her hands on a kitchen towel and again on her humble wrap-around sarong that always looked so pretty. I could tell she was so happy to see us. Instead of greeting her daughter she would pick me up and kiss me, dropping everything as she did. She had the most beautiful skin, I thought it was the whitest and softest skin I had ever seen; later on I understood why they liken some people's skin to porcelain. Hers was like a china doll, so white, shiny and smooth, and her dimples were just as deep as mine. She always wore a traditional *kebaya* blouse, nothing fancy, but always clean. As I am writing this, I can see her vividly in my mind, such a beautiful, sweet and humble lady with the kindest smile and voice.

"Mamah"—my sister would call her, in her excited

voice. After greeting us she would open her small refrigerator and my eyes would light up as I saw what was inside. I tried to be coy about it but the array of contents made me wildly excited. She made all kinds of *Es Mambo* ice lollypops for a living. They were made of green mung beans, chocolate, vanilla, mango, durian, black or white saké and 'guanabana' —yet another of my favorites. As kids, we were always told by our parents not to eat *Es Mambo* unless made by my sister's Mom. The ice lollipops made by others were dangerous, since they were made with tap water that was not potable. My family knew Wewe's Mom used boiled water, besides they were super tasty and made with really natural ingredients; she was famous for them in our town. I never failed to gobble up a few of them at one sitting.

Mami Wewe would then tend to us, but especially me. I knew she adored me, as she would treat me like a little prince, grabbing me and putting me on her lap and feeding me *Es Mambo* and all the other snacks she had. Sometimes she would send your aunts or uncle to run and buy some snacks from the other local vendors to welcome us, but mostly I thought it was for me.

One thing I always noticed when I was at their humble house, it was always immaculately clean and well organized. Part of the floor was tiled in simple charcoal-black tiles that kept the house cool, and they were always clean and seemed to have been polished till they shone. We would sit around the dining table that was pushed against a grate window. The small rectangular table was always covered with a bright colorful plastic tablecloth with floral prints. I remember the bright red, yellow, blue and green of it, and it was surrounded with simple wooden chairs and plastic stools. Next to the dining room was a living room, but we rarely sat there. That table only fit four persons when pushed against the wall towards the window, or six maximum if pulled into the middle of the room, which hardly ever happened. At meal times, Wewe's Mom would insist that we sit at the table while she sat in the kitchen on her floor stool, but of course your Mom would drag her back to the dining table to sit with us.

Your Mom has an older brother named Nyen Nyen, and three younger sisters, Tutung, Susun, Cicin and her youngest brother is called Aphat who they call Apat. He was always being funny and silly and he was about my age, or perhaps a little younger. I love your aunts, they too are like my sisters. They were kind and sweet and adored me, playing with me as if I was a doll, and always included me in their activities. We used to go walking around the neighborhood to get snacks, or sit at home sewing, knitting or just lying around on the cool floor napping. Of course I loved it when we would play with dolls and makeup. They let me play with their hair. I always felt I was welcomed with open arms in their house. Another thing that I remember fondly was how peaceful they were. There was no yelling and screaming, only small and silly bickering among the sisters. They all knew I was the son of their father's employer and their oldest sister had been adopted by our family, but they were also aware your Mom loved me as her own and I was her favorite and as a result, they always treated me with special care.

When it was time to go to bed, if my memory serves me right, there were only two rooms in the house. Your grandpa shared the room with your uncles and the women and children slept together in one room. They shared a bunk bed and a separate pullout bed. When your Mom and I spent the nights there, they always insisted to give up their bed for us and they slept on the floor on a rollout mattress or mats. This always made me feel bad until now, but it showed me how loving and generous your Mom's family was. They didn't have much but they gave all they had for us. While your Mom has become a part of our family, I can see now how she learned her good, kind, and generous, loving manners. Your grandparents, who looked after her for the first six or seven years of her life, set such a wonderful example.

I still keep in touch with all of your aunts, although I haven't seen or talked to your uncles for many decades. A year or two after your Mom passed away, my husband and I saw your Auntie Tutung. As usual, she was so generous. She insisted on driving us around and gave us a lot of coffee beans from her business to take back home to San Francisco. It was also she who took us to you while you and your Nanny were at a public pool. I know you were not too sure who we were and why we were there. I gave you a hug and you complied. You looked so much like your Mom and Grandpa. I tried so hard not to cry but I couldn't stop myself, although I made sure you were not looking, and pretended it was the water from the swimming pool as you were still wet.

We didn't want to scare you or make you confused, as we knew your Father wasn't keen for you two to see us.

After that visit, Auntie Tutung drove us to her old house—your Mom's parents place. No longer did we have to walk up all those stairs and climb the mountain. Now a car can drive right up to the front door. The house has been painted white with a light green accent. Uncle Stephen knew how emotional I got as soon as I entered the empty house, he gave me a hug and your Aunt Tutung said that she knew how much your Mom meant to me and she was worried this would make me sad, but I thanked her. I was grateful just to be there with my memories of your Mom.

The house was completely empty, there were no furnishings left except for a few needlepoint pieces of art on the walls that were made by your Mom. There was one of a cross and Jesus' hands praying. As I started to roam the house, no one spoke, as I sobbed noisily, remembering all my sweet memories of this house, which now has a tiled floor, and all the walls that used to be made of woven bamboo have been changed to solid cement walls.

One thing I still noticed was the old window grill where the dining table was. I went there to look out at the roofs of the neighbors before I went to the kitchen and for a few seconds I thought I glimpsed your beautiful grandma with the porcelain skin, her hair in a chignon and wearing a *kebaya*, smiling at me from the kitchen stool, her dimples deepening, as she handed out an *Es Mambo* popsicle to me. My hand stretched out to receive it, but she was no longer there.

I turned around to continue my meandering and entered the bedroom where I used to spend the night with your grandma, your aunts and Mom, and last of all I went out the back door from where I had used to enter the house. From there I looked back for the last time, hoping to grab your Mom's hand so we could walk back down the muddy stone road together one more time.

~ *empat* ~

"The center of my universe..."

One day not long after I had started writing these letters
to you I went to a book-reading session in Menlo Park,
California that was given by a set of identical twins, Logan
and Noah Miller. It was about their promise to their Dad that
they would make a movie. They had written their book about
their Dad's life—an alcoholic who lived in the outskirts of a
small town not far from the Golden Gate Bridge. Because of
their father's chronic addiction problems, he was homeless
and lived in the bush.

One member of the audience asked them why they had
wanted to write about their Dad at all. I don't remember
his exact words, but I didn't like his tone. It was as if he had
said '*Why the hell did you write about your Dad? Who the f...
do you think you are or your Dad was?*' I am not sure exactly if
he meant to be so insulting, but it surely felt uncomfortable
to me. I remember his unfriendly, contemptuous expression.

Perhaps I took it a bit too personally, as I was writing
about your Mom at the time. I was worried that someone
would ask me a similar question about my book and your
Mom. But their reply put all my fears to rest.

"Everybody has a story," they said, "and their own
universe too. Dad was the center of our universe, and this is
our story!"

Well, I had a story to tell about my sister and my sister is
the center of my universe too, and this is her story. Ever

since that I continued to read their book, *"Either You're in or You're in the Way"*,[2] and I have found it inspiring, to say the least. They promised their Dad to make a movie, but it was too little too late. They always told him, "One of these days Dad, one of these days…." and at the end, they made a vow holding their Dad's cold corpse in a morgue.

The amazing thing is that they kept their promise and made the movie *"Touching Home"* within a year. Well, to their standard, I am already three years late. As I write this, it is now May 31, 2009 and my sister died on May 24, 2006. But I promised your Mom that I would write her story.

This past week, I have been super motivated to continue my writing that I started two years ago, almost to the date. But somehow, I am stuck again, looking for the best format to tell my story in. I have found that there are too many options, and I have too many ideas. I seem to be sifting through too many unfocused ideas. Perhaps I am trying too hard to find the best angle.

While I am thinking about the nuts and bolts of it I find it most difficult to continue my writing. It's always the same thing: I want to tell the best stories, but I get stuck thinking what's the best format, then I end up deciding that our place is not a conducive place to write, and doubting if I can do any justice in telling the story anyway, so I stop, and to start again is so difficult, as it brings all my painful memories flooding back and I get caught in the same loop over and over again.

---

2. *Either You're in or You're in the Way: Two Brothers, Twelve Months, and One Filmmaking Hell-Ride to Keep a Promise to their Father*, by Logan Miller and Noah Miller, HarperCollins Publishers, 2010.

I would hate to make this story sound more like a diary, but when I read the Miller Brothers' book I became more and more determined to write my sister's story. I have so many memories of Wewe and at random times they come back to me. I always think about her.

Today I remember her hair. How it looked—her haircut that sustained her signature style—the boyish trim with a bang, a soft gamine look. The way her hair looked as if it grew naturally, just as if it had been planted that way, all her life. I had the feeling that it must have looked that way from the moment she was born and remained just perfect right up till the end.

I never remember her having any different haircut. Well, there were two versions of the same thing. It was either what I called the casual oval 'bob', or a shorter version. Always short, never below her shoulders. Her bangs usually always got in the way of her eyes. It was one of those styles that no matter what she did: after a shower, after school, in bed, just when she got up, at church, at a party, at a funeral, at a picnic at the beach, it always stayed the same—low maintenance, just the way she was.

She could shake it, comb it, blow-dry it…anything… and it still looked the same. To the best of my memories, I have never seen her go to a hair salon. Believe me, I would know. This was completely the opposite of my other sister and my Mom, who were both regular customers at a few beauty salons and so was I. I can not ever remember her demanding or asking for anything new, not a new pair of shoes, new clothes, not even new hairpins.

Our Mom always provided her with her needs and it always felt more like 'forcing' her to choose and select what she wanted or needed. Eventually Mom would just buy stuff for her, because your Mother would refuse if she asked her in advance, she was so determined not to be a burden. She had such a considerate nature and never wanted to bother our parents or burden them in any way. This always raised her in my esteem, and I saw her as possessing a saint-like quality. At that time my brother and I were the brats of the family, always asking for new toys, new clothes, new shoes. I also remember how Wewe used to wear our Mom's hand-me-downs, even when they were outdated; she always preferred wearing them to the new clothes that my Mom wanted to buy her.

I believe she felt she had to know her place, but she also gave us a wonderful example. Besides simply being the amazing person and human that she was, this thought of her feeling that she had to be in the background and not bother our parents always made me sad, as I know she deserved just the opposite. I always felt that your Mom deserved better.

Throughout my adult life, Grace and Zef, your uncle Jonathan has been labeled with so many descriptions, I can scarcely remember them all. Nor would I want to. I have been called too bold, too intense and too anal, among other things: I am too American, too westernized, too Asian, and not Asian enough, sometimes I am not even American enough—perhaps you get the picture. Some of the things I have been called I would rather not describe them to you, as they are just plain rude and unkind. However, the point I am trying to make is that people think of me as a person who knows what he wants, and goes for it. I pursue my dreams till they become reality. I am the A-type personality they say. Generally speaking, a person like me is considered to be able to do what he pleases. I am expected to be the kind of person who suffers no regrets, or at the very least has only minimal regrets in life.

Well upon face value, obviously that appears to be true. However, I have come to the conclusion that there is not anyone alive in this world that has no regrets. Everyone has regrets in life, and the older you live, the more regrets you tend to have.

As I grow older I have become more realistic, and I am no longer immune to regrets, although for the longest period in my life, I thought I was. Funnily enough, I still feel proud of my own life; not proud in an arrogant way, but proud to have had a life that I shaped myself, finding my own way. I am content with how I lived my life so far.

The exception to this in my case is when I think about your Mom, Wewe, my dear sister. When I think about her I know there are two major regrets that will haunt me for the rest of my life and they are well deserved.

I know now that I should have spent more time with her in her healthy years, but I did not. That is one of my greatest regrets.

These were the years when I was still the 'rebel' in the

family, a time when I always thought I needed to get away from what I considered to be my bat-shit crazy family. It was also the time where I needed to find myself after a breakthrough during my therapy sessions. It was almost as if, in trying to liberate myself from all of my perpetrators, I also abandoned my protector, your Mom. Perhaps this was a result of my rush to cut my connection with so many others in my past. I am afraid that in my attempt to escape my own stories of the darker periods of my life I lost sight of my sister, the most important person in my entire existence, ever since childhood.

I am concerned that I might again sound self-serving and selfish, but in many respects I have to admit I was. To call me a brat was an understatement. For many years in my adolescence I lived the idyllic life of a young prince, relatively speaking. Moving between Switzerland, Paris, London, Milan, and the U.S., I was so self-absorbed in liberating myself and asserting my own independence from my family and relatives, especially those who had tried to control me all my life, not only physically, but also mentally. Those 'perpetrators' included my cousin and her husband in California, who did their best to prevent me from having friends other than Christian Indonesians or Asians in order to be able to force their beliefs and their religion and faith upon me. I had to get away from them and from it all to find myself.

But in the process, I forgot the one person who loved me for me, the most non-judgmental, kindest, loving soul who raised me and had so much positive influence on me. Well, forgot is not exactly the right word. She was sacrificed to my needs to be independent and follow along the rocky path to my own self-discovery. In saying so, I feel a sense of guilt for making these excuses, for coming up with these reasons of why I didn't spend enough time with her. Isn't that what regretting is, after all—a constant feeling of guilt? Or even worse, remorse for something that cannot be undone?

One thing I know, I have never forgotten her, not even during the years when I was away from everyone. I missed her then as much as I do today. It was during a hard time also when my parents had lost all their money. They had been tricked by another 'adopted' son, and lost everything. I was practically rendered homeless while still at college. I had the option to go back to Indonesia at that time, as my parents could no longer finance my tuition fee nor my living expenses. But it was also during this time that I was just coming out, accepting my own sexuality and I needed to process that and find a way to survive.

Those were the years when civil unrest broke out in Indonesia as the fanatic Muslims taunted the ethnic Chinese, scapegoating them for the many social problems in Indonesia. The nightmares in our growing pain as a country made international news. Ethnic Chinese Indonesians were kidnapped and raped, their parents murdered, businesses and houses burned. Even your mother's small stationery store was burned down. I was scared and confused. In fact, during this time, I made up my mind. Rather than be forced to go back to Indonesia, I would commit suicide. I could not imagine what my life would be like in such a repressive country where I knew my sexuality would continually expose me to life-threatening situations.

I was determined to stay, and I knew there would be a point that I would have to make a choice. If I stayed in the United States I would be homeless, literally, as I could not afford a roof over my head. And what could I do to be able to finish my college education?

When Professor Jenning Hansen, my accounting teacher at USF found out I had to drop out, he took me aside and asked me what had happened. Besides being one of his best students at that time, I also had an overall great grade-point average. To cut a long story short, he pulled some strings and nominated me for a scholarship. Between him and my Business School Hospitality Management department, they raised enough money to give me a full scholarship until I graduated. What was more amazing was that I had no idea who else contributed towards my tuition, and I still don't. There was no way the scholarship alone would have been enough to pay the expensive private Jesuit university fees. Clearly, Mr. Hansen is another hero in my life along with other people who anonymously took care of my tuition.

That left me to figure out a way to raise funds for my living expenses—rent, food, books and transportation. For the next two years of my college life, I figured out a way to survive. To be poor after you were extremely wealthy, in my opinion was a lot tougher than if you were born poor and stay poor for the rest of your life.

For the first time in my life, I had to work and I was only allowed to work on campus because of my foreign student status. I applied to all departments but the one place that would hire me was the Audio Visual department, located at Campion Hall of USF, down in the basement, with no window at all. It was a congregation of foreign student workers, with all kinds of accents, mostly from Asia, run by a few nerds who embraced us and showed us the ropes.

Our boss Mary was a petite chain-smoker who was a straightforward kind of woman, managing what typically then was a male-dominated department. She was always in her office behind a closed door. Her room was full of cigarette smoke that billowed out and travelled all the way down the hallway. I never liked cigarettes and the smoke always gave me terrible allergies, resulting in watery, itchy eyes that continually made me sneeze and left me moody. But she was sweet and kind to me and hired me. She gave me my first job ever in my life at $3.25/hour. I had to push around metal carts loaded with TVs, videos and slide projectors, and an array of pullout screens that I hooked up according to the needs of various classes that had made reservations ahead of time, or had standing reservations during the semester or school year.

The irony was I could barely understand how the AV equipment functioned, let alone set it up. Imagine me struggling to set things up, sweating profusely after carrying and pushing them all over campus. Sometimes I had difficulty finding the locations, which was no easy task in those days before Google maps were invented. There were many locations that were hard to navigate, with lots of steps and grass access and some of them not well paved. To add to the injury was the fact that at times, all eyes were on me. Hundreds of pairs of eyes would stare, laugh or joke about the uncool foreign student who got a job in what they called the loser's department—the only department that would hire me. No matter. I needed that money.

I worked every Monday, Wednesday and Friday and I attended my eighteen to twenty-one units, or around seven classes per semester on Tuesdays and Thursdays. I had arranged to attend the classes from 8 am to 10 pm, so I could do my homework in between classes or on Saturday and Sunday or at night. I made a total of $260 to $300 a month minus tax. Essentially every month that first semester I had to survive on about $150.

This was the story that always made your mother and our mother cry. I started out sleeping on the sofa or in the dorm rooms of my kind girlfriends and my old roommate until I could save enough money for the deposit to rent a room. After a few months I could move into a room that cost me $125 a month. I bought 5 kg or 10 lbs. of potatoes every month and dry pasta as well instant spaghetti sauce. I could not afford the meat sauce, as it cost about 45 cents more. I soon realized that one Idaho potato was big enough to make me feel full. I got it down to a routine and developed my own formula: I washed the potatoes, scrubbed them clean and took the eyes out, and I took one for lunch per day. At school

I poked it evenly with a fork, wrapped it with a clean wet paper towel from the school restrooms or break room before nuking it in the nasty dirty microwave provided in our break room. I soon knew how long each side needed to be cooked in that weak microwave, depending upon the shape and size of each potato. I would devour it with ketchup, Tabasco sauce, salt and pepper or other condiments I found for free.

On lucky days when someone could not finish their lunch I would eat whatever they wanted to throw away, along with my lonely potato. On a super-lucky day, my coworker would bring me lunch, knowing I was a desperately poor student.

At night I ate either the same pasta and tomato sauce I that I made every Sunday for the week, alternating now and then with instant Top Ramen. Later when I could treat myself a takeout, I would pay $3.95 for a Chinese meal that I could split into 2 dinners or I would split the cost and the meal with a friend who was also poor at the time. More heroes in my life, my friends Andi and Kris would periodically take turns to feed me with Top Ramen or popcorn or brownies, all homemade in their dorm room. Andi would help me by correcting my English papers, Kris would lend me her computer, and both of them fed me whenever they could.

A semester later, a lady named Eliza at the Bursar's office felt sorry for me and gave me a chance to work in the office where students paid their tuition and sorted out their financial matters with the University. Eliza became one of the surrogate mothers I had in that office, and I still call her

Mom—I am so grateful for her kindness. I made a little more money working there, and the women in that office adopted me as their brother or son or nephew, knowing that I was hungry and broke, they always brought some food for me and we did a lot of 'potluck' meals.

One woman in particular, the lovely Chinese-American Kirsten Chow, took me under her wing. She was already out as a lesbian, and understood what I was going through. She became my mentor in helping me to accept my sexuality. Kirsten also helped me to be more aware of human rights, equality and what gay pride truly meant. She always brought me food or treated me to meals at Chinese or Thai restaurants, and she taught me LGBTQ history, whilst becoming my all-round role model. She reminded a lot of your Mom, except Kirsten was not so shy about her emotions and anger, style or sexuality. She was out and proud. She also always bought me gifts—small tokens of her love and care picked up on her travels from New York or Amsterdam, the two cities she loved. Her roasted pine nut and sugar cookies were my favorite and she always brought the entire office the pastry from a local Chinese bakery everyone loved. But she always put pork buns and custard buns aside for me, knowing they were my favorites and she made sure I could take some extras home, knowing how hungry I always was and how little money I had. After I graduated we kept in touch and she continued to treat me as her little brother, except now I could take her out to show my gratitude and to try to pay her back in whatever way I could for all her compassion, kindness and generosity during my desperate years. When I opened the store that carried my last name, J.Rachman, it was near her house. She came in and without my knowing she purchased a big gift certificate with no other reason but to support my business and me, discreetly.

A few years ago when I was lounging in the pool with your uncle Stephen, in Hawaii during our annual Thanksgiving holiday around my and her birthday (our birthdays are only a few days apart), I received the saddest message from Sally. Her wife Kirsten had unexpectedly died after a few days in the hospital. Sally told me how proud Kirsten had been of me, and that she was still bragging to the nurses about me in the hospital about my successes right up to the day before she died, she even showed them pictures of me and my store. Needless to say, I was heartbroken: another sister, protector and heroine in my life left me too soon. My heart ached for her. They say that the good ones always die young. I am happy to say that Sally, her widow, and her brother have kept in touch. We see each other annually—usually around our birthdays to celebrate her life. During these luncheons, attended by 10-15 friends and family I insist to pay or I pay ahead to avoid any arguments at the table, and to honor her love; without her I wouldn't be here. She fed me, and nourished my heart and soul—just like your Mom—for so many years. In a way it was Kirsten who continued to raise your uncle where your Mom left off, when I was far from home, and lost touch with your Mom. Both women had the biggest and most generous hearts, always ready to share what they had.

Looking back, while I had no idea how I survived my last two college years, I also know the answer: it was the love from so many people and strangers who have become my friends and *ohana*[3] that made it possible for me get through some of the toughest years of my life.

I made a vow to myself to never feel hungry again the way I had during those years. The pangs of extreme hunger are hard for any human to experience, and I believe no one deserves to feel the way I did at that time. While I am not happy I had to go through that, it has helped me to be even more compassionate about world hunger. I know I can't save the world from hunger, but I can certainly help a few people from suffering the pangs.

Between getting lost in trying to finish my college under the toughest of circumstances, coming out, surviving and finding myself, I neglected the one person I should have never abandoned, my sister. That is my biggest regret of this life. I only saw her every few years. My parents could no longer send the money I needed for my travel back home, and I had to manage my own finances responsibly. But, every chance I got, I would fly back to visit them with Stephen, who was finishing his graduate studies in psychology to get his Ph.D. and soon to become a licensed psychologist.

Both of us were financially limited due to our responsibilities. After the crisis in Indonesia I had to find

3'. **Ohana** is a Hawaiian term meaning 'family'. The term is cognate with Māori kōhanga, meaning 'nest'.

a way to support my parents. As soon as I could, I started sending them what I could and Stephen helped me. As I write this memoir, I realize Stephen and I have supported our parents as a couple almost as long as we have been together. He never once asked me how much or what the money is for and it always came from our joint account. I am blessed to have a husband who also has the biggest and most generous heart, just like your Mom. They say you marry someone who reminds you of your parents or the people who raised you. Stephen definitely has a lot of qualities that remind me of your Mom and I couldn't be more proud of them both.

The other biggest regret of my life is not being with your Mom while she was dying. I know I should have been with her. Just a few years after she died I was blessed to be one of the main hospice caregivers to Stephen's Mom, as well as his Dad. It changed my life, but it also added to my guilty feelings for not taking care of your Mom in her last days. I can make up a lot of excuses for not being there: your father, our responsibilities in California, my work, money difficulties—and while these were all valid reasons, the fact of the matter was I should have taken the time and made the effort.

Could have, would have, should have are words of regret and these conversations played over and over again in my head. Why didn't I go, why didn't I take care of her, why didn't I made her more comfortable in her final days, why, why and why? These questions haunted me. As

I question myself, my troubled heart refuses to accept this absence of mine.

I understand self-forgiveness is important for us to be able to move forward as well as to grow. This is something I have to learn also to live with. I need to forgive myself for not being there.

- *lima* -

"When I was small and needy..."

Another thing that has helped me make peace with myself and eased my regrets is the simple fact of how well I know your mother. Besides her love and compassion and her enormous heart, she was also gifted with the rare ability of not getting angry. I never once saw her angry in her lifetime and that is a fact that I can vouch for and I am sure many people could attest to this statement. Neither was she able to hate anyone. This was another trait that she possessed which was truly angelic. I knew in my heart that she would always forgive me, usually she would not even think I had done anything wrong—and that made me both feel better and worse all at the same time. That too, I know is the nature of my regret. Yes, I forgive myself, but I will never forget, and that is something I will live with for the rest of my life—and I have accepted this is all part of remembering your Mom.

She was, is and will always be the center of my universe in my heart and mind, and I know I was hers. Can you imagine what it was like, to have a sister who was always there for you from the moment you woke up, and got you ready until it was time to go to school, and after school there she was again to pick you up? She was always ready with a tin of steamed rice and my favorite Indonesian spam—we called it 'ham and wurst'—a type of preserved ham and sausage meat that came in round cans. She would slice it and cut it into quarter rounds that she fried and placed on top of the rice.

She would alternate it with flossy dried pork called *Abon* to top the rice. It was often still warm when she opened it and started feeding me in the car after kissing me and hugging me. She was always there for me.

There were two incidents in our childhood that I will never forget. These are more examples of your Mom's love for me as well as her selflessness. For her it was always about other people first, their needs, their safety, their comfort, their feelings…my dear sister always put herself, her needs, safety and emotions last and mine first.

The first incident took place on the evening before the Thursday prayer group that my family always attended when we were young, which you will learn about later in this letter. But there was one specific evening at dusk when your Mom and I were being driven by a driver whose name is Pak Reggeng. I remember vividly that we were not in our usual green Land Rover that evening. We were in a Japanese land cruiser he wasn't familiar with. I think our Land Rover had been lent to my father's friend for hunting. I believe we were going home from shopping, passing by a movie theater area which was by a store called Toko Jelita (Beautiful Store) which was our family favorite and one of the best known stores in town as it carried everything but food.

I'm not exactly sure how to classify this store, but it was our family's favored place to shop on a street full of street food vendors, ornamental fish sellers, next to a movie theater called Queen. It was dusk so the light was failing, and the road was narrow. The sidewalks were uneven and the parking area was never properly designated and could be tricky to get in and out of.

The street was not well lit, and we climbed in the front seat next to our driver. In Indonesia they drive on the left side of the road, so the driver was on the right, and we got in on the left. The car had been parked on a lower part of the road, just off the street. It was near the stores area and to drive out of there the driver literally had to take the car along a sidewalk that passed over a creek with a few uncovered surfaces. At times cars had got stuck there, as one wheel would sink into the creek We got into the car—there were no seatbelts in cars at that time[4]—and closed the door, or so we thought. It was a heavy door and hard to close. There was a manual gear-stick shift between the driver and us. The driver obviously had driven us many times in this area, so this was nothing new. We were in familiar terrain. He knew he had to accelerate to gain momentum to climb out of our parking spot back up into the street as soon as we sat down and closed the door, so he pressed on the gas pedal.

The next thing I knew both Wewe and I had somehow flown out of the car and landed separately on the rough concrete surface of the makeshift sidewalk that passed over the creek. We were both screaming at the top of our voices and I must have cried out hysterically because there my sister was, may be five meters away from me, and she was injured. Bystanders shouted and tried to help our driver, who

4. Seatbelts were not yet installed in cars, and the wearing of seatbelts was not enforced legally by the Indonesian government until decades later.

was shaken up, and trembling as he got out of the car.

Oblivious to everything else, your Mom crawled towards me, yelling out my name and crying, sobbing, something I had never seen before at that point of my life. In spite of her injured arms and hip, she grabbed me and soothed me calling out my name again and again.

"Yoyo…! Yoyo…! Yoyo sayang…!"

There were tears, blood and sweat all over her and she continued to try to lift me. Miraculously I was only scratched on my lower palm and arm and leg on one side. Considering the impact and what could have been, it was a miracle that neither of us had been badly injured and we both remained fully conscious.

What happened next still baffles me. Wewe lifted me to the car and cradled me, wiped my tears, blood and sweat with her T-shirt and instructed our driver to go home. Clearly we were not hurt badly; at least there was no major injury, although we remained shaken by the accident. The driver was not just worried about us but also about his job, he probably thought he would lose it when my parents found out.

When we arrived home to our family they were shocked to see the state we were in as we got out of the car covered in blood and injuries. It looked like a murder scene. My Mom was hysterical and cried so much that we joined her and cried all over again with her, but Wewe instantly took full responsibility. She blamed herself for the incident, telling our parents she mustn't have closed the door properly, so it was not our driver's fault. In all fairness, it was no one's fault: the door was heavy and hard to close, the driver thought we were all safe and ready for him to get out of that tough spot, and he was steering a car that he didn't regularly drive.

After we had cleaned up and been inspected by our parents it was decided we were all right, so off they went to their prayer group. My sister stayed with me to make sure I was not in shock. I was most probably only four or five years old, and she would have been fourteen or fifteen, so this was before she became a nurse and she would have still been in junior high school. She fed me my favorite fried spam with rice and sweet soy sauce and made me her famous cold sweet milk before bed, the drink that I loved so much. Then she cuddled and cradled me all night long—all these were things I would much rather do than going to the boring prayer group, and now I have my sweet memories of the evening after our near-disaster.

There was also another event, which has remained imprinted in my heart ever since it happened—an incident that always makes me think of your Mom and her loving and considerate nature. It also affirms how she was—not just as a human being, but as my sister—the one who always put my needs, emotions and wellbeing first above those of anyone else, even if it put her in an uncomfortable spot or made her an uncool person among her peers. Because of this incident, I always use her as my benchmark, standard and point of reference. There is a famous acronym that has become popular, you will see it as a bumper sticker all over the U.S.—WWJD: What Would Jesus Do?; well my standard is WWWD: What Would Wewe Do.

We went to the beach where the locals loved to go, a beach called Pasir Putih, which means 'White Sands'. We usually went there on a Sunday afternoon after church or super early in the morning on a holiday to claim a spot. Typically we would go with our family relatives or to entertain guests, as this beach was a local pride. We always brought the locally woven *tikar* mats that were made out of natural materials or plastic thread, to sit on. We took our picnic food and supplies from home and we liked to buy the famous spicy chicken wrapped in banana leaves along the way in Pandjang neighborhood. The back of the car was filled up with large vessels of fresh water to rinse off with after swimming, as there were no shower or public bathroom facilities back then.

Wewe always brought towels and our change of clothes. Typically we would drive there in a convoy of three to five cars, it was quite a circus. Indonesians love to do everything with as many people as possible. We called it '*ramai-ramai*' which describes a happy crowd of people doing something together. The trip would take at least one hour each way in those days as not all the roads were paved. Now it only takes around twenty minutes. There was a section where the road suddenly took you over a bump as we crossed a river, and I remember that if you drove at the right speed, it made everyone's stomach feel tickled and we all laughed and laughed. After that bump we knew it wouldn't be too long before we would arrive at our beloved beach. We would stay all day long, playing in that large expanse of nature; our parents never found it easy to drag us back to eat or to go home. We usually would go home at sunset, just before it got dark. I still have some pictures of it from my childhood and later when I went there after I moved to the U.S. and went back to visit, always with fond memories. Except for one.

On this specific trip, curiously it was only our sister Edna, David, Edwin (this was a rare occasion) and his friends, plus Wewe and I, no more than seven or eight of us, all piled into the Land Rover; I don't remember if our driver drove us or was it our elder sibling. I wasn't sure where our parents were or at the time, or if it was an unplanned trip spontaneously carried out by the teens in our group. I believe it was our elder sibling's idea as he was home on vacation. We arrived pretty late in the afternoon but it was still bright and the beach was not very busy. We did the usual things— swimming, playing on the low-tide sandbar, and we had some food. I was left to play on the sandbar on my own, as was fairly normal. The older guys were not too far way and could keep an eye on me. The next thing I knew when I looked up I couldn't see them at all, and I continued to play with my water well. I liked to make moats around my sand structure and watch the water rush in to fill them up. The next time I looked up it was close to sunset when usually we started to pack up to get ready to go home but no one was there so I started walking towards our parked car and looking for our *tikar* mat on the beach where the clothes, water vessels and food were usually left. Not only was there no sign of our belongings, I could not find our car, nor my siblings and their friends. I panicked, instantly feeling abandoned and alone, and I thought I must be in a bad dream. I started to cry and ran everywhere, looking left and right in a panic. I thought I would pass out from my heart beating so fast, unable to believe that I could not see them. Strangers tried to talk to me but I would not listen or stop crying and I kept wandering around like a lost child. I felt truly lost.

Suddenly my car came out of nowhere, zooming past me at the top of the beach. It passed in front of me, but it continued on. I ran frantically after it, as fast as I could, feeling so helpless, and I ran until I thought I would die from running. Remember I could not do sport and I did not like to run either, so I had no idea how to keep going. I felt like my chest was exploding and I could not breathe; my shortness of breath made me feel even worse. In my poor mind I really thought they had forgotten me, and they would leave me behind.

You have to remember this was in the early or mid '70s. In those days there was no public phone, nobody had cell phones, and there was no way of knowing how I could get hold of my parents or family if they left me or I was lost or 'forgotten'. In my mind I thought I would be left there forever, or perhaps I would even be kidnapped. I could starve and I would become a homeless child. We witnessed children in this situation quite commonly in Indonesia in those years. They would be naked, or wear shredded clothing, and they had the saddest, most desperate look. I was going to be one of those dirty, homeless children. For certain, I thought. That would be me.

Then I saw them again. As I screamed and waved, running naked, desperately pleading and trying to get their attention, I could see your Mom's faced plastered onto the back glass window of the car. She was crying and while I could not understand the words she uttered, I could tell she wanted the car to stop, she was begging them. Her hands reached out to me—while David and the other teens were laughing.

I most probably glimpsed this for only a few seconds or at the most for half a minute, at a distance of a few hundred meters, but it felt to me like it stretched into hours, a lifetime. I kept on feeling that it was a nightmare and hoping I would wake up from a loop that played over and over again as no one stopped for me. I screamed: "Wait for me, wait for me please wait for me…I am here," and I called out Wewe's name over and over again. It truly felt like the worst nightmare anyone could imagine, except it was real.

The car suddenly stopped and as I continued to run towards the car Wewe flung the door open and jumped out, then fell, as she cried and screamed my name. She got up and ran as fast as she could—scooping me up off the flat damp sands, hugged me, and calmed both of us down, wiping my tears and hair and kissing me and hugging me so tightly, while our siblings and friends laughed and laughed at us from the car. Ignoring them, she grabbed a towel from the car to wrap me in and warm me up. By this time I was drenched in cold sweats. I was not only relieved that I wouldn't have to be a *gembel*—the local slang for a homeless child—I was also elated to be reunited with my sister. I could not have been more furious with the rest of them, and that anger stayed with me for a long time.

Later I learned that they did not intend to abandon me for real. They had started out to teach my sister Edna to drive, a common thing to do at that empty beach. Yet they thought it was so funny to scare the shit out of me with a mean prank, the kind of trick they could only play upon such a little boy. I also thought perhaps that was why they didn't tell my parents or maybe they had planned it, so it would only be us, as it happened not on a weekend but during a weekday, at rather an odd time to visit the beach.

I knew it wouldn't have been easy for them to make Wewe join them and leave me alone at the beach. They must have put some kind of pressure on her, or tricked her as well. I wasn't surprised that my older siblings and their friends wanted to play a trick on me, the sissy boy, especially those boys. In a way it was a cruel joke on both your Mom and me and I still don't find it funny, even now as an adult. Nor could I at the time it happened. Cruelty that was played out as a prank in childhood is still cruelty, and it left me scarred for life, with a deep fear of being left behind.

I don't remember the rest of what happened then, there was only one thing I knew for sure. I was all right and I felt safe, secure and calm as soon as my sister hugged me. After such a traumatizing experience my mind was not capable of making sense of what had actually happened at the time. Her presence, voice and tender laughing touch had an instant affect on me then and it always would. With her beside me I knew everything was going to be fine again.

My sister was as upset and devastated as I was. For her to see me in such a state and have to fight so desperately to be able to rescue me—which she did—was very hard. I have no doubt that it would have shaped part of her character from then on. From my perspective then, and my point of view, even as child, I knew she had to beg and scream for them to stop and to let her out to help me, judging from her look of pain and their laughing faces. For them it was not a big deal, but for Wewe, who knew me so well, and could tell that I was as distressed as a little bambi separated from its mother, it was a different thing altogether.

That feeling of not knowing if we would ever be reunited again—although our actual separation did not happen until decades later—left an image that stayed in my head for the rest of my life. I finally found out, when my sister, who loved me so much and had always fought for my life, successfully rescuing, soothing and comforting me, that in her time of need I could not be there. All I could do was try to watch out for her and desperately try to reach her. I imagined seeing her face filled with so much sadness and pain, and yet I could not help her. That was my recurring nightmare.

Regrets are the penance I pay for not spending time with your Mom in her adult years, yet, no matter how long she has been gone, no matter how long I have been married to my husband, your Mom, my sister, is still the center of my universe and for that reason and so many other important reasons, I must tell the world this story, of her love and life.

During her last year of her life and ordeal, as well as the time just after her death, there were a number of seemingly random things in my life that continued to remind me of her. That year when I learned she had been diagnosed with stage-four cancer, Stephen and I had been watching a HBO TV network series called *Six Feet Under*, produced by Alan Ball. Every episode opened with a focus on someone who had just died. While the series itself was about a family that ran a funeral home, there was a death in every episode including members of that family. The series ran for a few years, up until the time that your Mom passed away, and carried on after she was gone. In a way I felt that watching it had prepared me—not that I would ever be ready—to face what I was about to experience with your Mom.

The ending of this series is still one of the best, if not the best finale of the series, which ran for a five-year span. In it, the youngest sister was now on her deathbed, already in her 90's or even older. As she was dying they did an amazing flashback of her driving as a teenager in her Dad's old car, a hearse painted an acid green color. As she drove she looked back through her rearview mirror as one of the most beautiful songs by Sia, '*Breathe Me*' played, perfecting the finale scene. In my mind, I'd like to think about your Mom, hoping she too had a pleasant flashback as her soul left her body. She deserved to be uplifted by wonderful music, and I knew that she was physically in so much pain and misery.

I am hoping her mind was able to escape that pain. The scene of this finale will always hold that fantasy for me, as I cannot bear to think about the alternative reality—the one that my sister actually had to experience, that there was nothing I could do to change.

There is a part of the lyrics of Sia's, *Breathe Me* that speaks both to her and me and it felt like my plea to her while she was dying, I was so desperate for her to stay.

> "Be my friend, hold me
> Wrap me up, unfold me
> I am small and needy
> Warm me up and breathe me
> Be my friend, hold me
> Wrap me up, unfold me
> I am small and needy
> Warm me up and breathe me."

Apart from my love of music as a reflection of my moods, music also speaks to me in various ways and it has often helped me to get through tough times. One of my favorite bands is Depeche Mode and I have been to some of their concerts. There was one song called *Precious*[5] which was out around the same time in 2005-2006 and for me this song is not only about your Mom but I would like it to be for your Mom from me; it speaks to me about us. Read these lyrics and see if you understand why this song is perfect for the way

---

5. *Precious,* by Depeche Mode, released in 2005.

I think about your Mom:

"Precious and fragile things
Need special handling
My God what have we done to You?
We always try to share
The tenderest of care
Now look what we have put You through
Things get damaged
Things get broken
I thought we'd manage
But words left unspoken
Left us so brittle
There was so little left to give
Angels with silver wings
Shouldn't know suffering
I wish I could take the pain for you
If God has a master plan
That only He understands
I hope it's your eyes He's seeing through

It describes my feelings for your Mom as well as our
state of mind at that time. Not only does it capture the
state she was in, my regrets and my sense of helplessness, it
also embodies my frustration and the anger that I felt with
this God I was told to believe in. It is complex I know, but
this song captures my emotions at the time of your Mom's
suffering and after. I interpret it as a form of plea and it

describes what I wanted to tell her in a poetic way, expressing feelings that I find difficult to verbalize.

Certain songs and music do that for me, so I want to share some of them with you as a way of expressing my feelings, in the hope that you will understand our relationship better. I hope it will give you a window into parts of your Mom's life that you may not know about. Every word and line in the *Precious* lyrics hit the spot in my heart, and I feel as if those words could be coming from me to her. I especially love the lines *"Angels with silver wings, Shouldn't know suffering... I wish I could take the pain from you...."*

I want to tell you about the time I had to go to Jakarta without my husband, something that has rarely happened in our life together. As I write this, we have been together as a couple for twenty-six years, four months and eighteen days, and we keep track of how many times we have been separated, such as when I travel for my business or the times in the past that Stephen drove his grandparents back to their home state in the Spring, after they spent a hard winter in a less harsh climate. To date, we have only been separated twenty-one times, and adding all those times up this comes to a total of 71.5 days.

Every time we share this information with friends and family they are surprised and impressed for several reasons. Firstly, we know exactly how long we have been a couple. Secondly, we keep track of how many times and the total number of days that we have been separated. And lastly, they are amazed that we have hardly ever been away from each other as a couple.

Yes, actually we don't like to be apart from each other. We are completely in love still after all these years, and our motto is: *Eternity is too short.* Or *Eternity is not long enough.* I like to quote Elvis Presley in his song about how I feel about my husband: "*Ku-u-i-po I love you more today, More today than yesterday, But I love you less today, Less than I will tomorrow…*" But that's for me to tell you another time, as this letter is not about Stephen and me.

Anyway, this was the first time I had to go back to Indonesia on my own for my work and it also happened to be the first time I had to go there alone after your Mom passed away. It was a short trip, yet an emotional one.

As a family we tend to acknowledge our sadness without verbalizing it, and customarily we always try to get together over a meal so I invited my siblings and their family, our parents and cousins to come out and gather as a family. I try to do this every time I visit Jakarta as our relatives mostly live around the area and I rarely go there. I prefer to go to Bali. We all gathered the night before I was due to leave, ate our meal together as usual, yet this time it felt different. The atmosphere was more somber than usual and more low-key, as all of us were in a rather somber mood. There were no visible tears but it's the kind of sadness that's unspoken. We all thought about your Mom but we were not ready to discuss it and openly mourn again as most of them had already done at the funeral.

Suddenly, the very next day, it was time for me to leave, with an early departure to the airport. As usual my parents, David and his family and Edna and her family all insisted on driving me to the airport to say goodbye.

This was when I completely lost it at the airport and we all did—even David, who is rarely moved to tears. I could fully sense his sadness when he said goodbye to me, most likely affected by the shadow of your Mom's death hanging over us. It highlighted the fact that we might not see each other again and this could be a final goodbye. As it was always, this was the moment we as family were served up our portion of reality on our platter. It might not necessarily be my turn next, or anyone's in particular, but as a result of your Mom's death, we were more aware of the possibility that our family might lose someone else between now and the next time we saw each other again. The prospect that one of us might not be there in the future now loomed; saying goodbye in our somber mood was like putting the punctuation at the end of the sentence. We said our teary goodbyes as usual, but it was harder, and—as I recall—even louder than usual.

I checked in, wearing my sunglasses to conceal my red and puffy eyes. The kind airline staff offered me tissues, with a sympathetic tone of voice. I nodded to thank them for their kind gesture. Immigration was next, and whereas usually I find immigration agents worldwide to be standoffish, cold and rude, this time it was different. I understand their attitude is a survival tactic, some kind of self-preservation and distancing that they find necessary in their line of work. However this time, upon looking up at me after officiously grabbing my U.S. passport from my hands, the uniformed gentleman, slightly older than me and presumably of Javanese origin, softy mumbled to his colleague in the next booth, not realizing I understood him.

"Little brother, this one is very sad...I feel sorry for him."

The 'little brother' looked at me and I only sobbed louder as they whispered to each other in Javanese "Oh, he understood?"

They both wished me a "*Selamat jalan*—Bon voyage!"

Next was the lounge. When I am not in such a sad mood, I often gorge whatever food is available at my last point of embarkment, especially when I am at an Indonesian airport, even if it's not the best food. I worry this could be my last chance to eat Indonesian food for a long time, or until the next time I come to Indonesia, or even—this might be my last time! Unfortunately this has become a kind of obsessive-compulsive-disorder routine that I first began when I left my home country, and it has carried on all my life. My clients always insist I travel first class, but this time instead of enjoying myself, and the delicacies available in the airport lounge for first class travellers, I sulked and proceeded to drown myself in sorrow.

I got up to get some water and passed the food area. Now I think you already know I am very sentimental, but at times I get super-soppy and sensitive. As I passed some food displays, I noticed a standard buffet of Indonesian food. There was *Nasi goreng* (fried rice), *Soto ayam* (chicken soup), and an array of *jajanan*(market snacks). I just lost it! My tears were uncontrollable—no sound came out, just tears, but I was inconsolable, and to make things worse my nose was stuffed up. A sweet lady offered me some paper napkins and told me she too was leaving her family to go back to Australia said she knew just how I felt, but I refrained from telling her the additional reason for my sadness, although I managed to thank her for her kindness.

The walk to the airplane felt like a death march, as if I was about to be executed. In the past, before the tragic 9/11 World Trade Center incident, family, friends and well-wishers could watch from a nearby balcony, even accompany me up to the gate, but that was no longer allowed. I still looked back, hoping to see them there, waving from the Soekarno-Hatta airport departure gallery. I imagined my family and your Mom were all there, waving their goodbyes as they did in my childhood, and this did not help my stream of tears.

As I got on board the plane the sun had just started to rise, and the flight attendant in charge of my section brought me a box of tissues along with my beverage. She handed me the box with an understanding look and a light touch on my shoulder, ever so gently and kindly, and put her palm on her heart with an expression that said "*I understand, I am sorry*". No words were exchanged, but I understood the universal sign language of kindness and compassion.

I must admit, I am a neurotic traveller and flyer. I have a number of obsessive compulsions I joke about, and I have some routines I follow when I travel to make myself feel more at ease. I wear certain things and carry particular items in my favorite carry-on. The sunglasses I choose are determined by the weather at the time, my outfit, the locations and destinations. My noise-canceling headphones are always with me, especially when I am not with my husband, and I always carry his framed picture in its heart-shaped frame in my front pocket so I can take it out at takeoff and landing to hold in my palm. During cocktails and meal times I put his picture on my dining tray again, just in case it is the last thing I see in my life.

Music is another special component of my travel routine. I have my 'waiting in the lounge' music, my 'taxiing' music, my 'taking-off music', my 'sleeping' music and my 'landing' music, and these are all determined by locations and destinations. I nearly always reserved seat number 1A, which was my favorite seat.

As the air bridge moved away I would put on my headphone and listen to the music Stephen and I had shared when we were first together. It was James Blunt's *High*. As the airplane pulled away from the terminal, the sun was rising slowly and the song that I used to listen simply because I liked the tune and melody which put me in a certain mood suddenly had a different meaning to me, one that I would treasure from that moment on, and I am sure this will endure until the rest of my life:

Beautiful dawn—lights up the shore for me
There is nothing else in the world
I'd rather wake up and see (with you)
Beautiful dawn—I'm just chasing time again
Thought I would die a lonely man, in endless night

But now I'm high; running wild among all the stars above
Sometimes it's hard to believe you remember me

Beautiful dawn (beautiful dawn)—melt with the stars again
Do you remember the day when my journey began?
Will you remember the end (of time)?
Beautiful dawn (beautiful dawn)
You're just blowing my mind again
Thought I was born to endless night, until you shine

Needless to say, in my state of mind and mood, the music, the view from my airplane window the smell of the cabin mixed with a tinge of aircraft gasoline was a deadly combination. Apparently I cried and sobbed so loud (with my noise-canceling headphones on) to the point where an Asian lady in the middle of the row got out of her seat and came over. She touched me on my shoulder and asked if I wanted her to sit next to me.

Seat 1B was empty, except for my box of tissues, and I simply nodded my head, not trusting myself to speak. She held my hand as if I were a child as the plane took off, and

I fell asleep. I was so engrossed in my sorrow that after my polite and sincere "Thank you…" we said our goodbye at Singapore airport and she gave me a hug. Rather un-Asian behavior in some ways, to be so nurturing and motherly to a stranger, but I knew that what your Mom would do the same for someone in my situation and it was as if I felt her presence in that kind lady. I wish I had kept in touch with her and had a chance to thank her for her generous and lovely gesture.

With each take off and landing on that journey my family, Indonesia and your mother felt further and further away. We flew from Jakarta to Singapore, Singapore to Hong Kong, and then Hong Kong to San Francisco. As happy as I was to see my husband waiting for me at the last airport as I rolled my luggage cart out of the arrival gate, when I ran and hugged him I couldn't prevent more sobbing, more tears. Tears of joy upon being reunited with him were now mixed with tears of sadness at separation from my loved ones and my home country. This is the story of my life that I know I must endure—the life path I have chosen as an immigrant means living far away from those I love.

Perhaps now you will see why all these songs, certain music, and even particular fragrances serve as triggers for my memory, especially those that will always be associated with your Mom. There are days when I am walking around the neighborhood and a whiff of the Javanese jasmine transports me. It is so powerful it can literally make me turn around, thinking she must be just behind me. No, there is no Javanese jasmine in California, but the blooms of the Pittosporum have a very similar scent. I react similarly to the sight of a deer by the freeway, or birds in our villa on our Bali vacation, or fried spam over rice. These are just a few of the constant reminders of your Mom and the time I had with her. Each element, sight, smell, or note of music instantly makes me think of her. Memories are very powerful and while some make me sad, others make me happy. She is always in my mind and heart and yes, she is still the center of my universe.

~ enam ~

"Yesterday once more..."

The taste and aroma of certain foods always brings back sweet memories. On the evening of 29th October, 2019 we were having our usual Saturday Steak night, with a side dish of purple Okinawan sweet potato. I shared with Stephen how the word of sweet potato or yam in Indonesian is *ketela*, which includes almost any tuber that's not potato or cassava. We grew *ketela* on our land in Lampung where I grew up, and we used to steam or boil the tuber roots as snacks. They are naturally sweet—we would boil them and eat them on their own, or stir them into a concoction of thick coconut milk broth sweetened with Javanese palm sugar and cinnamon, adding a *pandan* leaf or two for aroma. It was called *Kolak*. Sometimes we added thickly sliced bananas or plantains in, along with the *ketela* or cassava.

Stephen's side dish of sweet potato made me think of your Mom of course, as well as the rest of our family. True to my sentimental nature, I played the music of the Carpenters during our meal, which usually reminded me of my sister Edna as they were once one of her favorite bands. But that night it made me think of your Mom, my dear sister Wewe and the way things used to be: '*Yesterday Once More*'[6]

---

6. Songwriters: John Bettis / Richard Lynn Carpenter. Yesterday Once More lyrics © Universal Music Publishing Group

When I was young I'd listen to the radio,
Waitin' for my favorite songs
When they played I'd sing along, it made me smile,
Those were such happy times and not so long ago
How I wondered where they'd gone
But they're back again just like a long lost friend
All the songs I loved so well

Stephen and I sang along and as I stared at the flowers reflected on the wine and water glasses by the light of the candles, a shadow came over me and tears streamed downed my cheeks.

"It never occurred to me that I would never ever see her again in my lifetime," I sobbed.

This awareness hits me periodically, leaving a deep residue of sadness, and it is usually triggered by something simple, such as that song performed by the Carpenters. Almost 14 years have gone by already, but I am still missing and mourning for the kindest, sweetest person I have ever had in my life. The feelings those lyrics induce always hit me at the core.

Sadness often turns into anger, and I find it hard to accept that the one person I have ever known in my life without a drop of hate in her soul was snatched away from her loved ones, especially her kids—you, Zef and Grace—and me, even though I know we are only three souls out of so many whose hearts and lives were left with a gaping hole.

* * *

Michele is my cousin, and he was born in our rental home in 1976, which practically made him my younger brother. Actually his mom is my cousin, the daughter of my aunt from my Mom's side, so I guess he's what you would call a 'first cousin once-removed'. In my family we don't differentiate. I called her 'Ci' Siong, meaning, elder-sister-Siong. Her father is 'Ko' Irwan, or older-brother-Irwan was my cousin's husband. Both lived with us at my father's invitation. They became the architects of our future mansion and ranch.

Michele was the cutest, sweetest little boy and everyone paid a lot of attention to him, as he was the latest addition to our family. His father, Irwan was a harsh, hard man who not only yelled, but also hit his son as a toddler. When he was in foul mood, everyone was scared of him: his wife, his son, the baby sitters and maids, and me. I was not only scared watching him, I was also a victim of his so-called 'machismo' and perceived it to be manliness. He participated actively in calling me unkind names and bullying me, just like the mean bullies at school. Mind you, he was in his late 20's or early 30's. In his mind, my elder brother David was the good boy. My mean and bullying brother was a boy after his own heart.

The two of them used to gang up on me, making me feel so small, smaller and more frightened than I should ever have felt in my own home. That was my memory of how he was, anyway. I never felt comfortable with him around the house. His wife, my cousin, always lived on the edge—I could clearly see her fear, even as a child. She was sweet and kind, and one of my parents' favorite nieces. I always felt sorry for her. I remember Irwan scolded Michele harshly at such a young age, and used corporal punishment on him. Michele would cry and cry and there was nothing his Mom could do as his father would not let her comfort him. I don't know what the story was behind this, but I had a feeling that if she tried, it would be her that her husband would be after with a stick.

Your Mom, however, had a way of saving Michele from the wrath of his father. Wewe would play dumb. Trust me, you, she wasn't dumb, she was anything but dumb, and she had a mission. She simply talked to Michele in such a soothing way, to a point that he stopped crying, and she would just swoop him up and walk away with him, and get him as far away as possible from his father's bad mood. Her presence simply calmed everyone involved; I figured that just her being there was enough to make the evil spirits within the human feel so scared, knowing there was an angel among them. She would slip out of the house with Michele and take him to the back or front yard to continue to play, and I would join them.

While Michele had his own nanny, it was your Mom who sheltered him whenever she could. He was her next 'baby' after me. Later on she continued to visit him when he and his family moved back to Jakarta. Recently I asked Michele what he remembered about my sister and while he could not specifically remember a lot of things from his childhood, he told me how she was always nice and warm to him and was never mad at him. How telling, I thought. I too, used to bury the bad memories from my childhood until later in my life. He remembered the gifts she would later gave him as a child, though.

His younger sister Annette told me her memory of your Mom was her soft voice and how loving and helpful she was as a person. I know that her memories of your Mom are identical to so many people who knew her, either within our family, relatives or mutual connections, who I find again and again have nothing but sweet memories to tell of your Mom.

Recently, my other second cousin William visited us from Vancouver, Canada, where he has made his home for over a decade. He is Michel and Annette's cousin, so technically, he is also your second cousin I believe, as he is your Mom's cousin, Lely's son? The last time I saw him was in the early '90s. This was the first time William met my husband, your uncle Stephen and I since he grew up. It was also the first time he came to share a meal with us at the table where I was having the *ketela* conversation. We started talking about our family and the past, and inevitably we reminisced about your Mom.

William is now 34. When your Mother passed away he was already in Canada. To the best of his memory, the last time he saw your Mom was when he was around fifteen. He told us how nice and kind she was and how he remembered her sweet smile and the glasses she was wearing and yes, of course, her trademark 'bobbed' hairstyle.

That smile I mentioned, it was the kindest smile, one

that revealed her soul and her heart. They say that the eyes are like a window to the human soul. Well, for your Mom, besides the intensity of her eyes, it was also her smile that did the magic. It is a smile that instantly made you feel loved—such a sincere smile, with absolutely no hidden agenda or pretense. For me that smile was an oasis which equated to safety and peace, especially during my childhood. I have hinted earlier that to be away from home with your Mom was for me always a wonderful escape from our family who were full of drama, fights and screams.

In spite of this internal turmoil our family was well regarded and respected in town. My father, who came from a very poor family, had managed to work hard to earn his wealth and was one of the wealthiest persons in our province. Over a period of time, our family had earned a reputation for wealth, style and success. People used to come to see what the fuss was all about—not only invited by our parents—sometimes they would invite themselves to the property, and they liked to copy some of the elements of the architecture. In spite of the large size, (it covered over 1.5 hectares of land), our entire estate was fenced with metal and concrete fences more than two meters high.

As I mentioned before, the house itself was designed by our architect cousins, Michel and Annettes's parents, but they modeled it after my father's cousin's luxurious house. He had one of the first Mercedes dealerships in the country. The house was shaped like a Q with an open courtyard in the middle and a koi fishpond, with its own man-made waterfall.

From the gate to the entry of the house was quite a distance. A maid had to run to open the gate and it would take her a few minutes to get there. To the left of the entrance there were cages of imported dogs. It is sad, I now know, for animals to be kept caged like this, but my father lined the entryway into the house with imported boxers in caged kennels.

Our garden was like the grounds of a hotel—the manicured landscape had been commissioned by my father to a noted designer who had also done my father's cousin's garden in Jakarta. Imported grass was laid in perfect lawns out of which mini man-made hills of green emerged. A prized red palm tree was the centerpiece, just next to the entrance veranda. Between the front yard and the gate, were a row of fishponds that housed carp, locally known as *gurame,* and other fresh-water fish that were not only for our visual enjoyment and relaxation, but also for our consumption in elaborate meals prepared by our cooks. On one side, my father decided to build a casual and humble hut over the pond, just like those found in the countryside and on the rice *padi* fields all over Indonesia.

Instead of being a simple structure as he had imagined, it was overly designed by the architects—not just structurally, but also in style. By the time it was completed it was complete with screened windows finely painted with fancy paints, a built in table and day beds, and had a roof to match our mansion. One could not blame the architects; our father always wanted the best of the best. Structure-wise, I believe it would withstand a strong hurricane or earthquake. The same crew who had built the house was summoned back from Jakarta and the best local craftsmen employed, including our previously noted ethnic Chinese 'uncle' who was a carpenter.

This garden pagoda or 'balé', became our favorite place for various leisurely activities typical of a wealthy family at that time. We often had Sunday brunch there after church, followed by an afternoon nap and tea, all served by our live-in maids, cooks and house-boys. It was perfect for our extra-curricular academic activities as well. Our friends from the same socio-economic background would come over after school and we had various private tutors come in who taught us mathematics or English, or other subjects deemed necessary for us to excel in at school.

The dreadful irony of it all for me was that there was one extra, unplanned 'activity' that I, and no one else that I am aware of, experienced in this beautiful place. I was molested there. Not just by one person, but by several different people. This structure was in the garden, far enough away from the main house to be quite private, and I had no idea as a child why I was lured there by one specific gardener.

It first happened when my parents were away. I loved company and attention, and the gardener would pretend he was working late, so he could lure me to walk with him at night through the garden, and then he would entice me into the dark balé. I would be afraid, and cling to him, and he would stroke me and hold me tight, and then do what I now realize was a violent criminal act. As a child, I thought at first that he was being sweet and nice and once it had happened I knew whatever he did to me was a secret I should never tell anyone.

It was not until I was already in my teens, long after the damage had ben done by him, and perpetrated by other offenders, that I knew I had been abused. Sadly for me, this place was not the first, nor the only place where I was molested. It would happen again, not only at home, but also at school and church. As you read these letters, you will learn more about my unfortunate childhood. Not a single person then or now would suspect any of it happened to me.

Back to our mansion and its beautiful garden—the house was surrounded by five layered beds of roses, all of different varieties, many of them imported. My father hired a rose specialist from Bandung, a cool climate town in Indonesia known for its gardens and horticultural beauty. My mother loved all kinds of flowers and exotic plants, she still does. This garden was created as an expression of love from my father to my mother. It was no secret that my parents were in love. To this day they still are like two lovebirds, renowned for their loyalty and love for each other. My father was always very open about showing his affection towards her in public, which is quite unusual in Indonesia.

As a child I was so in love with the roses, with all their different shapes and varieties, colors and sizes, but I was especially mesmerized by the intoxicating fragrances. I would poke my nose from rose to rose to smell them, compare them and I absolutely adored their individual fragrances and personalities. I would often be found assisting my mother cutting her roses for the house—or better yet, for Sunday service at church. Every week on Saturday afternoon, after sundown so it would be cooler, or early on Sunday morning, my Mom would prepare floral arrangements for the altar, showcasing her roses every week. We usually made two matching arrangements for the altar or one big centerpiece.

Later when my Mom travelled or was away, the task fell on to my older sister Edna or my favorite cousin who lived with us, Ci Tian, we called her. I always loved assisting them both with this task. I was so proud when they let me do it my own way—the 'sissy-ness' in me came in handy at last— and I was in heaven. Decades later, much later, I became the florist for celebrities, and that was my launch pad as an interior designer. I still blush whenever people refer to me as a celebrity designer.

Back in those days, when I first became obsessed with making flower arrangements, I had already started to mix different types of flowers together. As well as the rose beds surrounding our mansion, there was a special part of our land dedicated to orchids. I loved the cattleyas, the dendrobiums and the cymbidiums; they were all so colorful and full of fragrance. From our dining room glass window, even though it was tinted to keep our house cool, and the house was air conditioned, we could see a patch of gladioli, and further down in the distance the vegetable gardens, full of green beans, peanuts, tomatoes, eggplants and other local vegetables.

The land was also surrounded by various trees and plants which produced fruits: star-fruit or *belimbing*, local cherries, guavas, jackfruit, breadfruit, pineapples and avocados as well as other rare varieties, so many that I didn't even know the names of them all. I recall one particular fruit called *kedongdong*. It was a much smaller size, but of similar shape to mango only rounder in shape, with a pit that looked like a giant spider. The quickest and dirtiest way of enjoying this one fruit would be to crack it open by putting it in between the door and the doorjamb, then pulling the door back against it; once it was cracked, we would devour it, puckering our lips as it was so sour but refreshing. We enjoyed eating it with salt and spicy hot chili, or sometimes our maids or my sister Edna would pickle it.

Our estate was so lush, filled with a luxuriant mixture of flowers, vegetable gardens, trees and exotic plants, including a variety of grasses, some as tall as the adults and as sharp as razors. There was even a giant bamboo. Later in life I learned the English word 'verdant', and every time I read or hear that word it makes me think of our estate in Tanjung Karang, under the Palapa Hills.

My father has always been a bit of a bird freak. He loves birds. I remember his collection of birds in our rental home in Teluk Betung before we moved to our mansion in what we liked to call 'our ranch'. There we had many birds that he kept in traditional birdcages made out of wood, bamboo or metal. Some were simple cages, others more elaborate, and there were even a few that looked like little houses, delicately hand-painted in the Chinoiserie style. They were charming!

He had some exotic birds in his collection and it included Mynah starlings, pheasants, colorful parrots—one in particular was limping and could not fly. There was one particularly gentle creature my friends and I liked to feed with a ripe fat plantain on a stick, and a loyal cockatoo that lived indoors, just above our laundry. The word cockatoo in Indonesian is *Kakatua*, which is an abbreviation of 'elder brother'. This little elder brother was sweet and cute, with soft white feathers and a yellow Elvis-style hairdo. Sadly, he was chained to a frame; no walls blocked his view, but he was limited in his movement to a decorative little swing that essentially moved just a few centimeters in either direction. In some ways he was free, as he was in the open air, but he could only move from one side to the other, or dangle from his chain like a circus performer. No one knew how old he was. Some cockatoos live up to one hundred and fifty years old, I was told. This cockatoo was everyone's favorite, but he loved my Dad and Mom most. He would be freed from his tiny chain to climb over their shoulders as he was petted. He spoke a few words like 'hello' and his own name, 'Kakatua', which he would say in such an affected way.

"Kakaaaa tuuuuuuuAAAAAA" he would shriek.

Later on, during a dark period of my childhood, this bird was one sweet elder brother to me. Forever ruffling his beautiful wings, he would keep me company while your Mom was away. I would say we had anything up to thirty birds altogether, plus a good ten to fifteen roosters at that time. Our father knew each one of those birds personally, too. He would feed them, pet them and play with them, and he even chatted with them. It always cracked me up to see him talking to birds as if they were humans. There was also one member of his staff who took care of his pet birds daily. If one of his birds escaped or died my father would be in a foul mood, and everyone at home would tiptoe around him. His sadness and anger would be expressed in a booming voice that made us all scared of him. If a bird died or escaped its cage the person in charge, Abang Sabri, and his brother who helped him, would be so crushed and so apologetic. It was almost as bad as if someone in the family had passed away.

My brother David was the exact opposite of me. He was wild and rambunctious and naughty, the exact masculine behavior expected in a boy. He took after my dad in the hobbies he loved as well, and already had his own collection of doves, pigeons, cocks and he loved *Betta*, Siamese fighting fish. His obsession with the latter drove us crazy. He kept fish in jars under the beds all over the house; at times they would stink, especially when some of the fish died and were undetected for a while as he was often distracted by something else. Male *Betta* fish are very aggressive, and attack each other if left in the same tank for a while.

It wasn't just the *Betta* fish he competed with, he also liked to participate in the neighborhood cockfights, and he would gamble on winning. I used to be so disgusted by the cockfights. I just could never understood what he called fun, and I felt sorry for the beautiful birds when they squirted blood or were mangled in a fight. I still don't understand. Sometimes the birds died in a public fight and that was the reason people cheered, as when one died another one won. It actually made them happy. I almost always identified with the loser, probably because I was the biggest sissy of them all, always being publicly humiliated and abused and shamed.

When David participated in the *Betta* fish fights the colors of his fish brightened, and they puffed themselves up, growing bigger when they were provoked, even if they were in separate clear jars, or if one was placed in a pool of *Betta* in its own jar. The boys in the neighborhood would challenge each other using their best fishes and roosters as proxies. I could not stand these boys or my brother. I thought they were cruel, heartless cowards. The doves and pigeons were the only pets of my brother that I deemed as tolerable, as they were not fighters, and I thought they were pretty. Instead of fighting them, he would pet them or mate them. He trained them to 'release to come home'. I found their homing instinct sweet and cute, but their excrement was still nasty, and they dropped it all over the backyard and roofs.

Once he had made his fortune my father took this hobby to a whole new level. Basically he went out of control. It was like his hobbies had exploded proportionately with his means, filling our ranch and mansion and taking up all his attention. He spent all his money, on doing exactly as he wished, like a child in a candy store—or should I say, in a candy factory—that sounds more appropriate.

Lets start with his bird kingdom. Next to my parents'

master suite, on the side facing the back yard, there was a lineup of individual, custom-made cages on metal stands, all their roofs designed to match our mansion's roof, in various sizes. All of them were perched on a wide pad of bricks that had been laid by experts—a platform almost as big as a normal house in size, just for the birds. In this area, our old birds resided—apparently they too now had their own retirement mansion. Next to this area, however, my father not only indulged his own hobby, but that of my brother too. He built a large aviary, designed by our cousins, the architects of the main house, the ones who were responsible for it being bigger than most other houses in our neighborhood.

I can't exactly remember how many birds or the types of birds that this aviary housed. Not only was it extra large, it was about as high as a two storey building. What I remember most about it is that it had its own pond, a little forest and cute individual family bird's houses, all arranged in miniature bird neighborhoods. There was a pigeon neighborhood, a parakeet neighborhood, and even one special area for the bigger birds. My brother practically lived there the first year we moved to this ranch. He was so proud of having his own aviary that he invited his friends to join him for hours inside the aviary. From my point of view, I thought they looked like chimpanzees in a zoo. David also had his own staff to help him care for his bird zoo; he was so privileged that he only played with his pets but did not do anything to take care of the aviary.

Luckily my 'elder brother' Cockatoo now lived inside

the courtyard of our mansion, directly in front of my parents' suite. His status had also been elevated. Now he ruled the roost and the courtyard. My dad also kept some of his favorite roosters and birds in in the courtyard too. Birdcages were lined up all the way along the outside walls of our family room and the dining room.

The birds were only the beginning of my father's collection. Next came the chickens, the turkeys and a number of other random creatures. As the number of roosters and hens grew, to be honest, I had no idea why suddenly my Mom and Dad started ordering hundreds of laying hens, and our ranch suddenly turned into an egg farm. I think it was their over-actively entrepreneurial minds wanting to be productive. We started with a few hundred hens but ended up having more than 5000 chickens in the following year or two. Two areas in the ranch became dedicated to egg farming, each one assigned to a member of staff who doubled as our gardener, and each of them eventually had their own assistants to help with the work. One of the rooms in the staff wing was converted into an egg storage room, where thousands of eggs were stored, cleaned and sorted by my Mom and her staff.

At first I enjoyed assisting and roaming around the chicken farm area of the ranch, but then a few awful things happened to me there. A certain damage was inflicted upon me by the two lead farmers, our original gardeners, and these were things that should never happen to any child or person. This part of the property always brought back bitter memories to me.

I would have thought the chickens were a big enough addition to the ranch—then for some reasons unbeknown to me, my parents purchased some turkeys as pets. I was not sure if they intended to farm them or eat them, but either way, that intention soon evaporated after an unfortunate incident took place. The way I remember it, we had about half a dozen 'starter' turkeys. They were caged in a large area next to the orchid garden with wire fences, and they seemed to have enough space to roam around fairly freely. This was the space next to the children's rooms. Now, what I haven't mentioned yet was the large number of dogs we also had in the house.

Before I tell you how many dogs we used to have, let me tell you about how the dogs were divided into three castes in our household. First there were the dogs of 'royal lineage', that lived indoors with us within the courtyard area and veranda of the house. This area was where the formal living room, the master suite, the bedrooms, the family room, the dining room, the kitchen and the staff wing were located. Essentially it was the inner part of the large Q-shaped building. These dogs were so honored as they were imported purebreds from the western world, and they came with a high price tag that was comparable to designer leather bags. They even had their own passports, birth certificates and imported dog food that looked like small dried meatballs and was purchased especially for them.

Lord knows how much it cost to feed them, but I am sure it cost more than our human food, especially in those days. The 'royal family' consisted of a large German shepherd and six or seven mini poodles. Later, Astor, our beloved German shepherd became the stud in our town to breed other pups with another 'good family' who owned a German shepherd bitch. She turned out to be a bitch in its true sense, while her owner was a bitch in another sense. Out of the eight or nine pups, we were only given the runt, who we called Asta after a famous dog character of a popular children's comic in Indonesia. This was the foundation of our family of royal pups. Next came the imported guard dogs, I called them the fancy palace guard. Sadly they were kept in cages and rarely taken out. Their cages faced the gate, between our front veranda and the overly designed balé I told you about, over the fishpond, so it must have been torment for them to see everyone passing by.

This pair of boxer siblings, Aaron and Alfina, barked a lot, but they were sweet—until they went crazy from being perpetually caged. I am sure any person or animal caged day in and day out would go crazy. We were totally ignorant about these things, and now as an adult, looking back, it makes me sad to think of them and their miserable life as prisoners in our vast estate. They could have roamed around and had a wonderful time, instead their lives were a true nightmare. The two of them would bark incessantly. I now believe they probably went mad. Please note these imported royal dogs were named with all the regal, western style names of their pedigree.

The last and most lowly group of our dog kingdom consisted of the Indonesian mutts who, ironically, in my opinion, had the royal lives. Anything from around twelve to sixteen mutts roamed around the property freely at any time, spending their time outdoors. If I look back at my childhood, we probably had a grand total of anything from twenty to thirty dogs at any given point of time.

Unlike the 'royal' dog family, the native dogs were fed rice, bones and other leftovers from the meals cooked for us by our maids. When they cooked the dog food all mixed up in one giant pot, the smell would travel the property. I always detested that smell and I could gag just thinking about it. While I could not keep track of each dog, or their names, we had a maid who was in charge of them and who fed them daily—Sutrisni was her name. Sutrisni knew every single dog's name. These dogs roaming around our gated property within the high concrete fence had two purposes in life. First was to scare away any potential robbers and burglars, and second to scare away the snakes. I will have more stories to tell you later on both of these subjects, but I haven't yet told you about the incident involving the mutts.

One afternoon I was in the car driven by our driver Abang, or 'bang Kasan, which means Bro Kasan, in modern slang. As usual, we stopped at the gate to ring the bell, as the horn was not always loud enough for the maid to hear. I would sit next to him up front and the live-in gardener's children would sit in the back of the van or pick-up, truck or car—yes, while our car collection was not as many as our dogs, we had plenty of them too. One of the children would ring the bell and we would sit and wait for someone to open the gates. On this particular afternoon, as soon as Nus, one of the gardener's sons got out to ring the bell, he was distracted by a commotion inside the gate. We had no idea what it was until we drove on towards the house.

There, on the front veranda, I saw my cousin, who was wearing her doctor's coat, surrounded by Dad, Mom and a few of the other staff. She had blood all over her white coat. My heart pounded, and the car had barely stopped before I jumped out, everyone following suit. Since my Mom and Dad looked fine, I knew it had to be someone else who was hurt, and I thought it must be one of our staff. However, it turned out that it was two of the turkeys. Our dogs had mauled both of them, and my cousin who was a medical doctor had been called instantly to put her skills to treating their wounds, acting as a vet. She had just finished performing surgery and suturing two turkeys.

As a child and even now as an adult, I have always been squeamish about blood, so I simply watched from afar, but I could tell one of the turkeys neck was barely still attached to the body, although it was still alive. The other one seemed to be in better shape, as the dog had only bitten it in the stomach. We had no idea how many dogs had ganged up on the turkeys. Perhaps they were aiming to have an Indonesian 'thanksgiving' turkey dinner that afternoon. Later that day the poor turkey with the mangled neck died as expected and the other one survived. Needless to say, their cage had to be re-enforced, and once the wire was doubled we had no more incidents, but the turkeys never multiplied, in fact they slowly dwindled in numbers as they died of natural causes. I always wondered if the bloody murder attempt had not taken place, whether my parents would have purchased more turkeys and turned our ranch partly into a turkey farm. If I am not mistaken, it wasn't till much later that my parents thought they would like to have peacocks on the ranch but luckily they refrained. I doubt if it would have been a good idea.

There was another incident that I would never forget which involved the outdoor mutts. Don't forget, there was an entire pack of them, maybe around twelve dogs by then. On that terrible day, Sutrisni, the maid who was in charge of feeding them daily, must have fed them late. I only heard about it from the other staff and my parents, as I was away when it happened, thankfully. Apparently when she went to the back yard between our house and the chicken farm to feed them, they jumped up and tried to get to the giant pot before she could portion the food out individually for the pack. One thing led to another while they were fighting to grab the food, and she tried to break them apart. Instantly, they turned on her and attacked her. She was badly bitten, and once again my cousin had to perform a medical emergency procedure at home. This time she had to clean and stitch something like twenty-six wounds.

I could hardly believe how brave she was, as my family told me that while she was mending, she continued to take care of the dogs, never once showing any fear of them. She healed without complication but the scars remained. Both of these incidents happened while your Mom was away in Jakarta studying to be a nurse, or perhaps she was already a nurse by then, working in a prominent hospital, I forget which. We would later tell her about these incidents and she would say the sweetest things about the turkey, making jokes about the funny noise they made, and their personalities, and I remember she made a point of talking about Sutrisni's bravery.

One more animal in the ranch stood out in my childhood: a fawn that was brought home one day. We named her *Manis*, Indonesian for sweet. Manis was given to my parents by my future brother-in-law's parents. I think it was a gift from them for my parents, as they knew about my father's passion for keeping wild animals as pets. They were another wealthy and prominent family who shared the same Chinese last name as ours—Tan. Their son later married my sister, your aunty Edna. Manis was assigned a lot of land all to herself by the fishpond with the balé, and another light fence was added to keep her in that area.

Don't worry—none of the dogs ever attacked her. I had a feeling the dogs were scared of her and her hooves. I'm not sure how it works in the animal hierarchy but they left her alone, possibly because she grew bigger and taller than any of them. At first our Mom and I used to feed her with a bottle of milk, as the poor thing must have been quite young when she was separated from her Mom. That makes me think of you both! Little Manis would suck that bottle of milk with such a loud suction sound, it made me laugh—it sounded like a combo of 'nom nom' and 'chomp chomp'. We could only feed her occasionally, as she had to be fed often, and the staff, my Mom, your Mom, my cousin and I all took turns until she was old enough to eat fruit and veggies. As she grew older and more independent she could forage around the pond area on her own. Manis was a sweet creature who would greet me when I came back from school as she was usually close to the gate. She would nuzzle me with her nose, lowering her head towards me so I could pet her.

I can still hear how your Mom would call her.

"Manis....Manis....Manis...."

Then we would both stroke her. Her coat was not as soft as you would think in some areas, but she was a most gentle soul. She was also popular with the kids of our gardener who lived on the ranch with us, as they would often come and pet her as well. My friends who came to play with me or attended our study sessions in the building over the pond all adored her, and she was never short of attention from the children about the place. Manis was also the creature who witnessed me being molested, at least I knew she was by my side, as we were just separated by the structural wall of the balé. During that unthinkable moment, she made an unusual noise and kept on bumping the wall and door which now made me realize, it was as if she was trying get someone's attention to save me—at least I'd like to think so. At least someone knew about the sad part of my life at that time. Manis was the only one who knew.

Manis lived for a long time and when I was living in the U.S. during the late '80s—or was it early '90s? I was heartbroken to hear that she had died. It felt like losing a dear sibling. I wish I could have comforted her during her last days too. I don't know the details, but I imagined she died of old age, and I hope she was not injured or hurt nor sick. I also hope it was a quick and painless death.

Manis was a constant fixture in my life, not only during her lifetime but after she died. She was always at the back of my mind, literally or symbolically. Every time I saw a fawn or a young deer, I always thought of her. Shortly after your Mom passed away, every time I saw a fawn or a deer, it instantly made me think of your Mom. In fact, that day your Mom passed away, I was in California. I don't remember much after we heard the news. While I could not remember the minute-by-minute details of what we did, as I was most probably overwhelmed and mourning, I remember that day it was rainy and dreary. For some reason, Uncle Stephen had to drive me somewhere. In the depths of my sadness, on the freeway, sitting on the passenger side, I saw a young deer staring at me, as we slowed down in the rain. Just like that, I thought it was your Mom, saying her last goodbye to us.

After that day, every time I saw a deer or any animal, I always associated it with your Mom's day of passing and I'd like to believe it was her soul sending a signal to let me know she was around, somewhere out there. Or may be it was Manis and her soul letting me know that she was with your Mom? Either way, it always gives me comfort when I see wild animals showing up at sunrise or sunset in Bali or in Hawaii or in my hometown.

I'd like to believe this link I still have with your Mom is true, yet in the back of my mind, I still have no real clue as to where your Mom's spirit is and it makes me feel quite unsettled as I write to you.

There is one last important animal in my life that I considered to be both a pet and family member. I called him Kas and I'd like to share him with you. Kas was more than a dog to me. An Indonesian mutt, with a grubby blond coat, he was handed on to our family by a Dutch missionary family when I was a toddler. From then on, for as long as I could remember, Kas became my companion. He let me pet him and lean on him, both literally and figuratively speaking. I played with him and talked to him all the time. Yes, as a child, I talked to him. He was the only dog and pet we had in our rental house where I was born. His coat was blondish, rather on the dirty side, and he had a sweet doe-eyed face. His favorite spot was under the table next to our dining room, facing the open garage and badminton court. This is where he liked to sit, guarding us, well at least I knew he was guarding me and guarding the house. I often sat there and played with him, and I very often shared my naps with him, while waiting for my sister to come home.

Remember that story about my daily routine of greeting my sister when she returned from school? Kas would be there with us and your Mom would pet him along with me as he jumped up and down for affection and begging for some of my peanuts. I would let him have one every once in a while, as there were not many to share.

Kas was not only a dear friend he was also my protector, our protector. Once in a blue moon he would slip out of our gated house and find me playing with the neighborhood girls down by the dirty creek. It always felt like he had come to fetch me home or to simply let me know he was there, not far away. Every now and then the boys would tease me for playing with the girls, starting with the usual name callings, and after a while a few of them would be aggressive enough to push me around. That's when Kas would start to bark at them, and sometimes he would even attack the bullies. Then it became a spectacle for the neighborhood, as the other dogs would gang up on him in return. Kas might have been sweet but he was the bravest, strongest dog when it came to fighting back—he was not afraid, no matter how many were set against him. Even up to six dogs, or ten dogs were to attack him all at once. He would fight them off, including that mean beast, the alpha male stud of the neighborhood.

While most of the time he would win, unharmed, I remember a few occasions when he got mauled and bleeding, but he always recovered with scars that became a permanent mark of his bravery and chivalry. These dog attacks on my best friend happened several times a year over a period of seven years, and it always made me sad to see him in pain. I would cry and keep him company, so would your Mom. The three of us would just sit together under the star-fruit tree on a platform, or we would play around him on the unpaved ground of our front yard. Your Mom would make me dolls or soapy water for bubbles or feed me lunch as I was running around being a hyperactive kid as usual. Or we would all lie down together, contentedly. Those were the days when we had nothing to worry about, and now they give me something to fondly look back upon.

There was one incident where I thought we would lose Kas. One day he escaped out the gate when we let the driver and car in. He didn't come home for a while and a neighbor told us he had been shot by someone and was bleeding at the end of our street. Wewe dropped everything and ran along with the help of our driver to find him and they brought him home looking like something out of a bloody killing scene from a movie. Kas was bleeding in a few spots. I was ushered away by my Mom, but I kept on crying, calling for Kas, and finally cried myself to sleep.

Later when I woke up, I found him under the small table by the dining room, looking absolutely dejected, with two small puddles of blood still oozing from his underbelly. I am not sure what they did to him, if they took him to the only vet in town or the vet came to us, as she was our family friend. For the next week or two, I would stay with him every moment I could, day in and day out with your Mom, feeding him and stroking him, but he was so weak it felt like a miracle when he recovered. Kas was my Teddy bear, only better, as he woofed sweetly to me; he was everything to me at that time.

Although that incident had a happy ending, I wish I could tell you that Kas continued to live happily ever after like animals do in a Disney movie. When we moved to our fancy ranch and big mansion, obviously we brought Kas along with us to the new house. I was not yet an adult, so I protested when Kas was left outside with the other mutts, instead of being allowed to stay inside with the poodles and German Shepherd. I am not sure if it was a discriminatory action from my Dad's side, or for the safety of Kas.

Clearly, Kas had to adjust to becoming just one of the many dogs and pets we had at the new place, and was no longer our only dog, as he used to be in our rental home. Not long after we moved in, I think a few weeks or less, Kas left us there, slipping through the gate, and he never came home. We drove and drove, looking everywhere for him, me crying day in and day out, devastated as only a child can be at the loss of a pet. I didn't eat much, refused to go out, and I couldn't sleep, thinking and imagining Kas being out there all alone or worse yet, being attacked by other dogs or humans. I think the entire family was saddened by the loss of Kas.

This was my first big loss as a child, and it felt like losing my best friend, after all I considered Kas to be a family member. There was no closure then, and as often is the case with pets, no closure until today. For years after we lost him, every time I was out in the car I kept an eye on every dog I saw and there were a few times I thought I saw him, only to be disappointed.

Years later we heard from our old neighbors at the rental house, which was six kilometers away from our ranch, about our beloved Kas. Keep in mind, this was back in the '70s—in those days not every household had a phone or TV, and cell phones, computers and internet had not entered into our lives yet. News traveled by gossip or through visits to the wet market or during a holiday visit. Apparently, according to some of our old neighbors, Kas used to hover around our old house and at times he would just sit or lie down by the gate, as if he was waiting for us. The thought of him doing this, being so loyal and missing his old home broke my heart and my family's hearts too. Your Mom and I cried when we heard this story, and we all regretted not looking for him there. We felt sorry for not making him feel more at home at our new place. He must have thought we had forgotten about him. We felt so sad for not making him feel special the way he did for us.

Decades later, I would visit our home and I found a black and white picture of him in an old photo album in my parents' room. I started to sob, remembering how much I missed Kas all that time ago, as if it was yesterday. Even today, the thought of him, his sweet face and the feel of his coat still bring tears. If only I could imagine he was now with your Mom, keeping her company, and protecting her, wherever she is, then perhaps I could feel a little bit happier.

~ *tujuh* ~

"The staff and the village..."

Dearest Grace and Zefanya,

I want to tell you about some of the wonderful people who surrounded your mother and I in my early years. There is a common saying that *"it takes a village to raise a child"* and we were no exception. For the first seven years of my life, the time when we lived in our rental house, we had a number of female staff: Puji, Penny, Sami, and later other *'mbak-mbak'* we considered to be big sisters, who were our maids and housekeepers, and also doubled as cooks or nannies. While everyone multitasked to help my parents maintain our house, it was fairly obvious who was better at performing certain tasks. Puji was the main cook and nanny and the siblings Penny and Sami both cleaned, but Sami floated between 'departments'. The house was not terribly big but it had a large room that housed all the female staff.

It was in this room that my sister Wewe slept when she first came to stay with us in the early years. This was the room that I always felt most comfortable in. It was a cozy room with large beds that sported French-style mattresses, stuffed with kapok. Each member of staff had their own bed, complete with a mosquito net that draped down over it like a tent.

The room was lit with the old fashioned and warm low-watt light bulbs, different to the modern and glaring fluorescent light bulbs in other rooms of the house. Candles were always available and ready to light, as power outages were a weekly occurrence in our town in the seventies. When the power cuts happened, we never knew how long they would last. It could be anything from mere minutes to whole days and no information was available.

In the middle of the room was a cluster of furniture: a large table, several armoires and dressers. The room had two doors, one to enter from the interior side of the house, past our 'elder brother' the white *Kakatua*, then there was an exit door towards a communal bathroom and restroom for the staff, and an outdoor area where they did our laundry by hand on wooden washboards. In this area, we also had a few pet turtles, a number of my father's birds in individual cages, as well as some beds of flowers and other tropical plants.

On a sunny day, Wewe and I would hang out here, chatting with Penny or Sami, and keeping them company while they did the laundry. Sometimes our Grandma would come out with her lunch and she always brought us all treats. This area was also accessible from the dining room and the kitchen, so it was like a little hub, a very convenient area where people liked to congregate. The staff room, dining room and kitchen were all in the same row. There were a few water storage tubs that we call *bak* in Indonesian. They were part of a water cistern system; the tubs held clean water for bathing and laundry. There was no shower. Each bathroom had an open-topped water tub from which you scooped up the water in a small pail and poured it over yourself. I loved to take my shower in the laundry area and when no one was looking I would jump right into the water tub, which was the size of a large stove or even bigger. Once they found out I had done that, they had to empty it out and replace the water before anyone could use it again. I loved to treat it as my personal tub, and my sister used to let me have fun in it, while the maids would chase me away—it created more work for them, as my dirty bath-water could no longer be used for other washing, especially after I had jumped into it dirty feet and all. Yes, I could be a brat.

I spent a lot of time in this area of the house. Besides being close to my sister Wewe and the maids, I felt safe and protected there, as my evil brother David usually played elsewhere with his friends, in other parts of the house, doing their 'manly' things. It was almost as if my survival instinct told me to stay away from him and his friends, who I considered to be beasts that would hunt, humiliate and torture me. In fairness, some of his friends were actually quite kind to me, but David was the alpha male in the group, and a mean one.

It was also in the maids' quarters that I observed, listened to and learned from the female members of the family. My grandma, my mom, my two sisters, my cousin and the maids constantly gathered in this part of the house, moving between the kitchen, the outdoor laundry area and the backyard while they were cooking, preparing for church gatherings or parties or simply doing their daily chores. The place was always buzzing with activities such as peeling huge piles of shallots, cleaning or rinsing the rice or pounding some type of grain with a large mortar and pestle to make flour, or wrapping hundreds of sweet treats in banana leaves for special occasions. I watched, or tried to help them in my child-like way. More accurately, I suppose, I distracted them, but whatever it was they were doing, I always felt welcomed and included, and I was never harmed. This was where the women in my life started to nurture me, especially your Mom, and these women were responsible for my informal education.

The stories that I listened to here were kind words of familial advice, interspersed with snippets of gossip that they shared as they worked. I listened attentively, and received my 'education', whether or not it was intended for me.

This was also where I learned to rinse our staple rice before cooking, again and again until the water was clear, to make sure that no small grains of sand, tiny pebbles, or unhusked rice remained in it before cooking. I learned to fold a banana-leaf plate shaped like a half boat and secure it by stitching it with a single sliver of bamboo. I loved making puddings, with sweet creamy sauce, and learned how to grate and squeeze the milk from the white flesh of a coconut—being ever so careful not to scrape my fingers on the crude metal grater.

It was here that I learned to make my first instant noodles with tomato, cracking an egg directly into it. I enjoyed eating it with the local chili sauce we called *Sambal Lampung*—a garlic-flavored, bottled sauce made from natural ingredients—so popular it was sought after by Indonesians from all over the country. I often watched the ironing being done, and learned how to iron simple items like napkins and table cloths or the one I still can't do well—long-sleeved shirts. As I listened to the conversations there I also learned about female monthly periods, sanitary napkins, and heard stories both happy and heartbreaking about childbirth and I first learned about the meaning of death, coffins and funerals.

Your Mom and I at this time were virtually attached at the hip; wherever she was, there I was too. She would constantly hold my hand, hug me and carry me around. Our Mom would ask her if she was tired holding and carrying me.

"Isn't he too heavy for you? It's fine to put him down."

But she always refused: "No Tante, it's fine," as she stroked and kissed me on my cheeks or hair. This was still during the early period where she still called my Mom Auntie and my Dad Uncle.

Speaking of hair, she was the only one who could stand the disgusting odor of my hair. I was notorious for refusing to wash my hair, or let anyone else do it. To say I hated my hair being washed was an understatement. Indonesia, being a country directly under the equator, is humid and hot even during the rainy season. It is customary there to take two showers a day, the first when one gets up and the other after work, or any time from 5pm until around sunset. Some people even take a few showers a day, as the humidity and heat can be unbearable on some days.

Can you imagine what I looked like? I was a little tyke with a mop of hair cut in the shape of a bowl. I had so much hair—they say I was born covered in hair, and that was why I was nicknamed 'monkey'—yes, they used the English word to refer to me rather than the Indonesian word *monyet*.

I was too young to remember much so these are stories your Mom told me later about my hair. Most of the time I refused to wash my hair, and sometimes I would hold out for an entire month. I would scream bloody murder when she or anyone tried to wash my hair. The same would happen when they took me to a barber to get a haircut. I would scream and cry and sob and wail as if I was being tortured. They had to bribe me with 'snow globe' ice treats, or *Es Mambo* popsicles and promise future gifts and treats.

As an adult, I realize it was the sharpness of my Asian hair that I hated. How sharp those little hairs were when it was cut—they poked me and made me itchy. Even nowadays, after a haircut, I still strip as soon as I can get to my bathroom and I always take a shower instantly. Now I feel ashamed to even think about how disgusting and smelly I must have been in those early days.

I was told one notorious story about my cousin Ci Pek and I. She was twelve, or maybe even fourteen years older than me, and I would stuff my hair in her face, and get a kick from her in reaction. The more she screamed and yelled and pretended she was suffocating the funnier for me it got, to a point where she had to hold her breath as I would continue to rub my hair all over her face until she cried. This story, too, is one that I have been told over and over again, during visits home, at family reunions or gatherings. People still laugh about it.

It was only your Mom who could coax me into washing my hair, relentlessly, and with her sweet voice full of conviction and love. Eventually I would give in and let her. Later it was also her who would treat my hair when there was an outbreak of hair lice in my school or in town. The treatment then was as disgusting as the epidemic itself. I am not sure what kind of lotion it was that they rubbed all over our hair before covering it with a plastic shower cap that we had to keep on overnight. The stench of the chemical in it still sticks in my memory. As a teenager, when I saw her later, your Mom was the one who would lay my head down on her lap to pick at any dry flakes on my scalp, one by one until all the nasty flaky stuff was gone. She also would oil my hair or treat my dry scalp with a special cream-bath. Then she would wash, dry and comb my hair, and massage my head until I fell asleep on her lap, only to wake up to her most loving smile.

The maids were always part of my life too; in fact they were also in some ways responsible for raising me during my childhood, and I was very fond of them. Sadly, my parents disowned Puji when she had an affair with a young pastor from our church, which infuriated my father. I didn't know what had happened at the time, but in those days, moral standards were strict, and premarital sex was considered a mortal sin. Although I did not know it then, they were both excommunicated from the church and expelled from our house.

It wasn't until a few years ago that Puji and my parents

and her husband—the ill-fated lover at that time—were reunited, and they embraced each other with a lot of love, compassion and regret. I last saw Puji during a memorial celebration for your mother ten years after she passed away. We invited you both on that occasion, but your father did not allow you to come.

Puji was replaced by Mbak Minah, a sixteen-year-old virgin from a Catholic convent, recommended by our Mom's old supervisor back when she was a teacher in a Dutch Catholic school. She appeared to be timid at first, but later grew to be the Alpha female after all the old timers had gone. It wasn't until much, much later that we learned she was actually not a virgin as her parents had claimed when she came to work for us. Contrary to all appearances and recommendations, she had actually given birth at the age of fifteen, after having an affair with a local boy. This always made me chuckle. Putting her in the convent had been the answer to her family's prayer, offering a perfect solution, a credible way in which to turn her into a 'good girl' and leave her past behind.

Mbak Minah turned out to be a savvy, quick learner and she soon became our Mom's trustee in all things to do with the kitchen, groceries and shopping for other household necessities. Much later in our lives long after she had left us to have her own family, she came back again, this time to help my Sister Edna with her noodle restaurant in front of my parent's house. Our kind-hearted parents have always been loyal to their employees who left on good terms, keeping in touch with them, and giving them a generous pension.

Anna was another newbie who came to work for our family shortly after Mbak Minah arrived, from the same convent, but with no scandal attached, either at that time, or later, right up until she died. Anna was like a female teddy bear; she was shy, sweet, giggly and nurturing. Later she became Mbak Minah's personal peon—at least that's how I perceived her. She was a good assistant to Minah and our Mom. As well as carrying out her duties as a maid, she doubled as my nanny but she was more like an unqualified governess.

I had a special affection towards Anna. Decades later I learned that she died during her second pregnancy. They said the cause of death was typhoid fever. It broke my heart when I learned about her death and I regretted that I never had thanked her for her dedication, patience and love towards me, and all of our family. My only consolation was that her younger sister Mbak Tini, who she introduced to our family, stayed on for many years to help my parents and later went on to work for my sister Edna and her family.

Your uncle Stephen and I wanted to show our respect for Mbak Tini so we offered her and her children and husband some financial help when they needed it. She would still show her affection to us when we visited her, and always expressed her sadness when we had to say goodbye to go back to the United States after each visit, sobbing openly when we hugged her to say goodbye.

Then came Sutrisni, the girl who was mauled by the

dogs in our big house. She was distantly related to Penny and Sami, I am not sure how, I think they were cousins of some sort. Sutrisni was the darkest Indonesian I had ever seen as a child, she had the most beautiful charcoal colored skin that glowed as if it was almost luminescent.

She was a character in her own way, very reserved, stoic and almost eerily antisocial. A woman of very few words, she seemed to always be a loner and always angry—in retrospect I would classify her as full of some kind of internal turmoil— but of course it was not until I became an adult that I interpreted her behavior in this way.

I noticed, as a child, that Sutrisni kept her distance from all of us family members. She might have been a bit friendlier to those who she considered to be her own pack, the other maids. Practically a child when she came to our house to work, she was probably only about thirteen or fourteen, well, fifteen years old at the most. She did not bother to conceal her moodiness.

One time I saw her fighting with my brother David who was not much younger than her. I could not remember what the specific reason was for this fight, but she and my brother got into a heated verbal exchange and later that escalated to physically fighting each other, right there, in the maids' quarters. Years later she also had a fight with my sister Edna in the big ranch house, after newly-married Edna moved back to our house, having refused to live any longer with her parents-in-law as was customary in the local culture.

I only heard about it from my Mom; Sutrisni defied

my sister's request or something she had ordered her to do when my parents were away and my sister was second-in-command. It was almost as if Sutrisni hated being our maid or being in the social class she didn't choose to be. Her anger was the first inkling I had as a child of the social class system in our part of the world. I also heard that she eventually ran away with our young gardener, Amat, who I called Mat, but this happened long after I had left home to go to school abroad.

The irony was that Amat was the only older male on the staff that I had a sexual relationship as a teenager when we lived on the ranch. As he was not much older than me I did not see him as a predator. We were of a similar age, two lustful teens expressing our physical desire—so it happened fairly regularly and often. We would hide in his room, or in a barn, where no one would ever find us, as it would be in the middle of the night. We never discussed or exchanged a word during our escapades. We had a simple mutual understanding that what we did was not to be shared with other people and it was our own secret. I wonder now if he and Sutrisni are still together, and if Amat continued to have affairs with men. I just hope both are happy and well.

Sami and Penny were sisters. Sami left during our time in the rental house, while Penny continued to stay on and work for us. Penny was a silly, comical character, petite in her build. I remember her as being full of funny stories and good energy. I can't remember her stories now, but I remember the laughter she created for our family, not just her storytelling but more her silliness, which was completely harmless and innocent. She was such a neurotic cleaner that our Mother loved and trusted her with our fine linens and beddings, and she was also deemed the best ironer of all. No one could iron as perfectly as Penny did.

I also remember the time when she left us, but shortly after she asked Mom if she would be welcome to come back. Not only was she welcomed back into the fold, she was embraced with joy and relief when she arrived. Penny was much older than the rest of the staff and she married one of our gardeners, a man who was deemed mentally unstable as well as not very intelligent. I have a feeling, now that I have learned more about these things, that Rasilah, her husband—who was half her age—was perhaps autistic or had a lower IQ and some kind of learning disability, but we had no knowledge or formal proof of this other than the way he behaved. They met at our estate and we were so shocked to hear that they wanted to get married, but my parents and family being the loving and generous people that they were, they helped them to go through the paper work, arranged the church ceremony, paid all the expenses and even hosted their reception at church and home. Penny made a cute bride with a tea-length tulle dress in a light creamy yellow with a matching fascinator; all made up with the help of a professional stylist, hair and makeup artists. It was cute in many ways, as he was considered to be a simpleton and she was like the family clown: together they made an odd couple, and at times they were mocked and made fun of by their co-workers as well as by our family members. Your Mom, being a kind hearted person and very educated in the sex education department had a chat with them along with our cousin, Ci Tian, to educated them about sex, family planning and all the important conversations adults need to have when they get married.

It broke my heart when I learned that Rasilah ran away from her later, I believe it was not long after they left my parents, and Penny died during childbirth. Another regret in my life is that I never properly thanked them for their dedication and loyalty to our family.

So, Penny, Mbak Minah, Anna and Sutrisni all came with our family when we moved to the Ranch and shortly after that Teresa joined us. Teresa also came from the convent and instantly became Mbak Minah's 'bitch'. Well at least that's what I would call her in today's slang, as Teresa became her constant companion, sleeping in the same room and same bed, even showering with her. There was nothing my parents could say or do. Lesbianism was suspected and bound to happen, just as inevitable as fights and dramas. Although they didn't really approve, they turned a blind eye, and life went on.

Those five maids, plus a few drivers and gardeners all cohabited and worked at our ranch. Let me count how many gardeners we had. There was Basri, with his wife and seven children, who had originally lived on the land in their own hut when my parents bought the property, either in late sixties or early seventies. He became our groundskeeper. When my parents built their 'mansion'—our large house—they also built Basri and his family a small house with its own well and garden in the far corner of the land, but still within the walled area of the ranch.

Then there were Suharman and Mastuarjo who were in charge of the chicken farms. They doubled as farmers and gardeners. Later, I will tell you about why these two were one of the main reasons I had nightmares for most of my early childhood and teen years, right up into early adulthood. There were also two others, Amat and another strapping lad I had a crush on later, a handsome, darker skinned gardener who was the same age as Amat, but I can no longer remember his name.

We had a night-guard who doubled as the bird-keeper, but he did not live with us. The night guard arrived after sunset, as soon as he had completed his evening prayers, as he was a Muslim. He left after he fed the birds, just after sunrise. His name was Pak Sabri. His younger brother also worked for us periodically, but I can't recall his name. Both men always wore a black velvet *peci* hat typically worn by the local Muslim men, and a sarong made locally in our island of Sumatra which traditionally has similar check patterns in subdued colors, similar to those of tartan kilts.

All these workers were deemed necessary for the safety and security of our property, as thefts and robbery were not uncommon in our area, especially at that time, when the ranch and our mansion were still the only household on our street. Now, I don't even recognize anything anymore, the last time I was there a few years ago, houses and commercial buildings had mushroomed rampantly.

Then there was another staff member who came later, after we had already moved in. His name was Aswan, and he was an ex-convict who my father brought home to live with us. My parents have always been generous, loving people full of good intentions, and my father went to preach in our local jail every Monday. Besides preaching, he and a few other church deacons went to visit the people incarcerated there and counseled them, as they believed good Christians should do.

Out of the kindness of my father's heart, he brought Aswan home when he was released from jail, and offered him a job. Besides gardening, he was expected to help with the farm. Handsome and tall in his build, he was popular with the ladies, and well liked by the lads of the property. He was charming and sweet to me and I liked the attention.

In fact, he was remarkably affectionate, constantly sitting next to me on the way to church, at church, at prayer groups and always putting his arm around me or on my lap. Weeks went by and he invited me to visit his living quarters along with a few of the other gardeners. Later I asked him to accompany me to get snacks on the street at night, as was the common thing to do. We would buy grilled satay and rice cakes, fried noodles or grilled corn together, and be driven or walk up the street together. He was easy to talk to, funny and full of joy. Later he became part of the night guard staff to help the older staff as word got out that there were more thefts and robbery as the neighborhood grew. He ended up spending the night in the fancy balé structure over the fishpond.

It was there that I would visit him, being now the only child left in the house. All my siblings had been sent away for school, either in Jakarta, Java or the United States, and Aswan became a sort of 'elder-brother' figure. I was happy to have a nice brother figure, as I actually did not have a nice brother. I was a child, a growing boy who needed company, naive and looking for affection. Aswan seemed to be gentle and kind-hearted.

When you read the next chapter of this book, you will learn about some of the demons and monsters in my life up to this point. Aswan was one of them. He turned out to be the opposite of what he originally seemed. Yet at that time I had no idea what he was doing or about to do was inappropriate. It was during this time that on our nocturnal visits Manis the doe would make a commotion on the outside of the wall, as if trying to distract us, or alert somebody, with unusual movements and noise, making a commotion on the opposite side of the wall just next to us, when Aswan was showing more affection to me than he should have. He basically had sex with me, a minor half his age and I did not know it was not right for him to do that, I only knew I should not or could not tell anyone.

What happened to me at that time would be classified as child abuse, although at that time I felt that I was a willing participant. Now, after years of therapy and being more educated about these things, I know better. It was simple really—I was a victim of child abuse and he was the perpetrator.

*   *   *

Remember the specialty carpenter, the Chinese gentleman I called uncle and I never knew his name, we simply called him Uncle Carpenter, Empek Tukang Kayu? He could have been my grandpa's age, but his skill and craftsmanship was top of the line. He was possibly the last skilled carpenter who immigrated to our island from China— his Indonesian was funky and rather limited and my father spoke to him in Mandarin. Our cousins the architects were frustrated a lot by him but recognized his talents. He basically was commissioned by my father to do all the millwork and prepare any wooden structural components for buildings in our mansion and ranch. Once the property was ready for us to move in, my father continued to keep him on the payroll as he was planning to build more structures on the property. I believe our family was his biggest client or possibly even his only client for the last twenty or thirty years of his life. While he never lived with us, he practically spent from five to six days a week with us, for anything from ten to fourteen hours a day. He was part of our extended family, a really soft spoken, mild mannered gentleman, and your Mom and I had a special spot in our hearts for him. In some ways, he reminded us of your biological grandfather, our driver,

Empek Edo. Uncle Carpenter converted to Christianity upon my father's persuasion, leaving behind his original Buddhist faith. As a result, we also saw him on Sundays.

Empek Edo worked for our family in two different phases. The first phase was before I was born right up until I was may be five or six years old, when we lived in the rental house. This was the time, from what I understand that your Mom started to come in with him to work, keeping him company or simply tagging along. Your Mom was born in 1960, my brother David in 1966. I think your Mom started to come to our house at the end of the sixties or early seventies, but I was too young to remember. I have heard this story all my life, how your Mom came to work along with her father, and David loved playing with her. At some point he asked her to spend the night—we would call it a slumber party these days, although their ages were quite different, her being six years older than him. He would have been four or five years old, and your Mom would have been about ten. One night turned into two, three four nights; then it became a week or two, then a month, and the rest was history. She never went back to live with her biological parents and became part of our family—forever. By the time I was born, as I mentioned, your Mom was simply my older sister. I never once questioned otherwise.

Empek Edo continue to work for us until I was in kindergarten I believe, and my parents always said how stubborn and temperamental he was and he pouted a lot like a child. Your Mom would agree and laugh—what else was she supposed to do? He resigned, but continued to be part of our lives as an uncle and still visited us. Years later, he came back to work for the family again when we moved to the ranch, and stayed with us there until he retired. I always wondered how your Mom felt as his daughter or if it put her in a difficult position. Yes, he was her father, but she was also the daughter of his boss. It was very complex and must have felt problematical I am sure, but we never discussed it.

I can only imagine how that might have played out in her head and his. Looking back, I wonder what conversation they had if any, as I had never witnessed any full conversation between them. They simply greeted each other, or spoke about the task at hand, or where we needed to go at what time. I did hear him constantly telling her to be a good girl, to listen to our parents and to be obedient. There is something I wish I could tell him now. I would like to let him know that he had nothing to worry about. In fact, Wewe was the best daughter anyone could have asked for, including my parents. She was the perfect daughter and sister, at least in my mind and heart.

Something about your biological grandfather and me that I'd like to share: I used to be called 'anak Empek Edo' affectionately by my parents, siblings and the staff. That meant I was the son of Empek Edo. I earned this nickname because of my strong dislike of collared shirts and pants as well as my signature pout. I would pout my lips so much I earned the nickname 'chicken-butt face' or 'monyong'. As for my fashion style, I preferred to wear my old raggedy

T-shirts with shorts, as the collared shirts made me itch terribly around my neck and the pants were too hot as well as scratchy, just like my hair, they made me itch terribly. Empek Edo, no matter where he went, church or out visiting with guests, even at parties or receptions, insisted in wearing his shorts. He might have changed to a nicer shirt but he always stuck to the shorts. When we flew, we all dressed up, at least the rest of my family did. They tried to dress me up until I cried and sobbed and begged to be changed to my 'monkey suit, Empek Edo's uniform'. I happened to love Empek Edo as a child and all my life, so I loved being called the son of Empek Edo. Besides the reason of our similarity in how we dressed, we were also both very childish. Well, I was a child, he on the other hand had retained his childish habits; and, just like father and son we both shared our similar facial expressions. If he and I were moody or unhappy, the entire estate knew, as it was so obvious from our 'chicken-butt' faces.

I also suspected it was like an exchange in some ways. I remember that your biological grandparents always referred to your Mom, Wewe as 'the daughter of her aunt and uncle', in other words, my parents' daughter. That was actually how they referred to her, although they were her own biological parents and family. I don't think she minded that, in fact, she was proud of it.

There were also a few different drivers as I grew up, other than your biological grandfather, Empek Edo. I remember Pak Reggeng, Bang Kasan and there was another driver, I can't remember his name, who was so mild mannered. The youngest driver was called Ada. They didn't all work for us at the same time but we always had two simultaneously serving the needs of the family and the church my parents supported, taking care of the vehicles and running us around.

One thing I remember well was how our staff would stay with us for a long time—years would pass once they came to work with us. For me, this was a testament to my parents' kindness and fairness in how they treated their employees. Besides their Christian faith, I truly believe that they are kind hearted, loving and compassionate people. I know families who treat their staff terribly, not just disrespectfully but also roughly. Some of our neighbors could not keep their staff longer than a month, let alone a year, and their staff employment record was like a revolving door. Our staff usually stayed for a minimum five to ten years, if not longer, and some stayed for a lifetime. Some, like Empek Edo and Penny, would come and go, returning again and again.

There was another male staff member who was considered part of the female contingent of the staff, as he was a housekeeper and he was known as the sissy one and got called the same names as me by everyone. His name was Mas Parjo, or brother Parjo. He was what I would now label as an effeminate man. I don't know how he came into our household; I think it was from some church connection or another. He came to work for us long after we moved to the ranch just before the time I had to leave home for school abroad. I have two things to tell you about him. The first is how he presented himself as a very sweet, God-fearing and bible-abiding person, but later he left our home having ransacked it and helped himself to a few of my parents' belongings. Essentially he was a thief. To read about the second thing I want to tell you about him, you have to wait until my next letter, as that's where his story belongs.

*   *   *

The last person I remember as part of our household staff is Mbak Ti. She was hired by my parents to assist my Sister Edna and her husband who moved back to live with us after they got married. Technically sister Edna was supposed to live with her in-laws in Teluk Betung, near our old house, the one your Mom and I always passed by to go to your biological grandparents' house. In short, when she was pregnant with her first son Ivan, around about her second trimester, she came home to visit us and started to cry uncontrollably, sobbing and begging my parents not to let her go back to her in-laws. It was simply a matter of their different way of living and family culture that she couldn't deal with. Her mother-in-law was a smoker and a gambler and had other very masculine traits, along with a strong and intense, individualistic personality. Also the household my sister had gone to live in was non-Christian as they had retained their ethnic Chinese beliefs. Our household was quite different—a Christian household that totally forbade smoking and gambling.

My sister Edna has a very strong and intense

personality as well, so that could also have caused clashes between her and her new mother-in-law, and I am pretty sure it would have been a classic case of the wife and the mother-in-law competing to control the husband and son. I think you get the picture? Anyway, my parents had to do the right thing for their daughter, which meant going to the in-laws and doing whatever they had to do to work out a deal, so their son and my sister could live at our house. This broke all the unwritten laws of patriarchy, but it lasted for twelve years, and it wasn't until three children later that they actually moved out to their own house.

My parents built a wing for them in our house, with the main entry through my sister Edna's old room. It had two bedrooms, a bathroom, and it's own nursery and sunroom—basically it was like an in-law unit. Not long after, being as thoughtful and as generous as they always had been in the past, my parents hired a special Nanny for my sister's newborn Ivan. Her name was Ti, and we called her Mbak Ti. She was a nervous, giddy, kind and sweet lady with a gift in handling babies, toddlers and children, similar to your Mom's. From the day she started working with my sister and her husband, she instantly became part of our family. I had a great fondness for her, as in some ways she reminded me a lot of your Mom.

Mbak Ti was a happy-go-lucky kind of person, always cheery and happy to help. Having trained as a nurse or nurse aid, she came with a certain set of skills. My sister relied a lot on her help and there were days that Mbak Ti was the sole caregiver of her newborn Ivan, as my sister at times got overwhelmed. Mbak Ti and I were like two siblings and we were always together with Ivan, who I considered to be the latest addition to my doll family, except he was a real baby.

I had discovered that I loved babies as much as I loved dolls. It came to me naturally to do my part of the nursery care. I could easily hold him, change his diaper, bathe and feed him and entertain him. There is only one thing I could not or would not do, and still cannot even today, and that was is cutting the baby's fingernails and toenails. The delicate nature of the nail and fingers freaked me out. I was afraid I might cut his tiny little fingers or toes in the process. I also was good at swaddling the baby, which we did a lot in Indonesia. Diapers were still made of cloth then, and there was no waterproof wrapping in those days, but I didn't mind that at all.

When your Mom came home during a holiday season or vacation, she would show Mbak Ti, our sister and I handy things to do for babies. She would tell us stories about delivering babies—she had a repertoire of funny, scary and sad experiences to share. Of course when she was home, I would follow her like a shadow, just like in the good old days. We would sit next to each other at the dining table and she would caress my head on her lap to get me to nap, or we would go around town together, holding hands. Ivan, my nephew, took an instant liking to her, just as other babies and children always did. She was so magnetic and charismatic in her own subtle way, especially with children. They say babies and little children, like dogs, always know a good soul—their instinct works like magic.

Because my sister had already graduated from college in psychology and counseling and her husband Ise married her in his senior year in college as an electrical engineer they spent most of their honeymoon driving from our hometown in Sumatra back to their college town in Central Java, a trip that took them several weeks. After their baby Ivan was about a year old, my parents gave them yet another gift, sending them overseas on a tour of Europe, the United States and Canada for almost two months. They left Ivan with Mbak Ti and my parents and I, and your Mom when she was visiting. We all became Ivan's caregivers. Mbak Ti became Ivan's Mom during this time, she would sleep with him and me and there were times we all would sleep in my parents' master suite on the floor on mattresses.

I remember one night, Ivan started to cry, screaming bloody murder all night long, no one could console him to a point we thought it was a bad omen and something had happened to his parents in their second honeymoon. Thankfully nothing had happened to them. When they finally returned we all picked them up at our local airport, but Ivan, who was barely two years old, did not remember his parents at all, and ran back to your Mom, Mbak Ti and me. My sister cried that day at the airport, when she realized that her son didn't remember them. We all laughed, but my sister didn't find it funny. It took my nephew about a week to get fully reacquainted with his parents.

There was a funny story I would like to tell you about when Ivan was born. Your Mom was with us when we visited him the first time at the hospital, the same hospital where I was born. As I mentioned before, Ise, Ivan's father, who was my brother-in-law, had unusual parents. As a couple they were known for having 'reversed' the traditional marital roles. He was, and still is, soft-spoken and gentle, whereas she has very masculine traits. Not only does she have a very manly build, she could almost pass as a drag queen, as she is tall and has big bones. Her mannerisms don't help.

Your Mom, often the comedian, used to say "*Ivan, please be sweet and gentle like your Grandpa and be strong and manly like your Grandma*" which made us all burst into laugher, including Ivan's Dad. Since then, we always quoted your Mom and we nicknamed Ivan's Grandma from his father's side as Ivan's 'third Grandpa', usually sharing a giggle whenever we did it.

Mbak Ti and your Mom bonded over Ivan and other children and sharing stories about working in a hospital as nurses. I was so happy during this time, as our family was joyful and peaceful, and I was surrounded by the favorite women in my life, your Mom Wewe, my favorite cousin who was the doctor Ci Tian, my sister Edna, Mbak Ti the Nanny, who was like another sister to me, and of course my Mom and her entourage of maids and housekeepers who were always kind.

There were only three other males living in our family

quarters at that time. They were my father, my sister's husband Ko Ise and his son Ivan, my first nephew. I will tell you more about Ko Ise in the next chapter.

Mbak Ti stayed with us until my sister had two more sons, who she named Sean and Alain. I believe she remained with us until Ivan was nearly twelve. The last time I saw Mbak Ti was when I said goodbye and set off to the U.S. She cried and sobbed in my arms and I did the same. Somehow I knew I would never see her again. Indeed, I haven't seen her again since, and I am now thinking about trying to find her. I would love to hug her and let her know how much she means to me, how I appreciated her company, care and love for our family and I do hope she is still alive and I am not too late, as I have been with some people who deserve my gratitude, including your mother, my dear sister, Wewe.

You may be surprised to hear that besides the staff of night guards, gardeners, carpenters, housekeepers, drivers, cooks, nannies and a few others I might have not included in this story, there were also a number of other people who lived in our estate.

My parents were the good Samaritans in a true sense. They always helped others, and they rescued and supported so many people, relatives and strangers alike. There were those people they fell in love with instantly when they heard their sad stories, such as the poor family with three or four children from church who lived in a house built by my parents especially for them, in our estate between our big house and the chicken farm. Then there were others they took under their wing, such as the single middle-aged man from north Sumatra who sold noodles and meatballs in the night market, the ex-convict Aswan, and a family friend's son who was suicidal.

They also supported various people from church and from their missionary work in the villages of Lampung, and a number of relatives in distress, both financially and emotionally, and the list went on and on. They were always generous with money and helping needy people. They gave from the heart, never expecting to be paid back or get anything in return, never asking other people to donate to help others.

All in all the number of people who lived on our estate at any given point ranged from thirty to forty people. It was like a small village, with living spaces spread through the four housing units; our mansion which housed our family as well as the female staff, the guesthouse, the male staff housing and the house for the gardeners and their families.

* * *

As if life wasn't crowded enough for me, even in the vast property we lived on, my parents were devout Protestants. Every week was always filled with church activities that involved lots of other people. I will give you a rundown of how I remember our average week.

On Monday evenings we had a multi-denominational prayer group that started at 7pm. Our drivers would pick up most of the people attending, and on a weekly basis we hosted anything from fifty to seventy people. Mom and the cooks and maids would be in the kitchen all day long preparing snacks to serve after the sessions ended, around 8.30 or 9pm, but people lingered at times till 11pm or so and then our drivers would take them back. It was a particularly long day for our drivers, who generally showed up for work around 6am to drive us to school or to take my Mom or cooks to the wet market.

Tuesday was the day on which I found it fun to go along with my Mom to the women's prayer or choir group from church. This typically took place at a church member's house, where gossip and snacks were served simultaneously. I was most likely the only boy there. If there had been another boy attending, he too would have probably been escaping being bullied by his siblings or friends, the kind of boy like me who liked to tag along with mother.

Most Wednesdays I dutifully went along with my parents to visit the sick at their homes or in the hospital. Usually I was bored to death, and I got quite scared at times, looking at people on their deathbeds amongst the stench and smell of the hospital and its grim outlook. Remember this was in the seventies, in Sumatra, where there was only one public hospital. Lets just say the situation in the hospital then was more like what you would expect to see in a movie from one of the early war eras. The hospital was divided into classes, and in the ward for the third class patients, they were put in rows on either side of the room. There would be anything from twenty to thirty patients in one long room. Second class patients had just a few patients in every room, and two first class patients shared one room. In later years they added some VIP rooms, which were air-conditioned and private for those lucky patients who could afford them.

Thursday was our day for the "rotating" prayer group, similar to the one held on Mondays at our place, but this one revolved among our Immanuel Methodist Church members' houses. We belonged to this church, so we would go to a different house every week, as was scheduled ahead of time by the deacons of our church. This outing could take all night long, as some of the houses were far away, and not easily accessible.

Of course my parents volunteered our drivers and cars to pick up any church members who would not go otherwise because it was too far and public transportation stopped running at night; others they picked up who were too physically and financially limited to manage getting there on their own. This kind of prayer meeting could go either way—if the household had other children I enjoyed hanging out with, it was fun—but otherwise, it could turn out to be a yawning session all night long for me. Mostly I couldn't wait for it to be over and to get back home. Not coming was not an option, we had to be good church members, or at least give the impression that we were, especially me, being the preacher's son. I knew my parents were always sincere in their intentions. They were always good members of the congregation, yet personally I felt I had no choice but to go with them. I only attended all these church activities because I was obliged to.

While I can't remember specifically what Fridays were for, I know that day always involved going to church, and I think it was for the choir practice that my Mom led. My Mom was not only a pianist and organist for the church, she was also the choir director. I would tag along as my Dad would go also—not to be in the choir, but to meet other lay persons and deacons of the church, to discuss anything from members who needed help to church renovations, to organize retreats, conferences and other church matters, or simply preparing for Sunday service.

I would play outside the church grounds with other children, usually the girls, or I would tag along with teachers or church members who were kind, especially those I perceived as being handsome—in other words, those I had a crush on.

Because our church was also a Christian school, there would be teachers who lived in the school housing at the property. I enjoyed visiting with them, both female and male teachers, as they knew me as the son of 'that rich family' and they treated me well, whether they felt obligated to or were entirely sincere, I will never know.

Saturdays were the same as Fridays. We somehow seemed to live at church, at least partly, and Saturdays saw me following my parents there again, either for another choir practice or to prepare for the Sunday service.

By the way, we used to go to school six days a week,

from Monday to Saturday. The idea of having a weekend had not yet been introduced in my childhood. School started around 7am and finished about one, except on Fridays when it ended at 11:30 am to allow students to observe their weekly Muslim prayers. Saturday was a normal day for school. I didn't mind so much spending a Saturday afternoon or evening on the church grounds. In fact I had a bit of fun playing 'doctors and nurses' with other children, some who I still see when I visit my hometown, and we always have our mysterious Mona Lisa smiles plastered on our faces, but we never talk about it.

That leaves Sundays. Where do I even begin? While other kids slept in, my parents would wake me up early for Sunday school, which took place at home from around 8 am, led by my Sister Edna or a teacher from our Christian school or sometimes by my Dad. I hated Sunday school. Firstly, I just wanted to sleep in, secondly I would rather not spend another day praying after having done that all week. To make things worse, this was only the beginning of the day's religious activities. Once Sunday school ended, we went off to church for a Sunday service, or, at times, two!

If my father, the preacher, had to give his sermon twice, we would stay at the church for two services which were back-to-back. Dad prided himself for not giving the same sermon twice, and he delivered every sermon with passion in his booming voice. I couldn't wait for the service (or services) to be over so I could play in the church grounds with the girls while—why, what else you may ask—another choir practice was held, for my Mom, or a meeting among the deacons for the minister, my Dad as they made plans to keep everybody busy throughout the year.

On particularly lucky days we would get home just in time for lunch and we would watch *Little House in the Prairie* on TV or we would go to the beach until sunset, which was a real treat, with picnics, and carrying fresh water to shower with after soaking in the salty and sticky ocean water.

That was how my childhood 'church life' passed me by, its cycles repeating themselves again and again for what felt like an eternity, a groundhog day that never came. I thought that was what my life would be for the rest of time: me, trapped in a loop of daily church activities and 'church people', forever.

Speaking of prayers, I am going to try to count exactly how many times we were supposed to pray in a day during my childhood years. Our first prayers were supposed to be made as soon as we got up. Then we prayed before we could eat our breakfast. At my private Catholic school we prayed when class started, as well as when it ended. That was supplemented with weekly obligatory Monday flag-ceremony prayers. Whenever I got picked up from school, my Mom or your Mom or one of the nannies or maids would be with the driver, and they would have brought me a snack to eat in the car. Of course, they would make me pray first before I could enjoy my snack. When I got home the table would be ready for lunch and we prayed before we started our lunch, and then later again before dinner. The night ended with a prayer before bed. Did you manage to count all those prayers?

For me it was that prayer before bed that provided the sweetest memory. If my parents were home and I spent the night in their bedroom I would get to watch them pray together, their palms intertwined and they took turns to say the night prayers. If my Dad prayed tonight, it would be my Mom's turn the next night and so on. As soon as I heard the word: "Amen!" they would open their eyes and kiss each other gently on the cheek, sniffing to breath in the scent of each other. Then they would go to sleep. This routine was never skipped as far as I could remember either in sickness or in health, in richer or poorer times. Even if we were fighting fiercely the minute before as young children, my evil brother David and I would join my parents regularly in their nightly prayers and we would kiss our parents before bed. I will always keep a few sweet memories of these times close in my heart.

~ *delapan* ~

"Evil monsters that lurk..."

How do you write a personal story that is painful, sad, and traumatizing? I constantly debate with myself whether or not I should be so open, blatant and honest about what happened to me as a child and a young adult. I worry day and night about this decision. Will I hurt people by telling the world about what happened or what they did to me? Will people think that I am selfish? Or will they call me a liar? What if they challenge the details or the facts of what happened? I have tried to write everything down exactly as I remember it, and I have changed the names of the victims and perpetrators, for the sake of their families. Would it ruin people's perception of those who played a role? They might look at me as a freak—or will they accuse me of being an attention-seeker? All these questions run through my head, but in the end I find the answers by asking myself '*What would my sister think, say or do?*'

Wewe, I know, would think only of supporting and embracing me with love, and she would let me do as I wish, as she always did. It is her presence that gives me an answer to all my questions in the strong and honest way she lived her life and her love for children and others. She guides me to persevere with this path of my story. It is her selflessness and generosity that pushes me to be honest and to share my past and my stories so I may help other people, especially children. Wewe would have taken care of all the children of the world if she could, in her own special way. I want to continue her legacy by telling my stories in the hope of raising awareness to the dangers, so that other children may be saved from the misery I endured as a child.

It is my hope that by the end of reading these letters, this book, all those who read them can learn from my sadness, pain and sorrow. Then perhaps my horrendous experiences as a child will not be repeated in other lives. In telling my story I yearn to find empathy, and I continue with it in the hope that it will awaken some sense of awareness in people around the world and enable them to acknowledge that these nightmares happen when they should not. None of these things should happen to any child or human.

We need to openly acknowledge and face the demons, not make them taboo to talk about. It is important to discuss and educate people, and only by doing this in the public sphere can we prevent them from being repeated. My sister Wewe's love for children and humanity gave me the permission to tell the world what happened to me, and what can happen to other children if we are not aware. Her love prevails, and it always will, as you will see.

My daily life as a child could easily be categorized as blessed, a childhood in which I was loved and well taken care of. To all appearances I was well provided for. I always had enough food, more clothes than I needed, and as you have learned, a series of enormous dwellings to live in with my family. In fact I lived in luxury far beyond the imagination of most Indonesian children. Heck—most children in the world could never imagine the comforts I experienced in my childhood. I lived in an environment absolutely dripping in luxury of the kind that you only read about or watch in movies. Who amongst you wouldn't want to live on a beautiful estate with housekeepers, gardeners, drivers and nannies, no budget limitations in their daily allowance, and be able to go to almost any prominent store in town without any cash and select whatever candies, snacks and toys you liked? To say I was coddled would be an understatement. I was one very privileged kid.

While I have never had any unfulfilled needs for material stuff, there were certain things I lacked in other departments of my life, not immediately apparent to anyone.

Before I get into telling you about the monsters in my childhood, let me share with you a bit of background about my parents and their dedication to their religion and faith. You have heard about our weekly religious and church events and the prayer groups we attended when we were children, as well as the prayers our parents scheduled and habits they abided by. I am going to ask my father what made him decide to become a preacher, as this was a turning point in his life. At a certain point of his life, when I was just a toddler, he let his business partner run his business for him and he became a passive partner in the company.

As a child I only knew him as the Methodist church preacher. He was so active at church that people thought he was the pastor, when in fact he never even went to a seminary school and as far as I know he was never ordained. Yet, he was a known and respected figure not only in the church itself, but also throughout the entire Indonesian Methodist organization.

We used to listen to his stories about how he became a devout Christian when I was a little boy. But it has been so long since I heard him tell those stories; my memory most probably combines a few different excerpts into one. I would like to tell you a few of the stories and some different versions that I may have been confused about. There are some important sections I still remember quite clearly.

One particular story that comes to mind was of my mother's brother having a vision. Apparently our uncle, who was formally ordained as a Protestant pastor, was staying with my parents, and on that occasion he got up in the middle of the night and woke my parents up and to tell them of his revelation. My father's calling was to be a messenger of Jesus, he said, and my father was to leave his old life behind and start spreading the 'good news'.

Another version, which I think is closer to the truth of how he came to dedicate his life to Christianity, was when they lost their baby. I was around ten or twelve years old when my cousins Enchong and Noni took us to visit a graveyard. Up to this point of my life, I had called their mother Tante, or Auntie. They had three other younger siblings, Toto, Meilan and Lucky who I assumed to be their brothers and sisters, my cousins. When we arrived at a graveyard, nothing was explained so I assumed that we were to visit one of our relative's graves, which was true. Later I found out, it was Enchong and Noni's biological mother who was buried there, my youngest aunt on my mother's side. Her Name was Kwie, had she been alive, I would have called her Ie Kwie. Ie is a word in ethnic Chinese Indonesian that describes her position in the family tree on my mother's side: the younger sister of my Mom.

The woman I called Tante Giok or Auntie Giok turned out to actually be Enchong and Nori's stepmother, and the biological mother of Toto, Meilan and Lucky. Her husband was the father to all five children, and he was my biological Aunt Kwie's widower. My Ie Kwie had died at the age of twenty-seven from diabetes coma, I was told. Apparently, her widower, Om Giok Die remarried after she passed away, needing a woman to care for his children. Enchong and Noni were left by their mother at an even younger age than you were, Zef and Grace, when my sister left you.

According to our family legends, this Auntie Giok was God-sent. She would breast-feed Toto, her first-born at the same time as carrying and feeding her stepchildren who she carried on her back. She used to tie them all to her with several long pieces of cloth wrapped around her body, known as *selendang*—these are sarongs that can be used as a baby carrier. To me, she was always a favorite aunt. I never met the biological mother of my two cousins.

Back in the graveyard, next to my aunt's gravesite there was a small, unmarked grave, just a hump of dirt really, with an old wooden cross. One day Noni innocently told me that was where my elder sister was buried. I was so confused to hear this that I went home and told my family that I had been to Ie Kwie's graveyard and my sister's too. At this time, my oldest aunt, Wak Ie Surabaya—her name is Betty but we always refer her by the name of the town she lives in—was visiting us. Wak Ie Surabaya is still alive as I write this letter, and turned 103 in July of 2020. She was the one who finally told me about my youngest aunt who died, the story behind Enchong and Nori's stepmother, as well as the story of my sister I never met. She was going to be named Debbie.

While my parents were not pleased that my Aunt told me this, it was clear that they could no longer hide our family's past history from their youngest son. She kept the story simple and straightforward about my aunt's death and cousins and half cousins relationship, explaining it in a way I could easily understand, managing to keep it age-appropriate. I was much more shocked when I heard that I had a sister who had died. As she told me what had happened I held on tightly to your Mom, riveted by our aunt's story. Clearly, your Mom knew about this event that took place before I was born, but she had learned, or perhaps she had been warned, that I was not supposed to know. She understood I was confused and I was a bit scared as for some reasons stories about death and funerals always scared me. As usual she comforted me with hugs and gentle strokes.

Many years would pass before my parents were willing to share with me what had actually happened. By that time I was pretty much grown up, and I assume they thought I would be old enough to understand the details and what it had meant to them to lose a child, and how they had survived this most painful phase of their lives.

My Mom was pregnant in 1967. I'd imagine it's what they would say an 'Irish twin' pregnancy as my older brother David had only been born in August of 1966. She was so huge at that time that people thought she must be carrying a set of twins. She has always been petite in her build, barely reaching 5ft tall in her shoes.

Apparently during her labor the baby would not move during contractions and that was when they found out that the baby's heart was no longer beating. They estimated she must have passed away about three days before my Mom went into labor. My loving father was always with my Mom during every labor; this time would be his fourth. They had no idea that the baby's heart had stopped, and my Mom began to be poisoned by the lifeless fetus, as it remained in her womb. She had carried to full term and she almost died. This was apparent from her blue extremities, a sign of her own imminent death. Then they actually learned she was diabetic and a C-section was not an option. In Sumatra in the sixties they weren't equipped with an operating theatre in the clinic where she had always given birth to her children, and even if they were, and she had the C-section, she would surely have died from infection due to her diabetes.

As my mother lay dying in the delivery room my Dad suffered the most unimaginable distress. I cannot imagine his state of mind, knowing that my mother might die at anytime with their dead baby inside her. It was during this time my father made a pact with God. In his words, he found himself pleading to his God that he could accept the irrevocable loss of his baby, as long as his wife's life was spared.

His prayer was granted when a Dutch nun—who was the midwife at the time—pulled the corpse of their lifeless baby out of my mother's womb by hand. Again, a scene out of a horror movie I'd rather not think about, but I had a vivid visual picture in my mind as if I was present there myself. After the gory labor, our Mom later told us that they had to bind her hips and they kept her in the hospital for nearly three months for recovery.

"Every time I tried to move it felt like millions of needles were poking into me" she told us, "such a pain I will never forget".

In my head, no matter how I tried, I could not imagine the unbearable pain that my mother endured during this most unfortunate event in her life. She told us this story a few times, especially after your Mom became a midwife. It is forever ingrained in my brain and heart. From everything that they told me I believe the stillborn baby was over 5.5 kg or about 12 lbs., an enormous baby for such a small woman as our mother. From this knowledge, I also calculated I was conceived only another year and a half after this horrific event, and they say I weighed around 4.5 kg (about 10 lbs.) and my mother was in labor for around thirty hours. I could not imagine that my Mom had to go through a similar painful experience to the one she had endured so recently.

I believe it was during this time that my father made

his commitment to become a 'servant of God'. It was also during this time that your Mom came to stay with our family, and I think there were many reasons that influenced that decision. My brother David fell in love with her and the idea of having a sister, my parents were mourning the loss of their baby daughter, who I later learned was to be named Deborah, Debbie for short. As far as I could remember, until I learned about Debbie's unmarked grave and the old cross, I never heard my parents utter a word about Debbie, a lost baby, a stillborn, nor did they mention a graveyard. Neither my older siblings nor I were sure if they had agreed not to talk of these things for my sake; I think perhaps it was simply too painful for my parents to remember and share the tragedy. It was a dark part in their lives that they preferred not to remember.

Much later in my life my father shared a story that touched my heart about the death of his baby. Mind you, my oldest sibling is a male, then my sister Edna and David, and their stillborn baby, who would have been number four, was a female. At church at the funeral service he told his congregation that God would replace their dead baby with a better one. When little Jonathan—which means 'gift from God' or God-given—was baptized, he lifted me up (at this time I imagine a scene similar to Rafiki from the Lion King lifting baby Simba) and declared to the congregation:

"You see, God kept his promise, he gave us a better baby—a perfect one".

My standard joke now is to tell people about my sister who never made it; had she been born alive, I wouldn't be here. I also tell people that my parents and their relatives and friends were hoping for a girl to replace Debbie. Well, they got one.

"I am a big girl in many ways," I tell them with a wink, "that's why I was always teased when I was a child." Now as an adult gay man I am able to joke around that I am a 'gurl' with tongue-in-cheek humor. In the early days it was not so easy.

Needless to say, I became the coddled baby, the favorite and the one that everyone thought was the cutest; I was born so fat I had to wear a three or four-month-old baby's clothes right away, and I had a delicate coat of fine hair all over my tiny body, which earned my nickname of 'Monkey'. Apparently I was the pride and joy of my parents, which was understandable. I am what they call a 'rainbow baby'—a replacement baby after a pregnancy that ends in miscarriage or worse yet, in stillbirth. Throughout my life, it was said that I was my parent's favorite not only because I was the youngest but I was that baby that brought them joy after a painful phase of their lives, losing a baby that mother carried to term. I brought the light after darkness. They called me the spoiled one, the coddled one. I remember all kinds of words they whispered or openly called me, such as *manja* (spoiled), *bungsu* (youngest baby of the family), and *anak aleman* (spoiled brat). I was also the one who was said to have the strongest emotional connection to both my mother and your mother. From the time when I was a toddler until much later in life, I was referred as *anaknya*

Wewe—Wewe's kid, a reference that I carried proudly, and still do, as a badge of honor.

I have a theory of why I have such a strong bond with our Mom. When my Mom was pregnant with me, I think I absorbed not only the nutrition she consumed but also all her emotions, and every emotion was so intense after the horrendous incident she had experienced prior to her pregnancy with me. I believe it is fair to assume that in spite of her fears, my mother was thrilled, happy and proud to be pregnant with me after her loss. In spite of what she had experienced, she was excited and joyful and full of determination. I know how brave my Mom was to be pregnant again, so soon after the nightmare she had been through.

Along with all those emotions came the fear of losing another baby, and in time this would make her melancholy as all of her feelings gathered together and overcame her periodically. I understood her feelings of shame and responsibility for losing her baby. While we are all now educated and intelligent enough to know none of this was her fault, as a mother, a woman, living during that time in a culture full of superstitions, it would have been hard for her. For sure, the gossip and whispers surrounding the loss of her baby must have been rough and hard to live with.

Even if shame was not a word that was openly uttered, I am sure my mother felt guilty for not being able to deliver a healthy baby, a baby that was alive. I can only guess. I imagine all the various emotions she would have felt during her pregnancy with me, as well as during the labor period, which lasted thirty hours from the time when her water broke. I am sure both my mother and father were terrified at that time, as they were still traumatized, after all it was just a few years since they had lost baby Deborah, and my mother had almost lost her own life. They must have both been terrified that it would happen all over again. Typically a pregnant woman's hormones influence both body sensations and emotions, amplifying them.

I believe that all these factors and reasons gave me an intense emotional connection to my mother and they also are partly why I became a very intense person. Essentially, I was simmering inside her for nine months, in a very intense physical and emotional condition within my Mom's womb, absorbing every single emotion she was experiencing—the good, the bad and the ugly. I strongly believe that had quite an impact on me as a fetus that manifested later in my personality.

On top of all that, once I was born, my mother and father's emotions, even those of your Mom's and my other siblings', and all those who cared for me were affected by the fact that I was a 'special' baby after what they had been through as a family unit. Understandably, in these circumstances, I was treated with some special esteem, as I was considered to be the baby who brought joy back into my parents' lives, into the family and therefore to everyone connected. Or so we thought…

Everyone, that was, except my older brother David. As

an adult, after going through years of therapy, I have learned
to understand his resentment of me as a child. It doesn't
take a genius to work out why David was not thrilled when
my parents brought me home. Not only could I see pictures
from a photo album how David would always act out in our
family pictures when I was in it, but our nannies and your
Mom have told us stories about how much he disliked me
as a baby. He was around four or five years older than me,
and he was the youngest child until I came along. Clearly
during my parent's ordeal with their stillborn baby, it was
hard not only on them but also on little David. Stories told
by your Mom and my nannies revealed how David would
come to the nursery and to my bassinet and would actually
pinch me when no one was looking, leaving black and blue
marks on me as a baby and later he even tried to suffocate me
with pillows. The stories were told in a light mood as it was
thought of how cute and naughty he was—it was only cute
until his behavior didn't stop—little did we know that David
would be a nightmare of a brother to me, and my nightmare
would continue for decades to come. In fact I had to endure
it for almost all of my life.

This is the reason why I wanted to share how my parents
became such devout Christians. Yes they met at church,
my father was translating from Mandarin and English to
Indonesian for the preacher and my mother was a pianist. Yes,
my uncle had a vision from Jesus—or it could have been a
psychotic episode—but I believe it was the loss of their baby,
and the fact they also almost lost my mother that brought

them closer to God. And later after they had me, the answer to their prayers, their faith became even stronger. So it was ironic that I became the strongest reason for their devotion, but in my mind, this justified why they made such a big commitment to their faith, religion and church. They were so committed that they decided to start leaving me, even as a baby, with your Mom, or my other sister Edna, the nannies, the maids and other adults they perceived as responsible. Sometimes they left me for weeks, or even months at a time, all in the name of their faith.

They had no idea of the danger I was in.

~ *sembilan* ~

"My big brother the Devil…"

I had random memories as a child of a time when David did not want to play with me as he considered me the baby, a child, and also a girl. I was like a plague that he avoided. I think he probably missed his parents too. It was also during this time that he started to act outrageously, his behavior reaching far beyond the boyish things others would do. He got into trouble with my parents for trying to drive at the early age of ten, started skipping school in fourth or fifth grade, and wouldn't bother to come home after sunset.

Sometimes he would pick a fight with our neighborhood kids or schoolmates. There was always a weekly fight or drama between my parents and him. He also wouldn't share anything with me, not his toys, food and especially not his clothes. He would be so angry if I even attempted to borrow his T-shirt. The irony of it was, as our Mom would say:

"He would give his head for his friends."

She couldn't understand at all when she found out he would not even let me touch his clothes, even though we shared a room and had our clothes in the same closet.

Nobody seemed aware that he had no affection towards me at all—on the contrary he went out of his way to show me hostility, humiliate and taunt me, and this grew into torture and abuse. In Indonesia traditionally it is pretty normal for elder brothers to boss their younger brothers around, but they are also supposed to take care of them. David was different.

He basically treated me as his slave and personal assistant.

It was: "Yoyo get my toy, Yoyo get my bag, Yoyo get me water, Yoyo get me food, Yoyo turn the TV on, Yoyo change the channel, Yoyo, turn the TV off!"

He also made me do other chores that he perceived to be my jobs. This happened very cutely in front of the adults, but behind closed doors or when my parents were gone, he would randomly start yelling at me especially if I refused his demands. It was never long before he began to kick me and hit me. If I refused, or I was too slow in doing what he asked, or simply deemed by him to have done something wrong, he would start insisting that I say sorry—not just once, but many times.

Depending how big my fault or mistake was, as perceived by him—and I never knew what the size of my error would be, because there was no baseline to measure my mistake in his mind—I would be asked to apologize by saying:

"I am sorry Ko…" "Sorry ya…" or "*Minta ma'af ya*"—"I am sorry brother…" "Sorry yeah…" or "Forgive me…"

By this time I would start to tremble and feel scared. I would say I was sorry ten times or two hundred times or even a thousand times.

"Ko I am sorry ya, sorry, sorry, sorry, sorry, I am sorry!"

And he would count the number of times I said the word sorry until he was pleased.

It wasn't long until I would be crying or sobbing and had broken out in a cold sweat. Nowadays I would describe that feeling as what they call 'being scared shitless'. If I didn't pronounce the word 'Sorry' or *'Maaf'* to his satisfaction, he would hit me or slap me or make me repeat them over from the count of one all over again. Out of nowhere he would add to my punishment indiscriminately if he was not satisfied. As I write this I can feel my heart pounding once more out of anger but also out of my PTSD—the post-trauma stress disorder brings back this instant physical reaction learned after years of torture. My blood boils whenever I remember his cruel behavior. If the apology session wasn't satisfying enough, or he was in an even fouler mood, I could expect a slap, a kick, a hit, or the next thing my head would be slammed into the wall or the ground.

No matter how the events proceeded, I always ended up crying, feeling sad, upset, helpless and frustrated. At the end I would find myself physically beaten and exhausted, but, as I mentioned before, I could endure the physical pain. It was the emotional torture that I found unbearable.

This happened from as early as when I was only four years old and went on until my freshman year in college. If I cried, he would continue the physical abuse or he would threaten me with even more severe beatings. He also threatened me with more abuse and torture if I told our parents or any adults in the house when my parents were gone. His wrath was more than I could handle as a child.

I witnessed the sadness and pain my Mom suffered when David started conflicts in the house. Speaking as an adult, I now can see that our Mother was a very emotional person and very reactive. During David's wildest years she was also at an age, I now understand, when she was most likely pre-menopausal and menopausal. It was a dangerous combination. When my Mom could not handle David being such a difficult and problematic child, and later a terrible teenager, it would end up in a screaming contest. My Mom would cry and tremble and she would beat her chest, saying she would die or join her Mother, our Grandma, in heaven. I was somewhere between the age of five to ten years when the worst arguments happened. My Mom would tell David that she might die in a coma from her diabetes or she would stop taking her insulin so she could join her mother. My father would get angry after all this emotional distress and a war would erupt at home on a regular basis. Your Mom and I would console each other, feeling sad to see our family in that awful situation, confused and not knowing what to do but cry. We would try to keep the peace, as well as consoling and comforting our Mother and each other.

As a child, I worshiped my Mother and I was scared of my Father, even if he never hit me or raised his hand to me or to our Mother. The sadness in my Mom's eyes, her emotional desperation and dramatic behavior made me feel so horrible that I would cry and try to calm her down, begging everyone to stop to no avail. David would continue to scream and yell at my parents, behaving like a degenerate who was raised by wolves, and acted out his anger, lashing his teenage rage at my parents. He would even challenge my Father to a duel or try to fight anyone in his way. As for me, I'd do anything I could to protect my parent's emotions and to keep the peace at home, even if it meant that no one knew what David did to me behind closed doors or whenever my parents were away.

Daily physical abuse was traumatic, but it was the humiliation and mental torture that got me so beaten and depressed. I became depressed to a point where I started having insomnia at the age of ten or eleven, and continued to suffer sleepless nights right up until my early twenties.

It was during this time that your Mom, my sister discovered what was happening to me. I was being regularly hit, beaten, and slapped and my brother David would not hesitate to spit on me, or slam my head and body into to the wall or floor. He was one raging, angry and violent person; even as a teenager, he could not control his emotions or behavior. I believe he took out his frustration at my parents leaving us personally on me. David was no longer the youngest child and he vented his unchecked behavior on me. I literally became his punching bag. He abused me on a daily basis for as long as I could remember, it felt interminable, until he left for Jakarta to continue his schooling.

My sister Wewe would beg him to stop during any episodes when she was home and found out what was happening, and sometimes she was successful. Although she was older, Wewe was much smaller in build than David. When David was in his nasty wrath and Wewe failed to plead her case to stop him, he would, without hesitation, push her away, shoving her until she fell sideways, but she would persevere, hanging on to me as long as she could. Or she would cover me, so she was the one who took his blows, both of us crying. Usually this happened while there was no one in the room or everyone was so far away in our vast mansion and estate that no one could hear us crying. Wewe would cry. She couldn't bear to witness me being treated cruelly, so she would cling to me when he got so angry, and he would hit her instead.

This went on for years and thinking about it now still makes me upset, less for me—in fact, not for me at all—but out of indignation that my evil sibling had no decency, at least not enough, to not hit our sister. My body was constantly covered in bruises and pain, and I felt like my soul was dying slowly. Only your Mom knew all the truth and she always comforted me. Later Ana and Mbak Ti would do the same. Your Mom and the other women in my life were the ones who protected me from my abuser. Just as your mother never demanded luxuries or money the way the rest of us did, she never told our parents what was going on. I think she didn't feel that she had the right as David was the biological child and she was an adopted one. The irony of this to me is that she in fact was always a better child and sibling than my own brother was—to my parents, to me, to all of us.

During what I called 'world war' and the explosive fights at home between my parents and David, I was always frantically trying to make them stop, going from person to person to stop or to comfort my mother and I would start crying, and become hysterical. In times like this your mother would rescue me and take me away, as far as she possibly could in our house or property so I would not hear or see what was going on. She would wipe my tears, hug me and console me in her motherly, soothing, calm way, while shedding her own tears. While I am not proud of my parents and family having these episodes, and have never talked about them, it is now time for me to share these stories. I want other parents or adults to understand and realize how such fights and displays of bad temper can affect their children.

I found some relief from the abuse from David after he left for school. Now he was gone most of the time, but during school vacations and holidays he came home and it started again. His school vacation meant my peaceful break from him was over. Now there were times where he loved hitting, spitting on, and slapping me in front of the neighborhood kids and his friends, with reasons I never understood. His justifications could be summarized from what I assumed to be my own inadequacies. I was girly, a sissy, I was like a girl, I was *banci, benchong* or I didn't do what he asked me to do. His demands started up all over again for me to do his chores or to get his stuff. If I touched or moved his things by accident there would be trouble. Another thing that people thought was cute but I also hated, was for him to demand that I massage his back and legs and body with his small toy cars. He would control the speed and where they had to go, essentially using his body as a racetrack.

Sometimes when he was in his insane mode he would yell and scream, trying to humiliate and physically attack me for no apparent reason—or with the excuse that I was simply annoying and a nuisance. I believe most of the adults in our house knew what was going on, but they each handled it differently. My parents were barely home with their intense commitments to their church, faith and religion—I think for them denial was a lot easier to live with, so they buried their heads in the sand. They already had enough trouble with him without me having to be considered as a part of the equation. Now and then they would reprimand him when he was a lot younger, but as he grew older and stronger he started to attack anyone who was perceived as his enemy, including my own father or the gardener, who tried to hold him down while he was full of rage.

It must have been easier for them not to have to deal with the real issue. Besides, they had no knowledge of psychological conditions or behaviors, and there was no such thing as therapy or behavioral education in those days that could help us to learn how to handle our situation. My sister Edna tried to interfere only to get slapped by David and she was seven years older than him. Wewe bravely continued to try to protect me, and later on the other women in the house who I mentioned before also tried. As a child, I had so much fear of loud screams I would shake and tremble easily, break into cold sweats, and my heart would pound so hard every time I heard any sort of confrontation or raised voices. I didn't sleep like other children or healthy children should.

Besides being disturbed by constant nightmares, cold sweats and difficulties to fall asleep, I used to wake up at intervals all night long, making sure any part of my body did not, by mistake, touch David. I was terrified of him kicking and hitting me in the middle of the night. In those years we shared a mattress on the floor in our parent's master suite. It was not unusual for my parents or the maids or David himself to find me sleeping on the floor a long way away from my parents' bed and far from our mattress. They would find me sleeping on the floor in my father's library or down by the bathrooms, and marvel at the distance from my original sleeping location without questioning it further.

It looked as if I had been sleepwalking, but I knew I had probably just inched my way as far as I could from my tormentor. He also demanded for me to be his alarm clock, one with a manual snooze button. I served as his alarm clock for many years, as he demanded I wake him up at certain hours during naps, or in the mornings. Almost every single time he would be so pissed that I woke him up—even though he had requested it—then he would tell me to come back in two minutes or five minutes or ten, whatever he felt he needed, and if I was too early or late by just a few seconds there would be hell to pay. All of these demands to wake him up happened regardless of the fact that he had his own alarm o'clock there, right next to him. I would get his wrath in verbal, physical or emotional abuse during his grumpy hours, and this happened for many years. Basically he treated me as if I was his child servant and personal slave. Even those without any formal education in psychology can see how his treatment of me resulted in my suffering from lot of emotional and psychological issues that lasted all through my childhood, teenage years and right up until early adulthood.

Apart from slapping, hitting, kicking, beating and slamming me to the wall and the floor he liked to play one particularly sadistic game with me called 'driving a roadster'. David has always been obsessed with hot rods and cars in general. He had remote control car toys and racing cars on tracks operated on battery and a collection of various hot rods. At random times, he would use me as 'his car'. My hands and arms became his steering wheel and my genitals substituted for clutch, brake and accelerator pedals just as if I was his car. He would make a noise that sounded like a racecar and would put pressure on parts of my body, using a kicking motion as if he was stopping or accelerating the car. Needless to say, the pain was unbearable but the more I screamed or cried or pleaded for him to stop, the more amused he was, and he would laugh loudly at times, with great hilarity. It was truly a sadistic act. Then when I was sobbing and least expected it he would punch me so hard that I instantly threw up, and this made him even angrier so he insisted that I eat my own vomit.

There were times I was in so much pain and emotionally drained that I simply gave in. My body would still be there and I would let my mind wander or switch off completely. During these episodes I could witness my own body being beaten or tortured. I basically passed out as a way of surviving my pain. It was so unbearable that I had no idea what had happened to me but I could hear and see myself, and my abuser, from high up above. Later I learned that out-of-body experience is a fairly common occurrence in child abuse. I looked it up online and found that an out-of-body experience, abbreviated as OBE or OOBE, enables a person to experience the world from a location outside their physical body.[7] One in ten people have an OBE once, or more commonly, several times in their life.

Being dunked by David was almost a routine whenever we went to the beach or pool. The more I fought him, the more he saw it as a challenge and it gave him great amusement. I can't remember exactly how many times I had to swallow the salty ocean water or the nasty chlorine pool water. I was always happiest when he paid no heed to me and he was with the swimming coach or with his friends. Being pushed under water and held there until my lungs were bursting usually triggered my OBE and I could see the entire pool from up above and not focus so much on my own struggle.

As a battered child I used to wish I could fly like a bird to escape to a new place and world, far away from all my pain and misery. When a movie called *Forrest Gump* came out there was little girl character in it named Jenny, who was also abused by her father. She used to pray as she ran away from her perpetrator and her words remain with me: "Dear God, make me a bird so I can fly far, far away from here…."

I cried and cried when I told my husband about my childhood experiences. Another really mean thing David

---

7. An OBE is a form of autoscopy (literally 'seeing self'), although the term *autoscopy* more commonly refers to the pathological condition of seeing a second self, or doppelgänger.

liked to do was to order me to bring him his dog, if only for the joy of watching his big dog Astor drag me on the terrazzo or gravel. He would laugh so hard and it seemed like there was nothing he would not do for his own enjoyment at my cost. He had thrown his books, bags, and roller-skates at me, he had locked me in a room in the dark, knowing I was scared of the dark. He had put a mirror in front of me while I was doing my personal business in the toilet, and made me wait for him while he was in the shower, forbidding me to go anywhere. He was notorious for being late for school and he would instruct the driver to drop him off first, knowing it would make me late as we went to different private schools.

My body was constantly covered in bruises, pains, and bloody scratches. My mind was a minefield, full of emotional bruises and pains that lasted for decades and left their mark on my life. I had been thrown to the ground countless times but I survived. Over the years I had been asked to apologize thousands of times. I was completely unaware that my monstrous elder brother had enslaved me, although it went on for most of my childhood. All I wanted to do was to keep the peace at home, to protect my parents and your Mom, and my sister Edna who he also taunted in his own ways when our parents were away and she was in charge.

Had we been living in a different country or time and era David would have been placed in some kind of therapy or a special behavioral school or institution. My parents would have been in trouble—in today's social system in the U.S. they would have been charged with child neglect. Sadly, it was culturally acceptable to do what David did to boss a younger brother around, and for my father to use corporal punishment himself on David was actually considered the norm. David too had been belted, slapped and even hung upside down by my father. He had even had hot chili rubbed on his face as punishment. I learned much later that my father had been physically abused by his father. Clearly this was permitted to happen by both cultural and generational mores at the time. I am determined to stop the cycle.

When I came to the U.S., I was in San Jose before moving to San Francisco while David went to school in Portland. At this stage his emotional power over me became even more detrimental in my life. In my first year of college he insisted for me to be with him for Christmas only to humiliate me in front of his friends and mine—who I had invited to come along as my safety measure. He could not conceal his anger and hit me in front of my friends, who left with me. His friends left too. No one dared to make a move or call the police. I had a horrible case of insomnia to a point that I only slept anywhere from thirty minutes to a few hours a night, affecting my general physical health badly. I was so distraught that he could be still hitting me at my age of eighteen—and he was twenty-three.

Technically I could have turned him in, if I had the courage. My fear of him was so paralyzing it actually made me think that he was my owner or my boss or slave-master, to a point that I felt totally helpless and thought this would go on for the rest of my life.

I had considered both suicide and a plot to murder him since I was eleven or twelve years old. Children of that age usually run around happily, but I planned to kill myself, or my elder brother. It got so bad that I finally sought help through University of San Francisco's campus health services where I received counseling. My first therapist was a PhD candidate in psychology from Stanford and she was another important woman in my life who helped me to survive and grow as a person. Her name is Karen Hayashi. She was the one who helped me for the first time in my life. I was eighteen years old, and I didn't realize I had been abused all my life and my brother was the perpetrator. I had no idea that he was mentally ill and he himself needed help. At this time I was desperate for help. I will always be so grateful for the knowledge and professional help I received from Karen.

The thing that triggered my emotions to a point that I thought I was going crazy, was David's trying to control everything I did. He started telling me what to do with my car, a vehicle that used to be his, and that grew into telling me what to do with my life: where to go during my vacation, what I could or could not do. This was in addition to my Christian-freak cousins in San Jose who had decided they could do the same, simply because they had let me live with them and helped me to come to the United States. The fact was that David, my cousin and her husband were overbearingly controlling, all three of them. They had decided I could only have Indonesian or Asian friends, preferably Christian, and I should go to Church, and it should be their church. Their power trip with me started to become more obvious when I began to break these rules, and my anger built up to such a boiling point that in the end I refused to see or talk to them again.

It was during my therapy session that I learned the perpetrators of my abuse relied on my fear to be able to control me. I felt so liberated by the thought that I was actually an independent human who need not report to any other person. For the first time I realized that here in the United States I was legally an adult, with all the freedoms of independence that adulthood involved, and no one owned me; no one was my master.

It was Karen who advised me that as I was an eighteen-year-old I needed no permission from anyone to live my life as I saw it fit, as long as I didn't break the law. For the first time in my life I felt so relieved, and I wasn't scared of anyone or anything. I finally understood that David had controlled me by using my fear, just as my cousin and her husband had tried to do. I felt a great weight lifting from me.

~ *sepuluh* ~

"The other monsters…"

It was around this time that my English professor at the University of San Francisco assigned us a research paper allowing us to choose any subject that we felt passionate about. She told us to choose our own subjects, preferably something we were curious or felt strongly about, and that touched us personally. I decided to write my paper on child abuse. Not only did it touch me personally, I thought, but this would also give me an opportunity to learn more about child abuse in general and to educate myself about my own life. It might even bring other benefits, I thought.

That was indeed what happened to me. I learned so much in researching this subject, and writing about it, although I found it difficult, it was quite cathartic.

I still keep a copy of the paper I wrote. To my great surprise, Professor Bright, my lecturer, gave me an A+ and she wrote a very sincere personal note on my paper, basically commending me for my bravery in writing it. She also let me know how sorry she was to know about what I had gone through from early childhood.

When she handed my paper back, she gave it to me with a hug. I shall never forget. I shared my paper and made a copy to send to my father, so he could learn what I had gone through. Now at last I understood it was not, and never had been, my fault. It was not easy to share what my elder brother had done to me with my parents, but I felt empowered to share my terrible experiences, not only about my elder brother who tortured me all through my early life, but also about the other monsters in my life.

Through my therapy and research, and talking to other members of my family I also learned how my brother David's behavior was partially learned from my father, who had also been a victim of violent abuse himself, by his father. It has been passed on from generation to generation. I am glad I have broken the cycle. Someday, I hope and pray, I will be able to write another memoir about forgiveness, to tell the story of how I forgave my brother David, after I disowned him for twelve years. I refused to have any contact with him until I was able to make up my mind to forgive him, after I realized that he too was a victim. I have tried to help him to be a better person, father and husband. I also forgave all the monsters in my life.

I finally decided to leave the University of San Francisco and move away, and went back to Switzerland to continue my course at the hospitality management school there, just to get away from it all. This enabled me to go away without David or my cousins telling me what to do, to take my life into my own hands and take charge. In this way I managed to rediscover my own self, as there had been so many demons and monsters in my life and I needed to work out how to deal with my past.

David was not the only monster of my childhood.

*   *   *

They say children can be cruel, but their cruelty is a learned behavior. I believe that there is no such thing as a 'bad" child, however there are a lot of bad parents, teachers, and adults. Most children learn their good or bad behavior patterns and attitudes from adults—especially those adults who raise them.

Throughout my childhood in Indonesia, the nasty name-calling usually came from my schoolmates, especially the older boys. Girls were typically kinder; they did not partake in the name-calling. Instead, they would befriend or protect me from the bullies. The bullying was endless, along with the name-calling, and regularly they also would physically harm me by pushing and shoving me to the ground or they would hit me and do their best to provoke a physical fight, although I would never retaliate. I was scrawny and effeminate, and clearly I was the perfect target for those kids who were angry, jealous or simply insecure.

The teachers who were good and kind would break up the fights whenever they could. I normally tried to avoid the usual suspects and stay with the girls or hang out with another one or two 'losers'. Yes, I was one of the losers at school. I might have had potential as the popular, smart, rich kid who sat in the front and became a teacher's pet, but it didn't work that way. I was unpopular and perceived as a loser by my peers and the older kids. The bad teachers would actually not only watch the abuse, they would also encourage the bullies to continue being mean by laughing, or worse still by joining them in calling me all the horrible names I have mentioned already.

A number of teachers called me inappropriate and abusive names, but that was only a part of it. There were three particular teachers I will never forget who not only called me terrible names but also physically abused me.

Pak Joseph caned me with rattan in front of the entire class while simultaneously calling me *banci* or *bencong*, adding to the physical injuries I endured. The humiliation of being displayed publicly in front of forty or so other students while being punished, simply because I was helping a classmate solve a math problem, was embarrassing. But to be called faggot or transvestite at a tender age while being lashed with a rattan cane was painful physically and mentally. The entire school heard about it, as all forty of my classmates quickly spread the news during recess.

This took place at a Catholic school and the principal of our school was a nun. No action was ever taken by her, in fact my misdemeanor was held up as a bad example of what not to do—do not be a sissy and do not try to help your classmate plus don't say a word or dare stand up for yourself. I was red from being humiliated and in pain from the rattan caning of my body. That day I counted two sets of ten marks, from the top of my head down to my ankles. This was at a time when our uniforms consisted of shorts and a short-sleeved, collared shirt. The marks left were there after school when my driver picked me up and he put ointment on them and hugged me and made me feel better. My parents were away on one of their frequent church trips; there were only maids and gardeners at home. They all tended to me and I saw their sorry faces full of compassion, but they had no power to do anything. After the incident, I tried to be quiet at school, and did my best to become invisible. I kept my head low and my grades declined. I didn't dare to look any teachers in the eye again after that.

That was not the end of my misery at school. When I was slightly older and my parents moved me to another catholic school, the same one that David attended, I was known to be David's younger brother and was expected to be like him. Huh! Were they ever wrong—we could not have been any more different. By this time David was already in Jakarta. But the fact that I was nothing like him, and unable to replicate his boyish, masculine ways, was the start of my trouble with certain teachers. The bullying got worse. Being a new student, as well as a sissy, girly rich student somehow marked me with a sign that said: "Please bully me or hit me or attack me!"

I expected no less, and going to school remained unpleasant for obvious reasons. The anticipation of being bullied and humiliated and hurt physically set in again, and the mental and emotional pains were worse than the physical pain I experienced. The daunting thought that this would continue in my daily life at my new school made me miserable and depressed, and I lived in fear. I was totally unequipped to deal with any of it and I was only a child.

Then there were the two other teachers, both of them called Pak Joko, who shared the same mean streaks. One was a Physical Education (P.E.) teacher and a coach, while the other one was an Indonesian language teacher. From the first time we met, both of these teachers zoomed in on me in a negative way. They both starting off by calling me sissy and *banci*, making fun of me publicly at every chance they had, in that macho way, as if their masculinity depended upon it. They behaved in a manner not too different to the behavior of the older male students. On several occasions Pak Joko the P.E. teacher slapped and punched me in front of my male classmates during a weekly volley practice, sending signals to all the students that this was an appropriate way to behave.

I had never ever been good at sports or any physical activities in a P.E. class, as you know. Being bullied and picked on didn't help me get any better. This Pak Joko character was always annoyed one way or another by the way I walked or talked and this got worse at some point when I could not serve the ball properly, or manage to do what he perceived every boy should be able to do. Basically, he punched me in the gut, just as he was calling me a loser, a girl, and all kinds of other nasty names. I must have said something to defend myself—finally, after he had been going on for some time—and that's when he lunged at me and hit me on my face. Yes, that happened at a private Catholic school with no action being taken to reprimand the teacher or to protect the minor.

The Indonesian language teacher, the other Pak Joko, constantly made fun of me in a similar way yet there was nothing he could do as far as my performance was concerned. I was a very good student academically at this point. However somehow I was always getting on his nerves, according to him. Yes he let the entire class know about this—I was like a girl and that irritated him. I spoke too much, I was a 'chatty Cathy' and I spoke like girls did, so I had no idea what I had done wrong in class, but the next thing I knew he simply slapped me a few times out of the blue, saying "That will make a boy out of you!"

How I wish I could go back to these ignorant unkind adults and tell them the effect their behavior had on me. I can't help but think about other students who have become their victims over the years, and I know from statistics that in every batch of students there could easily be one or two like me, who are particularly vulnerable.

To say that I dreaded every P.E. class and Indonesian class was an understatement. I experienced severe anxiety and insomnia every night before those classes, as I was dreading the humiliation and physical abuse. It was during this time I vowed to study abroad and I swore not to speak Indonesian ever again once I left this country. My resentment as a child to anything that involved sports or the Indonesian language grew stronger than ever. I began to study French and English, as I knew I wanted to study in the countries where those languages were spoken.

Later, I was so pleased that I was given a chance to live in the United States, Switzerland and France and I could achieve my goals. I had accomplished what I told myself I would do, and managed to get away from the monsters that were supposed to teach and protect me but did just the opposite. I was also extremely proud that I graduated from my high school in San Jose California with honors in English as a second language, although technically it was my third.

There were other demons and devils at school and around the neighborhood or at church but they were tolerable relatively speaking in comparison to the ones I have mentioned, and the ones I am about to tell you. As I am writing these daylight nightmares down, two things came to mind. First, I had never ever told your Mom, as I knew her heart would break and she would feel responsible, and I know it's the last thing she needed as she was going through her own torture. Second, I continue to ask myself which monster do I share first, or which of the sad parts out of everything I experienced should I share here. I battle constantly, as I write these letters, whether or not to share them with you and the world.

While my sister did not deserve the pain from these nightmares I knew she would have wanted me to tell her— and I am telling her and the world now for the reasons I have mentioned—to help prevent any of these things from happening to other children, to educate others and to spread an awareness of child abuse with the hope it will continue to reduce the incidents for generations to come. This always calms me down and makes it possible for me to continue to share my nightmares.

I would like to warn you that the next part of this chapter is going to be difficult for you and all those who read it. I still find it very hard to share, even now I am almost fifty years old. It somehow feels as though this was an experience that happened to someone else and I can hardly believe it actually happened to anyone, let alone myself. But it did, it happened to me, and I cannot change that.

To tell you this story I have to take you back to the time when we built our large house. Our two main gardeners, who were also farmers, started to work for the estate before the new house was ready for our family to move in. Out of curiosity, I used to visit the construction site, along with hundreds of random construction workers who were busy completing the house, mostly male workers.

I believe Suharman and Mastuarjo were friends who came from the same area in Lampung. These two men had always been nice to me. They were friendly and always welcomed my visits to their 'territory', which mainly consisted of the chicken farms and vegetable gardens situated at varying distances around the house. They usually worked six days a week from 8am or so till dusk, from Monday to Saturday. I liked to roam around the property when I wasn't at school on the afternoons when I had no extra-curricular activities or play dates with my schoolmates. I enjoyed visiting various parts of the land. It was always fun to play by the ponds and with our baby deer Manis, and I liked to explore the vegetable gardens, the employee houses and the aviary, although I would not go near it if I knew David was there with his friends. I would make these little visits to my favorite places when I was bored or trying to avoid David.

Suharman was quite tall, at least that was my perception as a small child. He was sort of silly and goofy, and I never thought of him as being mean or unkind. I used to help him harvest the eggs from the chickens or play around him as he was planting or gardening. He taught me a few tricks in planting vegetables or maintaining my Mom's roses and pruning branches, and I enjoyed being around flowers. Our land was so vast that if you were in one part of the property you wouldn't hear or know what else was going on in other parts, as each nook and cranny was obstructed from view by trees or some type of structure.

By this time I must have been around nine years old. I would follow Suharman around like a puppy. At some point Suharman took on extra duties, helping the night guards to keep an eye on the property for extra security, and he began to spend the night once or twice a week, roaming around the land to make sure the fences were in good shape and there were no intruders. He always carried a machete day and night. I continued to follow him around, even during the late hours after it was dark.

When my parents were away there were only a couple of maids in the house at night, as well as my cousin. At times there were no family members at all. I would follow Suharman in his rounds and would sit with him in the dark. He wore a sarong at night like most men in Lampung. One night I sat next to him in a corner of the backyard where my parents had built a structure for washing and repairing the cars. We had a lot of cars and it was designed so you could drive the car up and wash it or repair it easily.

It was a quiet part of the yard, far from the house, and no one was around there at this time of the night. I had become used to sitting close to Suharman in the dark, as I was very fond of him, and no words were usually exchanged. This time he seemed very tense, and when he grabbed me and led me behind the tall structure, which hid both of us from view of the house, I knew something was wrong. He put his hands over my face and he held me tightly from behind. The next thing I knew he spread my legs and pushed something hard in me. It was so painful that I groaned but he continued to cover my mouth, gripping harder as the shock and the pain grew worse, and then he grunted, a different kind of sound to the one I made. Somehow I thought he must be hurt too.

I was in such pain that I struggled, and tried to push him away, but that only seemed to make him tighten his grip and push into me further. All this time he was smoking a clove-scented kretek cigarette, taking a puff and then removing it from his mouth and putting it on the concrete structure, as if it were the most normal thing to do. I could see the smoke spiraling up into the air.

I don't know if I blacked out, but when I came back into my body I felt a sense of wetness, and he was done pushing me. I pulled my shorts back up and rushed to the spigot to wash myself in the dark. I wanted to cry but I was too afraid. He moved closer to our garage, motioning to me to go back inside the house, and he cautioned me with a long "sssshhhhhhh" while raising his finger to his mouth, clearly gesturing for me not to tell any one what had happened.

I went straight to my bathroom and that's when I learned I was bleeding…I was even more scared by the blood at that point than by the painful act of brutal aggression from Suharman, who I had thought was my friend. I cried and cried. When my maids asked me why I was crying all I could say was I missed your Mom and my parents. I think in my child's mind I thought I was dying and I might never see them again. The bleeding had stopped but the pain continued both physically and emotionally. And I did not die, although at times I wished I had.

I began to live in a daze where I was going through the motions of my everyday life, but I felt that I wasn't there in my body, even when it happened again. I was so confused that I didn't fight back, but I mostly stayed quiet. I witnessed myself being molested again and again from up above looking down on my body. I didn't know then, that I was having an out-of-body experience, and it only added to my confusion.

It got worse, as there was another monster in waiting. If Suharman did what he did to me at night, his friend Mastuarjo would do the same to me in the broad daylight in his chicken farm area. I had no idea if Suharman informed him or not. Perhaps there was a mark on my forehead that said 'molest me'. It happened roughly about the same time, not long after Suharman first did the unthinkable. In my state of confused oblivion I became an easy prey, and Mastuarjo was even more callous, to a point that I would just lie there on the ground after each attack, with my tears flowing and he didn't even seem to notice. Like a bird of prey he would appear out of nowhere, scoop me up and fall on top of me, crushing my immature child's body to the ground, his whole weight on top of me. Or he would turn me on my stomach first, forcing my face onto the gravel.

Both of those men had their own wife and a number of children. Not until I was an adult and I was in therapy did I even dare to think about their families, or question if they ever did what they did to me to their own children. I cringed every time the thought crossed my mind. For the sake of their children—I told myself I must be the only victim, and no other child had to experience what I did. Even now as I am writing this, it feels so strange to think that this happened to any child—it is so wrong on so many different levels—and I can hardly believe that I was that child.

Then there was Mas Parjo, the male maid that my parents hired from church who later stole household items when he left. He robbed more than silver and kitchen equipment. This he-devil reincarnate was also another human who robbed my childhood and innocence. As I mentioned, while he was employed by my parents his tasks were more that of a maid, he did things such as housecleaning and kitchen duties. When the other members of our staff who usually cleaned the house were on vacation he would be the backup to do their jobs. One day when no one was home he came in to my room and forced himself on me, performing oral sex.

The shame that I carried after that happened haunted me as I had been told oral sex was wrong and as evil as the sin of premarital sex or worse. My young mind had no capability to process the realities of the crime that he was committing and I simply focused on what I had been told. I was full of fear that I was no longer 'clean' or acceptable in the eyes of God and the church. The fact that I had an erection while he performed the act was the worst part of it. I felt that I must have somehow been complicit. While the original rape and abuse I experienced was terrible and painful physically, this new act was in some ways more emotionally damaging because of the shame and guilt it brought with it, which I carried for years. It was not until after years of therapy and working on myself with the help of a professional psychiatrist that I understood it was not my fault. One thing I knew, I would never let myself be in the same room alone with him ever again and he had no chance to repeat what he did to me.

As a teenager, when I was about fifteen or slightly older, I lived and attended school in Jakarta for a very short time in my life, although it felt like a century. Those who are familiar with me know I have an aversion to Jakarta, I call the chaotic capital city the 'armpit of Indonesia'. It was there that I met a pastor named Edan, who was also very sweet and cute. Most of his congregations were charmed by his personality and looks, so much so that I referred to them as his 'hypnotized herd'. He was a friend of a family friend of ours in Semarang.

I had just been through the most terrible time adjusting to what was considered to be the best private Christian school in the country. There were many reasons I found it difficult. The tougher academic studies made it hard for me to catch up, I was still being bullied, and the overall school culture didn't suit my more liberal, rather westernized way of thinking. Already I could not wait to move to the United States. I had a 'girlfriend' who was absolutely obsessed and in love with me, but I knew I was a homosexual and she was a convenient cover. The social pressure of behaving like a heterosexual to stop any rumors and to avoid the bullying was very difficult. I was dating this sweet girl who actually fell head over heels for me. Instead, I fell in love with Edan.

Edan came to stay with us and for me it was love at first sight, but I was barely sixteen, and he was most probably around twenty-eight, or older. We had a very intense affair that included having sexual relations. While he never forced himself on me in the manner of those adults during my younger years, I still believe what Edan did was inappropriate and wrong. I was practically still a child, and legally a minor. It was intense to the point of obsession and we would concoct hidden rendezvous, disguising our relationship as friendship and fellowship. My family seemed to be easily fooled, and they were so happy that I was close to a pastor. My parents had always hoped I would be one.

Most of my family members and friends simply thought I needed a role model and my parents could not be happier that a pastor and their son were best friends. But behind all that, we had a raw sexual affair. He was an ordained pastor of the Presbyterian church, while I was simply too young to understand all that it entailed to have a proper relationship and driven by my raging hormones. While I didn't classify him as a complete 'monster', I would put him under an even more dangerous category. I think of him now as a hidden devil, decked in the cloth of religion.

Sadly, this was not my only encounter with men of the cloth. I went on to repeat the same pattern as a freshman at the University of San Francisco with a campus ministry director, Father McLeod who was also the ordained priest of St. Ignatius. We fell in love, head over heels, became obsessed with each other, and for more than a semester we continued along a path of sexual encounters. He would smuggle me into his church housing. Later we even met up in the Philippines, where he did his sabbatical, as well as in Europe. While in Europe I found out he had cheated on me in Asia. He promised his faithfulness and loyalty to me, but broke that trust, in the same easy way he had broken his commitment of celibacy to his religion and church.

I was eighteen by now, legally an adult in age, but still immature, and the power and professional status he held in his position should have prevented him from approaching me, let alone having an affair with me for almost two years. I never reported him but I still keep all the memorabilia from the pictures, love letters, even a few other personal items. Originally, the reason for me to keep them was for the memory of my love, but now I keep them as proof of his inappropriate behavior and if I heard anything about him involving another minor I would not hesitate to report him. He was in his late thirties, a campus ministry director who should have been trustworthy, but he broke that trust with an innocent eighteen-year-old foreign student freshman.

Each of these men of the church now feel nervous around me, or when they hear from me. Both knew exactly what they were doing was wrong, hiding behind their robes, preying upon innocent souls and leaving psychological and mental burdens on people like me.

As I write about these nightmares I have to continually remind myself of those things I learned in my therapy, and practice what I learned to do to avoid getting caught up in the trauma all over again, or letting myself drift away into frustration and anger. Yet I can't help but ask, as I converse with this child inside me. "How did you survive such a horrendous childhood and youth?"

How does a child learn to cope with the monsters, demons and devils on this earth? To be a child in the coming-of-age period in itself is not easy, even without predators. We all suffer growing pains, they say, but growing up for me was beyond any comprehensible pain, of the kind no child should ever have to endure.

A few people in my life who know me well enough, to have learned about my childhood asked me how I could go on living after all the pain, torture and abuse. There were times when I didn't wish my life to continue, and even now I am grateful that I didn't end up dead, or institutionalized from a nervous breakdown, or even a drug-addict. My terrible childhood could have led to any of the above.

I would say that I barely survived. In fact in some ways I know I died on the inside as a child. At one point as a teenager I was so depressed that I became addicted to sleeping pills in Switzerland. When one pill didn't work, I took two, and if that didn't work I decided to take three. I couldn't remember how many I had taken when my co-worker at the hotel where I spent my *stage* internship during my hotel management school found me on the bathroom floor at 4:30 am one day. The owner of the restaurant where it happened had to take me to the hospital in the dead of winter when the roads were packed with snow. Was it an attempt at suicide or a cry for help? Perhaps a little bit of both, my adult self now tells me.

Another answer to my survival is love. The love I received from so many people in my life, and especially the love your mother showered me all her life, this is what has kept me going. I am a firm believer that for every unkind, horrible human, there are at least ten kind, loving and compassionate ones. Good does conquer evil, and your mother's kindness and love trumped all the evils in the world. In bad times, then and now, I could somehow survive and recover from those horrific events in my life by imagining your mother enveloping me with her warmth, love and affection. I simply closed my eyes and my mind would work its magic. I would think about the times she would climb up to pick star-fruit from the *belimbing* tree to get me the juiciest ones, ripe and yellow, and we would quickly run them under water and use our teeth to get rid of the greenest toughest edges, then devour them till the juice dripped down our faces and arms. Or we would get the green ones and make a ground-up salt and chili concoction to dab with our green star-fruit, or the rose-apple *jambu* that grew at our rental house.

I would remember waking her up with kisses in the dead of the night, and she would never once be angry with me, instead she would open her eyes, stroke my hair, kiss me back and she always knew exactly what I wanted—a glass of super-cold iced condensed milk, the special kind that she made so perfectly. She would get up and carry me or I would follow her in our drowsy walk with our sleepy eyes to the kitchen. Once there she would combine the perfect amount of condensed milk from a can in the fridge that had been punctured at two opposite ends, in a glass. She would stir it with water and ice cubes and I would lick the leftover condensed milk dripping on the side before I devoured the entire cold and sweet concoction. She then would carry me back to bed, usually already asleep, and the next thing I knew it was morning and she was waking me up to get me ready for school.

Getting ready for school was a ritual I won't forget, and memories of this carried me through my darkest times. Wewe would first wake me up with her kisses and carry me to the plastic tub—we had no bathtub in the old days—and she would have filled it up already, mixing the hot and cold water to a perfect temperature. She would bathe me, still half-asleep, then dry me off, put my uniform on and comb my hair. The last touch was always a handkerchief folded immaculately and put it in my crisp shirt pocket. She would then get ready herself while I either ate my breakfast or went back to napping again in bed. Then she scooped me up and carried me to the car and put me on her lap. She wouldn't start waking me up till a few minutes before we arrived at my school, and then she kissed me goodbye, handing me my bag and water canteen.

Another precious memory I would escape to was the time she made me my dolls and we played with them, her smile, her laughter and her clever hands crafting my favorite toys. Of course many times all I did was close my eyes and wait for her to come home from school. Sometimes my dog Kas and I would play in the front yard or on the badminton court, just sitting and lounging around until she came home. Together we would run to her and she would also run to us to scoop me up, then she would carry me, handing me my packet of garlic peanuts while hugging me tightly and showering me with kisses. There were times when things were bad that I just closed my eyes and pretended she was covering me, holding me, taking away the beatings or the abuse. She was the one person that gave me comfort in person, and even when we were apart her love always lingered and hovered around me, protecting my light from being extinguished by the evils and monsters in my life.

~ *sebelas* ~

"There were other angels too…"

Your mother gave me the most precious gift during my
unspeakably painful childhood. She supported me whenever
she could, not only with her physical protection when
possible, but also with her constant love. The memory of her
and all the things she did for me as a child, which may sound
like normal things in the caring and loving of a child, perhaps
insignificant to some, were in fact, larger than life for me.
They filled the darkness in my soul with a light that helped
me find my way through a labyrinth in my most desperate
and pain-filled times, and they continue to give me joy, a joy
that is infused with the sadness I feel as I miss her so much,
throughout every hour and every day in my life.

It would be inaccurate and untrue to say that your
mother was my only angel throughout my early life, and she
would have wanted me to share my stories with you about
the others who cared and comforted, loved and protected
me from the evil behavior I was confronted with in my
childhood. It was not a matter of whether or not they realized
that was what they were doing. My sister Wewe treated
everyone with kindness, never speaking ill or bad of anyone;
my sister Wewe always let others shine.

I would love to share a few stories with you about
those other angels in my childhood who made my life not
only bearable but also memorable for me, enabling me to
continue to grow and to be a stronger human. It's best that

I list them naturally as I remember them in my mind, with no order of importance, as each one of them was and still is important to me.

My cousin Ci Tian, who is a doctor, lived with us for over a decade. She is my Mom's niece, the daughter of Wak Ie Jakarta—an older aunty on my Mom's side who lived in Jakarta. She was one of the closest persons to me as a child and now still is, at least in my mind. I always remember the time when she lived with us, and she used to come and visit during her university years. She also joined us on vacations with our family fairly often. Ci Tian was not only a source of comfort and love, but many times she provided another extra source of serenity that helped stabilize our family besides your Mom, Wewe.

Ci Tian has always been calm, grounded and wise, unlike my parents and siblings who are always intense, dramatic and hysterical. Ci Tian's calm demeanor brought a sense of peace and normalcy to my life. She was much older than me, about twenty-one years older, and has played different roles in my life—that of mother, sister and best friend. When things got really loud, hard, tough and rough at our household, she would sneak me out of the house and take me shopping or to get local snacks in a car—we called it her ambulance—it was a real ambulance that she could drive herself around in when she was not using it for emergencies. Well I guess these were real emergencies as far as we were concerned. We would visit her friends who owned a batik store, or our relatives around town. Sometimes I would tag along with her to the local hospital where she was working or to her private practice, where she helped as a temporary replacement for our famous family doctor, Uncle Ong we called him, when he was away on vacation.

People around town adored Ci Tian as she was always sweet and friendly, humble and generous. She helped many of the poor and uneducated villagers in parts of Sumatra, using her time to care and educate them in health matters. All the time I was with her I observed and learned from her ways. She taught me with actions, not words.

Later during my unpleasant year in Jakarta when I had to live with my eldest sibling Edwin and his wife, who I could not get along with, Ci Tian and her husband Ko Tie would rescue me on the weekends, driving hours in the horrible Jakarta traffic to pick me up and they brought me back home at the end of the weekend. I was sad to be away from her but happy that during the weekends I was able to stay in their house, spoiled with home-cooked meals, and they often treated me with trips to a popular noodle and wonton house, or to the movies, and bought me ice creams and sweets.

Dear Ci Tian is also extremely talented in her own way. She made clothes for herself as well for others she loved, laboring over new patterns and purchasing delicate fabrics for my Mom and other sisters, sewing them late at night after a long day at work or on a Sunday, the only day she had off. We both enjoyed the fashion world and she is a stylish woman. She also has 'green thumbs' and had her own orchid collection. She would take me to buy her starter orchids or new hybrids coveted by the locals. We also did the flower arrangements for our church together when my Mom was away. She was a very good cook, and I adored her specialties. I still salivate when I think of her Dutch-Indo style *Pastel Tutup*—our version of Shepherd's Pie, *Sosisbrut*—a baked filo pastry filled with a mixture of spiced pork that we call 'Piggy in a blanket' in the U.S., her Date cookies and a few other of her specialties.

During our family fights, Ci Tian would take me away, removing me from horrible situations no child should endure. My parents often left her with the responsibility of managing the household when they were gone. There were plenty of times, during her dating years, when I became her mini-chaperone, but for me those occasions always felt like our special times together, and I got to know her dates better than anyone in our family.

Ci Tian was a source of comfort, safety and love for me; she knew what David did to me and would usher me away in a natural way without upsetting my abuser. She is seventy-one as I write this—my love for her is unconditional and I miss her as I miss my own Mother and sister. She has played a very important role in my life. I look up to her and her wisdom and I am grateful for everything she has done for our family and me. Her generosity and selflessness are similar to my sister Wewe's. In so many ways, they are so much alike in character and personality. I realize that they both have shaped me to be the person that I am today.

Ci Tian remembers your Mom with a lot of fondness.

She was there during her last birthday at the Dharmawangsa Hotel and on other occasions after that evening. She visited your Mom right up until her death. Every year, I communicate with her on your Mom's birthday as I know, she too had a lot of affection for your Mom and our feelings are mutual. Wewe had a lot of love and respect for our cousin Ci Tian; she was our role model in so many respects. Her taste and elegance were also something I remember and admire, and her intelligence and hard work were great examples for us. Recently she had a heart procedure and I didn't learn about it until later, as her husband did not tell us. I was saddened and concerned for her health. I cling on to our memories and hope to see her again in the near future. Those days cannot come soon enough. Ci Tian is an angel on earth for me and I know she is loved and respected by so many people. She has a very special place in my heart for the rest of my life.

I have mentioned a few of our maids, Mbak Ti, Ana and Tini were a few of my angels when I was a kid. Not only did they serve me because I was the son of their employer, as part of their jobs, but I truly believe they cared, loved and had a lot of affection for me. They witnessed David's cruelty and did whatever they could to protect me. I remember Mbak Ti would directly tell David how mean and cruel he was. Ana and her sister Tini were more discreet in their ways of protecting me. They usually ushered me away or removed me from being in close proximity to David. I believe Mbak Ti and Ana had their share of being pushed away or hurt by David while they were trying to protect me, just as your Mom did.

But besides being my protectors from the abuser, these women were also my companions and best friends, my constants in a world of absence from my parents, and other transient people who inhabited my childhood. They nurtured me physically and emotionally. They would keep me company, even sleep with me, as I was always scared to sleep on my own, especially in the big empty house when my parents and sisters were away. They would keep me company at dinner. They were the last people I saw before I closed my eyes and the first people I saw when I woke up. I felt closest to them—all the maids and housekeepers were my angels. I spent so much time with them in the kitchen watching them cook and prepare our meals.

Clearly, I was more at ease and felt safer with the women than I did with the men throughout my early life. These women were paid to do their jobs but their hearts were truly full of love and compassion for me, I am sure of it: my heart tells me so. There are days when I wonder what happened to all of them, each one I remember fondly, and some I know have died before I had a chance to let them know how much I appreciate them and I am grateful and truly love them. They filled a gap that was left by my own mother and father. So yes, they too, are my heroines and angels.

My sister Edna is another personality who has played a constant role in my life. I am definitely attached to her emotionally. She is so very different from your Mom and Ci

Tian. Edna is intense, dramatic, hysterical, moody and fierce, yet restrained by her own traumas. However, her love for me is definitive and strong and I am grateful to her. Although we often bicker and fight, which I attribute to some similarities in our traits, especially the emotional part, we know we love each other and our relationship is solid. We feel strongly and passionately and our emotions at times get the best of us. Sadly, Edna too has been a victim of our family culture in so many ways.

Being a second child, a daughter born after the first son in our family, was not easy. Edwin is my eldest sibling, who I don't get along with as an adult and didn't as a child either. In fact I barely know him, nor do I have the desire to. He was supposed to be the shining star, yet Edwin could not be any lamer than he was. Slow, insecure and lazy, he always behaved like a privileged, rotten brat. Edna was his first girl sibling, and she stood out and excelled in a way similar to me as the sissy youngest son, seconded to David. For this reason, I believe Edwin suffered a lot from jealousy and he treated Edna terribly—not physically, but verbally and mentally. I remember watching Edwin yell and scream at Edna and creating fights and drama in our life.

Edna would not succumb to male repression; another reason she is perceived almost negatively as a strong woman by other women in our circle and family. Edna always spoke her mind. She was not shy of showing her emotions and very expressive in her happiness, sadness and anger; another proof to me that we are similar. I personally have always, as a child and until now, loved and admired those qualities she possesses. Now I see Edna as what they call a 'bitch' in the U.S., which means that she is a powerful person, and I am so proud of her. She was my role model in certain manners.

Edna might have been a 'bitch' but she has the biggest heart, and she is generous to a fault. As number one in my mother and father's absence, she had to run the household and be the 'she-boss' of our estate. Some maids didn't like her simply because her style of management was different to that of my Mom's.

But I know Edna loves me as her own child, the way your mother did. I remember how she always took me to the wet market with her—even now we still go to the market together sometimes when I visit Indonesia, and she taught me a lot of things about food and cooking. She used to make me my favorite food, and still does. She is the only one who can imitate my Mom's *Lemper* recipe to perfection. This is a specialty snack, made of coconut and glutinous rice, like tamale, filled with aromatic herb-infused spicy chicken and wrapped in banana leaf, a delicacy everyone loves in Indonesia. I could eat ten or more in one sitting. Nowadays she always makes some to bring when she visits me when I am holidaying in Bali, or sends some when she can't come.

She also made me my favorite *Gudeg*, a famous local dish from Jogjakarta, Central Java, that consists of mild curried chicken and green jackfruit along with other ingredients like boiled eggs, tempeh, tofu and beef rind cooked in earthenware over a fire with teak leaves. The smoke of the teak leaves turns everything into a dark burgundy, purplish color. She is also famous for her *sambal,* noodles and *Kue lapis legit* layered cake. This is another sweet delicacy that takes all day to make, as each layer takes 30 minutes or so and there are countless layers in a pan. The more layers it has, the more prestigious this cake is perceived to be, and she makes the best kind, using Dutch butter. It melts in your mouth. Edna is also an amazing baker. After taking pastry lessons as a teenager she became the baker in the family that made us all our birthday cakes. I still have pictures of my birthdays as a child and I was always posed with Edna's cake, some of them had from four to five tiers to reflect my age. She made her own wedding cake, and it had around nine tiers, the bottom one almost as big as a round dining table and surrounded with dozens of other cakes.

Edna is always considerate, in fact she is the 'hostess with the mostest', a skill undoubtedly learned from my mother, that she developed into her own style. I took my husband to visit her, first in Sumatra, and then later on in Jakarta. Even before our arrival she would ask us what we would like to eat, and where we would like to go. Every chance she got, she always picked us up at the airport and showed us around town and treated us at her favorite restaurants which she knew we would enjoy, especially me, because she knows how much I miss Indonesian comfort food. She always tries to visit us if she can, when we avoid Jakarta by flying direct to Bali, our favorite island, and she always arrives laden with gifts, from lengths of *batik* cloth, to coffee beans and all kinds of sweets and traditional *jajanan* snacks.

It's important to note that Edna also makes the best *Nastar* cookies, the small round cookies filled with homemade pineapple jam that the Dutch brought to Indonesia. She has so many other specialties in her cooking, it will be no surprise to hear that she ended up owning several small food businesses, and caters for private events, as well as running a noodle restaurant, a sambal business and various other enterprises.

In her role as my protector she had no qualms in telling David to behave, and to be a good elder brother to me, when she caught him taunting me. But that came with a price. David would not listen to her—he became even less respectful to her, regardless of the fact that she was seven years older and his elder sister. I witnessed David hit her and slap her in his teenager years and that mortified me. It made me feel sad that I could not protect her as I looked up to her and loved her so.

I was so close to Edna that the night before her wedding to her husband Ise, I cried and cried and cried, sobbing most of the night at the thought of her leaving us, and I slept next to her on her last night, thinking she would no longer be my sister and would never love me again. I was proven wrong by her when she continued to show her love for me as strongly as she ever did before her marriage. I was their junior groom and best man and Reny was her junior maid of honor. We were the only two attendants at their lavish wedding.

She and her husband even asked me to spend time with

them one summer vacation in Salatiga, where we all slept in the same bed. I know that in Western culture that would be considered inappropriate or strange, but in our family and Indonesian culture it is not at all unusual to sleep with your siblings as adult, simply because we feel comfortable, and not everything is sexualized. That was one of the best vacations of my childhood, staying with my sister and her husband in a boarding house in the college town of Salatiga in Central Java, a holiday of lifetime for me to remember fondly. We argue with each other passionately, something that your mother never did. But we never lose confidence in our filial love.

To come to think of it, I never witnessed your mother fighting or speaking ill of anyone, or placing herself in a compromising situation other than the firm bravery she exhibited with others in her role as my protector.

Edna was one of my mother figures in my childhood. I remember her taking me in her arms when I was feeling sick as a dog, running a very high temperature, and my parents were away. She knocked on the door of our family doctor's house in the middle of the night, waking up Oom Onggo, as she was so worried. She used to stay with me when I was ill, even if my parents were around to comfort me, and she would cry, worrying about me and wishing she could make me feel better as my mother would.

She was the one who sat me down with Mom and Dad to give me a proper sex education when she felt it was the right and appropriate time. Edna is such a paradox: she can be set in her ways and makes it hard for anyone trying to make her see things differently, yet at other times she surprises us with her willingness not only to listen but also to ask questions and learn new ideas, perspectives and points of view. She can be testing in some ways but super fun in others. While our family are generally speaking non-drinkers, Edna has now started to dabble in drinking wine, beer and cocktails, and when she visits us in California we have fun going out trying new drinks, or Stephen makes her cocktails at our place. Other family members turn red after one sip of a cocktail, but Edna and I are blessed to share the genes that allow us to drink our night away, having a great time in each other's company without a trace of the 'Asian flush'.

It was Edna who first accepted us as a same-sex couple in our family. While my parents lovingly and amazingly embraced us when we came out to them, our Mom struggled to reconcile both our status as a couple and our sexuality with her Christian faith. Her instinct was not to talk about it or openly show us off in Indonesia's rather repressive society. Edna was just the opposite. Not only did she embrace us as a couple, right from the start she showed everyone how proud she was of us and she always welcomed us as she would other in-laws in the family. Edna loves hard and passionately—there is no in-between with her. Her fiery and intense personality has always stood her in good stead in facing her battles, but in the end, her love always prevails.

Every time we said goodbye Edna cried; she still does, as do I. It started with her leaving me when I was a child and she had to go to the island of Java to study. When she left the first time and after she came home for vacation and had to leave again, I sobbed my heart out at the airport. Back home I would bury myself in her room, snuggling into her pillow in her bed, staying there for days on end, wishing she could still be with me.

As adults we would both cry at the airport as if someone had just died. Edna was one of my best friends—she still is closer to us than any other siblings or in-laws. She trusts us so much that at some point all her sons have either vacationed with us or lived and stayed with us. All of her children were touched by and cared for by your Mom. Ivan, Sean and Alain were so fortunate to have known your Mom and her loving kindness.

It is impossible to talk about Edna without talking about her husband, Ko Ise—our 'brother' Ise. For me to call him brother is truly an honor and a blessing as he is in truth the only brother I had when I grew up. Ise and Edna started dating in Junior high school and they have been together ever since. Originally Ise started off as Edwin's best friend but that created a lot of animosity between them when he and Edna got married.

I have never felt I had a brother—how could I? The eldest one left home when I was only six—we never got along anyway—and the other one was the bully. Ko Ise however, was not only handsome and grounded he was also a calm role model, and the kindest, most polite, helpful and loving person you could ask for as an in-law. While he did not have an outgoing, chatty disposition, he easily made up for that in his willingness to help, his gentle good manners, and he always made an effort to contribute to our parents' household above and beyond the call of duty. While he lived with us, he was always helping with the chores, even if we had so many other people to help. He made himself available to drive my Mom and me around and was always ready to lend a hand with anything, even manual labor if needed. He was such a good craftsman and handyman that later on he became an electrical engineer and made a great career in a big company where he went on to become one of their top managers. He is friendly and well liked by so many, the kind of person that we call a 'good egg', a handsome gentleman. As a child I had crush on him, and I always felt safe with him. He never behaved inappropriately with me or anyone else. He is referred as the 'golden' son-in-law, or the answer to a mother-in-law's prayer.

When my parents lost their wealth in a tragic and ironic situation and our entire family business stolen by a trusted 'adoptive' son who I never met, my father had to asked me to split payments for my tuition at an exclusive boarding school in Switzerland. This was something unheard of in my life at the time, as he always paid everything in advance, in full and with cash. My school cost around U.S.$150,000 a year, plus my jet setting that had never been questioned. Suffice it to say I spent my weekends between Lausanne, Geneva, London, Milan, Amsterdam, Paris, Frankfurt and Copenhagen at that time, staying at the most lavish hotels available, with some of the wealthiest young people on earth. So when my father asked the school if he could split up the tuition fees into part payments, as you can imagine, I was alarmed.

It wasn't until years and years later that I learned that it was Ko Ise who paid my last tuition in Switzerland by getting a loan from his company. That's the type of person he is—helping selflessly without even wanting to be known—totally discreet. This was also the same guy who let me spend nearly a month with him as a newly-wed without any complaint, sharing the room he had rented for the two of them, even sharing their bed with me.

There are qualities to him that remind me also of my sister Wewe. In so many ways they both possess all the positive and good qualities a human being should have: kindness, gentleness, being helpful, willing, polite as well as sweet, humble, discreet and low-key, plus family is everything to them. I hate to use the word in-law when I describe him, as to me he is my true brother, the only brother I have ever had. In fact, I hate to say that your Mom was my adopted sister too. She is simply my sister. Both she and Ise have been constant angels in my life. In a way, Ko Ise and Wewe have been more like siblings to me than some of my biological siblings. Ko Ise continues to be an angel in the family. He is most probably the kindest to our elderly parents. He is always ready to come to their rescue if they need help, safety and security, and he is most probably one of the most kind-hearted of all their children. It's not that we are not kind to our parents, but I have to admit that we can be hard on them, all of us.

Earlier you have read about the devils at my childhood schools, but there were also angels too. I had some lovely girlfriends who befriended me and did not care that I was a weak, sissy boy nor did they care that I was perceived as a loser. I want to mention Juliana, Astrid, and also Reny, who happens to be the younger sister of Ko Ise. Keke, Natalia, Locetta and a few others have always there for me, as well as a few boys who took it upon themselves to include me in their circle—there was Afa, Wisnu, Denny, Benny, Uwan, Alex, Harsono and dear Engkus who died at only fourteen years of age from a car accident.

These kids were different to most of the boys I encountered. They were kind enough to include me in their activities, knowing I wasn't good at basketball. I sat with the girls, and I wasn't into car or motorcycle racing. I preferred just to cheer them on—and I was always miserable when they listened to their hard core rock music, but I stuck around.

I had fun with the girls shopping or watching sappy girly movies and going to beauty salons, styling them. The boys would ask me for my opinion on fashion and girls. Your Mom would always welcome these dear friends with her open arms and was happy that I had friends who did not pick on me. They have become my lifetime friends. Although everyone is now spread all over the world, social media has made it possible for us to keep in touch.

There was another angel at school in Lampung who left her mark in my heart. Ibu Theresia was an English teacher who was also a guidance counselor, the only nurturing figure

I found at school. She was so caring, kind and wise. She was not only gifted in the way she taught our English course, but she was also full of compassion, and she had an amazing way of communicating with students. I believe she always knew I was bullied and a homosexual. She always tried to protect me in her own way by making it known that I was her pet student, and she frequently coached kids about being kind and reminded them not to bully anyone, which was ahead of her time both in Lampung, and other parts of Indonesia. A sensitive, nurturing soul, she made it easy for me to go up to her and open up about my emotions and problems. While we never openly discussed my sexuality, it was understood that she was fine with me just being myself. While other teachers—they were 95% male—participated both passively and aggressively in bullying me when they perceived my mannerisms to be feminine or noticed I had more female friends than male, which was considered 'gay', Ibu Theresia never once said anything negative or unkind about me. To the contrary she praised my grades, my intelligence and talents as well as my good behavior, and her acceptance of me as I was helped me to survive my miserable time at school in the other classes. I always looked forward to her class and her 'counseling' sessions in our classroom.

When my friend Engkus had a horrible car race accident he was transferred from the local hospital to Jakarta, where he died. At that time my elder sister Ci Na was in charge at home, as my parents were travelling somewhere abroad, the Netherlands as I recall. My friends in our circle all decided to drive to Jakarta on their own, in spite of being under-age drivers. My sister, concerned for my safety, prohibited me from going with them. I was so upset and frustrated; I felt I was missing out not only on saying my last goodbyes to Engkus, who was one of my best friends at that time, but I also wanted to be with my peers during one of the saddest times of my childhood. It was the first time for me to have a young friend die. I fought my sister, arguing with her as hard as I could, and she still wouldn't let me go. I left the house with my driver and I knew I had to find Ibu Theresia. I arrived at school while classes were in session. I was beside myself and I had taken the day off for mourning Engkus, as well as to keep Uwan company at the hospital. He was also in the accident and still in hospital, his foot had been crushed and he was kept there under observation for weeks.

As soon as she saw me in distress she left the class she was teaching and gave me the warmest hug, letting me sob on her shoulder. It was not and still is never the culture in Indonesia to hug someone, but that too, was a gesture that I knew came direct from her compassionate heart. She knew how to console me. Love knows no cultural boundaries. Her heart had always been in the right place and I knew she always did and said the right thing. She stayed with me for a while with no words, simply being there for me. Once I calmed downed, I told her that Engkus had died and I told her how upset I was that I couldn't go because Edna my sister wouldn't let me. In her motherly, nurturing way, she acknowledged my emotions and validated my frustrations and disappointments—not to mention my sadness—and my overall state of mind. But in her signature calm, wise and sweet way she helped me to understand how dangerous it would be for me to be with my peers who were barely fifteen to drive on their own to Engkus' funeral and how in this case Edna had to be the adult and mature one to make that decision. While I still felt I was missing out, I trusted Ibu Theresia. Her words and wisdom helped me to process my emotions, and her warmth, kindness and love soothed my broken heart and soul.

She was one of the hardest persons to say goodbye to when I had to leave that school to go to Jakarta and Switzerland and later the United States. I was heartbroken to say goodbye to all my dear friends but to say goodbye to Ibu Theresia was like parting with another mother. I shed my tears and we embraced, knowing it would be a long time before we would see each other again. I have since visited her a few times as an adult with my husband. She is an important figure in my life and I wanted my husband to meet her—one of my angels, one of my protectors. Ibu Theresia is more than a teacher to me and I know, for so many of us have been so lucky and blessed to have her in our life. Today, she is a proud mother and grandma and I still keep in touch with her on the phone and I cannot wait to hug and be hugged by her again, my tears rolling down my face as I type these words. She will always have a very special place in my heart.

As you can imagine, there have been other angels throughout my life as I am now approaching my half-a-century milestone. Those who have played important roles in my life, no matter how small they are in other people's eyes, are my angels. While it would be impossible for me to write about every single one of them in my letters to you, I think it is important to acknowledge them. I wouldn't be here without all of their support and love; some are total strangers I may never encounter again such as the gentleman who found me distraught at a train station in Geneva when I had a panic attack about your uncle David, and helped me. I thought I saw David following me and he was about to hit me, as I was trying to get away from him at that time. This kind gentleman took the time to stay with me, offered to take me to a doctor or hospital and in the end he took me for a walk to ease my mind and gave me his contact details in case I needed any more help. I am sure I wouldn't have survived without my dear friend Emma who was always there for me in Switzerland during my darkest time, when I was feeling suicidal.

Then I think of how grateful I was to the teachers in San Jose where I was a foreign exchange student. I felt lost in a new culture and country and they made sure to give me advice and guidance on what was appropriate or not in my new place and culture. It was very moving to see how they welcomed me along with other students who barely spoke a word of English and made us feel welcome in our new environment. The same can be said of friends who not only made me feel normal and treated me as they would any other human, they also stood up for me in my college years when others started to make fun of me for one reason or another. And so the list goes on…

It is my belief, dear Grace and Zef, that for every unkind or evil person in this world, there are ten or more souls like your Mom. These are the people who made it possible for me to endure and survive my childhood nightmares and ordeals. Love prevails, always!

Throughout my life, after I felt comfortable with friends I have shared my stories and intimate details of what happened to me as a child, especially with some of my closest friends and family members. Mostly they wonder how I managed to survive my childhood. Now you know that your Mom and other angels in my life are the main reason that I am still here. The love, kindness and compassion that surrounded me were way stronger than the hate and evil that tried to diminish me as a child, as a human. But there is something else that I want to share with you, dear niece and nephew, and that is forgiveness.

I have forgiven every single person who wronged me as a child, every person who beat, battered and abused me, or sexually molested me. I have forgiven those who mentally and emotionally abused me as a child, including those adults who took advantage of me. I have forgiven those who have given me nightmares and insomnia as well anxiety attacks and anger. Forgiveness is such a powerful act it has helped me to delineate a stage in my life and has lifted my sorrow, wiping away the hatred and anger that would have consumed me. Besides forgiving for my own sake, I forgive those who have wronged me for their sake as well, as there is already enough anger and hatred in the world and I want to have nothing to do with those emotions. I want to only spread love and forgiveness, as I believe they need to heal too, just as the world needs to heal.

We as humans need to learn to be better, and let me be that child who can share with you and the world that what they did to me was wrong, painful and sad. Let us remember my misery and the misery of so many others as a result of their actions. No child nor adult should ever experience what I experienced and my forgiveness will be the part that will heal not only me, but those who have done all those horrible things to me, so they may learn, and step back from doing these things, and know that I will not be silenced. I want them to learn that although they tried to destroy me, I am still here, stronger than ever. But beyond that, beyond myself, I want their other victims to rise and to know that they are not alone and we are all still here and we are healing the world. I want my perpetrators to forgive themselves and by doing so, they will heal themselves and stop doing what they did to me or other children.

My abusive past does not define me. While I forgive, I will never forget what happened. It will always be part of me as a person. I am blessed and lucky to have all the people in my life who have loved me so much. Not only did I survive; I thrive.

I'd love to close this part of my letter by sharing with you what I posted on my social media today, inspired by your Mom and what she did for me, and also inspired by my husband, Stephen, who has been my companion for over twenty-six years now and he has not only seen my growth but he is the one person who is responsible for me continuing to grow, and the one person who accepts and loves me for who I am—not just for the good, but also the bad and the ugly of me.

"BE KIND please, to the boy who is a weak sissy, and could not finish the lap, the one who was picked on in the school yard or at PE class... Be kind to the boy whom they called 'faggot, *banci, bencong, PD*, girly, to the mommy's boy who loved to play with his dolls... Be kind to the boy who barely spoke English and was in ESL class... Be kind to the boy who always hung out with the girls because the girls were nice to him... Be kind to the boy who was bullied, beaten up black and blue.... Be kind to the boy who was pushed and kicked and bled... Be kind to the brown baby... Be kind to the Indonesian, the "isn't he just a florist", the guy who served you at a fancy restaurant, who made your bed at your hotel, and the guy who made your smoothies... Be kind to the immigrant boy... Be kind to that boy as that boy was—and still is—me.

~ *duabelas* ~

"Island of the Goddesses..."

This evening I just took a bath at home in San Francisco,
using a mini bubble bath sachet provided to me at the resort
we last stayed at, in Ubud, Bali.

It was left in the bathroom where I had my last outdoor
shower after I plunged in the pool before we had to leave.
Plunging into that pool in the midst of such a wonderful
setting is something I love so much to do, and when I saw
this unused bottle of bubble bath I couldn't resist packing
it. While I was shampooing my hair for the last time with the
view of rice *padi* fields, coconut leaves, hibiscus trees, bird
of paradise flowers, tropical trees and plants and the sound
of creatures I never heard in San Francisco, I took a whiff of
the fragrance in the air. Then I dried off and completed my
packing, along with the bath amenities from the resort.

I know this action was small and unimportant, and
it might sound incidental and insignificant to you, but to
me, within that small bottle of bubble-bath was the magic
I needed for my plan of trying to recapture the memory
of that last shower—the view, the warm humidity, the
sunlight and the sounds of a place I love. Remembering was
important to me, and I wanted to imprint the memory of my
favorite island in the world forever in my mind—along with
everything else that I knew I would miss when I was back in
San Francisco.

I am aware that the sense of smell is highly emotive and

closely linked with memory, as each time I take a bath in San Francisco with this bubble bath, especially when I miss Bali, I see the name of the resort, and smell the perfume of the bubble bath, and it always reminds me of that exact day, the trip I took with Steve and Bob, and the memories imprinted of that particular time of happiness, and peace come flooding back. This was such an important and healing time for me, knowing the people that mattered the most in my life were all close by. Mom, Dad, my siblings and their families, our cousins and the Balinese people we have met over the decades, and have become our *ohana*. I already knew then, when I picked up that little bottle and stashed it in my suitcase, that although I would miss the people I left behind, I could refresh my wonderful memories and return to them again and again when I was back in San Francisco.

Well, tonight I did just that. I revisited that special place from far away on the other side of the world, here in San Francisco. I picked up the plastic bubble bath bottle at the edge of the tub, opened it and smelled the fragrance then I poured it into the tub as I ran the water. I also lit some cheap candles that I had bought at the Ubud market, just because they were scented with a perfume called '*Bali*'.

All these actions served to bring back and amplify my memories of Bali. In the past I used to judge people who buy cheesy knick-knacks for souvenirs rather harshly, but I have now become one of them, and I will be less judgmental, as I understood why they do it. I was hoping that by taking home a little reminder of the place I love so much I could heal my homesickness and reduce my longings to be there. At certain times Bali is on my mind a lot, and at those times how I long to be back there. But tonight it seems that dwelling on my lingering memories has had the opposite effect to what I had hoped. It made me miss everything about Bali more than ever.

*   *   *

Bali has always been a part of my family journey since my childhood, and now it is has become part of my husband's and mine too.

My obsession with Bali started at a very young age. As far as I can remember I was still a toddler when I first heard the word Bali uttered by our parents. Many nights at my childhood home in Sumatra, especially when we had relatives visiting us, we would gather around the dining table after dinner, or sit together in the family room eating snacks and telling stories. Our family favorite 'talk-story' snacks were sunflower seeds or salted peanuts roasted in their shells. The aunts and uncles and cousins would reminisce on late family members or trips they had taken together and memorable events in their lives. This was before the advent of television. Our house would be filled with the noise of chatter, laughter and sometimes there would be tears and even sobs.

On occasions like this Wewe was somehow designated as the most efficient person in the family to pluck white hair for my parents. She would sit or stand behind them, one at a time, and she would search for any white hairs, which at this time were quite hard to find, and therefore considered to be most offensive, as my Mum and Dad were still in their early forties and not ready for such signs of maturity. She would patiently search through their hair for any culprits and use tweezers to pull out each white hair that she found. There was one funny incident when your Mom was so tired that while she was doing this she actually dozed off and dribbled on the offending head, I'm not sure if it was Mom's or Dad's. Ever since, that story has become a family classic to be told over again and again at family gatherings. She never lived that one down until the end of her life. I am pretty sure, even if I wasn't at her wake, that the story would be told and retold, and at first they would laugh, then they would cry, as they cracked salty roast peanuts from their shells.

Your Mom Wewe liked to clown around too in her own way. During our late night story-telling sessions around the dining table and in the family room she used to tell us all kinds of funny stories. Later after she became a nurse, she would tell us stories about her days at school, or her time in the hospital when she was a trainee. I'll never forget her story about the time when she had to stay overnight in the hospital morgue on her own. As a child I was always scared of dead bodies, coffins, corpses and anything connected to funerals. In this story she told us how she had to spend the night in the morgue as part of her training. I don't remember the specific reasoning behind it, but I think it was a tradition designed to toughen future nurses and to prepare them for the time when they would have to deal with death of a patient, and all the other difficult things that come with that job. It certainly wasn't for the faint-hearted.

I was so scared when she was telling her story that I clung tightly to her, until she wrapped me in her arms. She tried to teach me about death, explaining that the corpses can't do anything, they were lifeless and no danger could possibly come from them. It was the stench that she could not deal with but she had to, as there was no choice. The smell was an awful mixture of formaldehyde and sanitation chemicals used in the area, and combined with the awful stink of decomposing corpses that was hard to bear. She was not scared at all, she told us, and she was determined to get through it. It was not so easy for all, she said, as a few of her friends didn't pass or quit as a result of this exercise. Our cousin Ci Tian later confirmed that story. She had to go through a similar training in her medical school days. Then and there, I told myself I'd never seek any vocation in the medical profession.

Your Mom also told us many stories about her experience as a midwife, some sad—for example when a mother died instantly during labor of an aneurism. She had also witnessed situations that involved forced adoptions, and yes, some stillbirths when the baby was lifeless upon arrival. There were also some outrageously funny tales, that everybody roared with laughter at, but I didn't fully understand some of the humor because of my age, and probably also because I didn't understand the logistics or technicality of how a baby was made or born. Even the messy part of labor sounded very strange to me until she explained the physical aspects of how it happened. Our mother would nudge her and suggest she go easy on me as I was still young, but your Mom had a way of telling the stories and using them as educational tools for me, in a way that was age appropriate of course.

There are a few stories that remain stuck in my head and always make me chuckle every time I think of them. I still share them from time to time with my husband or special friends and of course within our family when we start talking about your Mom, remembering her silly side. One particular story was about the Indonesian woman who cursed her husband at every contraction so loudly and with the foulest language imaginable, all the while slapping and hitting him. She held on to him so tightly he couldn't get away and during her last push, she virtually choked him. The poor man was left gasping for breath. Wewe was so descriptive in her delivery that she made us all feel as if we were in the room with her as she delivered those babies.

It was during one of the visits to our home in Sumatra from our Aunt and her husband Wak Ie Surabaya that my parents recounted the story about their first Bali trip as a family. I say 'their trip' because I wasn't even born when they did it. The story was so full of fun and evoked a plethora of enticing, romantic and happy memories. It left an indelible mark in my heart. First it made me curious to know more about Bali. As young as I was, I fell in love with the idea of this little island, where the culture was so different to the rest of our archipelago. But listening to this story made me feel so left out—I literally felt as if I had been abandoned—or in today's lingo I was probably experiencing *fomo*, an acronym that describes 'fear of missing out', possibly even missing out forever, in the worst case scenario.

Can you imagine how I felt? In spite of the fact that I wasn't born yet at that time, because all my elder siblings were part of that trip, along with your biological Grandpa, my Empek Edo, who was also your Mom's father, I felt I was missing out on the all the fun, both then and now, with the conversation being about something I knew nothing about. No one seemed to know how I felt so alone at this time. I realized then that your Mom understood my feelings, because it was at this time that your Mom would put me on her lap as I sat next to her listening to their stories, both of us together as the 'outsiders'. She had not been part of that trip either. We listened to everyone jabbering about it for hours and they let me stay up until past 1am

The story as I remember it was that our family drove from Sumatra, taking the ferry to Java, where they met up with other relatives who then joined them on a road trip to Bali. This was in the late 1960's and the roads were still very rough.

To give you an idea of what it would take to go from our hometown to Jakarta, the capital in Java, during my time it still took anything up to six hours just to go to the port to catch the ferry, which then took around five hours to cross the Sunda Strait. It would take the same again to drive from Port Merak in West Java into Jakarta if all went well. Some of the roads in Sumatra and Java were unpaved and muddy all year long, and they were at their worst in the rainy season. Mechanical problems were pretty much always guaranteed with both the cars and the ferry, as well as delays, cancellations and unforeseen issues always arose in these relatively short trips during my childhood.

I could only imagine what it must have been like in the late 1960's. They told us how they liked to take more than one car in case anything went wrong. Travelling in convoy with friends and relatives was apparently how Indonesians travelled in those days, always in a group for safety. Sometimes we went in a convoy, too, and it could take anything up to five cars, to transport almost everyone in our entire little compound where we lived.

From Jakarta I suspect they would have driven the next leg to Semarang in Central Java. This was another grueling dangerous drive, which could take a minimum of fourteen hours if all went well or double that if it didn't. An overnight stop was necessary of course. But the drive was enervating for all the passengers, as there was not exactly any freeway. I guess 'freeway' in those days meant drivers could drive freely, however they wanted with no rules or laws to abide by, along narrow, twisty and winding roads that often mutated from two way to just one-way, especially at times when it was hilly or there were cliffs to pass. Fatal accidents, robberies and kidnapping for ransom were not uncommon in those days.

Once they reached Central Java, typically our family would meet up with other relatives who would join them on their trip, but first they would visit the rest of their family who lived there, before continuing on to Surabaya, the other big city in East Java. This took roughly the same amount of time as travelling between Jakarta and Semarang, possibly a bit less.

In Surabaya the routine of meeting up with relatives and visiting them took place all over again—indeed, it sounded like we had family in most major cities. Finally they would set off again and drive from Surabaya to the little port at Ketapang, and load up the cars on the ferry for a relatively short ride across to Bali's westernmost port of Gilimanuk. The ferry ride was only about 30 minutes, but then they had to drive from the port to the tourist enclave of Sanur, which I suspect would have taken another five hours in those days.

Imagine driving in a motorcade of heavily loaded cars, with women and children and toddler David in tow, over vast distances from our hometown all the way to Sanur. I estimated it would have taken them at least a full week to get there. Our parents and relatives who told us about the trip described it as travelling with an entire 'village' of relatives. My mom was possibly pregnant at the time with Debbie, our late sister, although she carried her toddler David constantly tied to her with a *selendang* baby-carrier sarong which was typically made of a long length of batik cloth tied over one shoulder on one side and under the child to support it on the opposite hip. The baby is supported and held in place by the fabric and the knot on the mother's shoulder makes it look just like the proverbial stork, except there is no beak.

Imagine a week of driving in a tightly packed car with a baby or toddler who was complaining and insisted on being only carried by his pregnant Mom. On top of that, David had a notorious attachment to a *guling* pillow, the kind commonly called a 'Dutch wife,' that served as his safety blanket. Shaped like a small bolster, it was his source of comfort, in the same way the famous Linus character in Charlie Brown Peanuts cartoons carries around a blanket. If anyone tried to get close to it or take it away from him he would be upset. The kapok inside it had long lost its fluffiness, and it had become flattened into something resembling a dirty rag. If it was grubby or peed on by him and my Mom had to 'steal' it away to wash it, he would go berserk and throw a nasty tantrum. Needless to say, that *guling* remained stinky and dirty. In fact it would become part of David's legacy, something that our family would never let him forget, and he still gets teased about it today.

Just imagine the appearance of this group of people from Sumatra and Java by the time they arrived in Bali. They had been driving for at least a full week in the equatorial heat and around 100% humidity, in a cavalcade of old cars with no air conditioning. Among the drivers there was one in particular who refused to dress decently. He was always attired in shorts and a raggedy T-shirt—yes that was your Grandpa, our beloved Empek Edo—plus a gaggle of parents, aunties, nannies, kids and a stinky child with his even more stinky *guling*. As my family described it they probably looked like a group of traveling *gembel* homeless people, or refugees from a war zone by the time they reached their hotel. This was the only hotel our father knew—the fanciest hotel in Bali at that time of course—called Bali Beach Hotel, the one built by our first President Sukarno, that usually hosted all the international celebrities and world dignitaries at that time.

They pulled in to the hotel driveway without any prior reservation. Our Dad was the ringleader of this circus—at least that was how our relatives described him whenever they told us the story, with everyone cracking up as they remembered the journey, tears running down their faces from laughing too hard. He went straight up to the front desk, to be greeted by a snooty front office supervisor and his uptight staff, and told him:

"Could you kindly provide me with a few rooms for my family entourage."

"Sir," the manager replied patronizingly, "in this property, the least expensive room costs x million rupiah per night!"

Clearly the well-dressed gentleman in his hotel uniform assumed the homeless looking man and his disheveled and grubby group could not afford his hotel, as this message was delivered with a laugh that was echoed by a number of condescending chuckles from the other front desk staff.

Father was well known for his short temper. Although he was usually kind and compassionate, he was short-tempered when provoked. Not missing a beat, he grabbed the front desk employee by his tie and collar with his left hand, while the right hand slammed down the front desk loudly, as he ordered the unkind and snobby staff in his worst Indonesian to:

"Give me the most f...ing expensive rooms in this hotel you have!"

Frightened out of his wits, the supervisor hurried away to call his General Manager, who came rushing out to sort everything out and calm down my father. To help you understand the level of wealth of our family at this phase of their lives, our father could have actually afforded to rent the entire hotel's rooms that evening, in fact he could have probably bought the entire property and company at that stage if he so wished. It's sufficient to say that this story has become part of my Dad's ongoing legend.

Even many years later, when I had already 'arrived' as the youngest in the family, and we took the car to Java my Mom, sister and I would cling to each other during those journeys, while my Father and David 'the menace' would have a lot of fun and adventures driving, and I would think of this story of the big family trip to Bali, and imagine myself a part of it.

Besides that story that has been shared, and retold in so many family gatherings, I heard other memorable stories of where they stayed, what they did and all the wonderful times they had. They spoke about the foods they had tried and loved and the best swims they had. If I listened to them intently, I could almost feel as if I was there, except I wasn't of course. I felt so left out, almost abandoned. Our entire family had been there except for your Mom and I, and this gave us another unspoken bond. As if listening to the stories was not enough, to add to our injury, they would pull out the photo album with its snap shots in black and white that my father had taken, developed in his own darkroom and arranged in the album. In those pictures I saw the evidence of the amazing time they had. I used to flip the pages, sitting on my own, and fantasizing that one day in the near future I would be there with my sister Wewe and our family, in that paradise!

Well, that eventually did happen, although not all at the same time. The Bali times finally came much later in life. My sisters Wewe and Edna and our Cousin Ci Tian, essentially all my surrogate Moms from my childhood, came to Bali with Stephen and I. In fact the most important women of my life, apart from my Mom, came to be with us in Bali.

There were times we went to Bali for my design projects there and other times we simply went to Bali because we loved it so much. I could write a book about my love of Bali and all the trips we have taken there. I have actually lost count, but I estimate that I have gone to Bali around fifty times now, and ninety percent of those trips were taken with my beloved husband Stephen. Bali is a very special spot on earth, and one of our favorite destinations. Besides the natural beauty, the culture and the religious ceremonies that the island is internationally renowned for, we have fallen in love with the people of Bali, as we find we truly connect with them. Yes, I am sure you must have heard how warm and kind they are, not to mention their joyful way of life, talent in the arts, and their hospitable ways. We have experienced all of those qualities and the sincere love they have shown for us, and some have become our *ohana*, members of our extended family.

It was in the late nineties, or perhaps early 2000 that the three women from my childhood decided to join Stephen and I for a few days in Bali. We had such a heavenly time together. My memories of that trip have been part of my consolation, a 'go to' whenever I miss those people or think about them and all the amazing things they each have done for me. That last few days in Bali will always stay in my heart for the rest of my life. Rather than trying to visit tourist attractions, which people usually do in Bali, we simply went there to be together. I felt so elated during that time. I was so full of joy, at peace with myself, and especially grateful and honored to be in the presence of these strong, amazing women. They have all played a special role in my life, somehow managing to compliment each other with their special skills, and each had their own different ways of raising, teaching and loving me.

Our family is intense, as I have shown you through my stories, and out of all of these three Edna wins the prize as the most intense and emotional. On a day-to-day basis she was always the one who had all the responsibilities and so she mostly acted in survival mode, playing a self-defensive role in the presence of other family and relatives. Yet, during this trip I got to know another side of Edna, and we had such a pleasant and peaceful time, in which we truly were able to enjoy each other's company.

To the best of my memories, that was the first and last trip we ever took as 'sisters'. I say sisters metaphorically of course. While I am their brother and male, I always feel that I am part of their sisterhood, as I feel more like a sister to the ladies in my life. In sisterhood we always helped and supported each other, just as we respected and loved each other—and we still do. Sadly, we had been raised in a rather toxic cultural environment that was overall very chauvinistic, a male-dominated household. This was predominant in Indonesia during my childhood, and as a result, women were constantly undermined and deemed to be the weaker sex. This situation always makes my blood boil, knowing how strong and amazing these women were, are and will always be. To me, they are superior to men as human beings. Women are always stronger by nature if compared to men, at least that's what I feel from my own personal observations and experience. That trip affirmed my belief in not only how amazing and superior they were but how wonderful they were to come together to support Stephen and me. It took a lot of effort for them to be able to leave their families to be with us, and I knew that they wanted to show us how important we were to them, and they wanted to be with us as well as to be able to spend time with each other. They each showered us with gifts and lots of snacks and food I had missed from my childhood. We filled that trip with sharing lots of meals together, enjoying strolls along the beach at sunset and simply being together and reminiscing our childhood and the bygone eras of our youth.

Out of the fifty odd times we have been to Bali, we have always managed to spend half of each trip with various members of my family or relatives, in different combinations. Some times it was just with my parents, and later with their nurse Suparni who came along as well, as they were older and more dependent on a caregiver. At other times we would spend our time with my parents and our cousins, and sisters or brothers and their spouses and children. Or if my parents could not join us then our nephews and their girlfriends would. There were so many trips I can barely keep track of the when and who of each trip, but we have pictures to remind us of them. Each trip was memorable in its own way, but there were a few that were extra special to me personally.

*   *   *

The first one that comes to my mind was a trip where our parents, Ci Na, Ko Ise and Alain, David and his beautiful and kind wife Rina all joined us as well as a cousin we call Ko Khing (pronounced Geng). On top of that, Bob, who is my ex boyfriend who has become part of our family also joined us. Bob truly is a family member. He is 20 years older than me and has had a wonderful relationship with my parents. My parents stayed with him many times, for months at a time in San Francisco when we lived in the ground floor of his house. Even after we moved out of Bob's, they would still stay with him. My parents treat him as one of their sons, while I treat Bob—interestingly—as one of my parents.

We stayed in Sanur at the iconic, boutique hotel Tanjung Sari. The beach in front is known as historic and legendary—it is said that this was the place where Nehru declared Bali to be "the morning of the world". At one time in the seventies people like Mick Jagger of the Rolling Stones and various members of The Beatles were likely to show up at the beachside bar for cocktails, and it was rumored that the Queen of Denmark and other noted individuals would gather here for discreet holidays. That's what we loved about this paradise-like tropical sanctuary, the romance and the discretion.

Stephen and I first went to Tanjung Sari for sunset cocktails on the beach at the invitation of two expats, Celia who I met on my flight to Bali, and her Australian friend Desley, who had lived in Bali for decades. Sadly, Desley later died of a brain tumor in Australia, and never managed to come back to Bali.

We fell in love with Tanjung Sari, not only because of the exquisite architecture and design, its verdant garden filled with Balinese sculptures and the seaside setting, but we fell in love with its old-school nature and the hospitable staff who made us feel so at home. It was our family trip that sealed Tanjung Sari as our favorite 'home away from home'. Each villa has a veranda or open-air bale and the interiors are decorated as if in centuries past. The overall feeling is one of traditional Balinese luxury, with attention to comfort and high cleanliness standards. No TV. Thatched roofs. The pool is overhung by a giant tree and shrubs form a hidden oasis next to the open-air library and living room, for guests to linger and relax, play games, nap or read.

We used to spend a lot of our time reading after breakfast, and then we would have more coffee and tea, lounging with our respective partners. I'd lay my head on my Mom's lap or sit on my Dad's lap or at times I would sit in between both of them, content, absorbing every moment as I knew this precious time would not last. Being able to spend time with my husband and my parents as well as my loved ones, all at the same time, has given me one of the happiest memories of my life.

Each morning we would get up to watch the sunrise before we joined the others for breakfast—either on the beach, or lying on the outdoor open bale pavilions together, or in the restaurant if we felt like sitting up to a table, or even sometimes in our parents' villa. Then we would simply relax for the rest of the day, spending the entire day around the property. There were so many spots to hang out: at the pool, the library, the bar or restaurant, or we took turns to visit the different villas our extended family and friends were staying in. To me, it was heavenly. I only wish your Mom could have joined us but she was no longer with us at that time.

My idea of heaven is a place where all my loved ones live in a peaceful neighborhood, or on a street where we each have our own home but we are always able to visit and to be with each other at will. Tanjung Sari will always be that place for me, like heaven on earth. It was here we took our first vacation as a family after your mother passed away, and we celebrated her life and mourned her as a family in our own way. We honored her memories by reminiscing about her, including her falling asleep while plucking grey hairs from my parents' heads and her silly stories from her time as a midwife. Together we raised our glasses and lit candles in her memory.

We have built so many memories in Bali as a family it is no wonder that we love it there. On August 3, 2007 we celebrated our parents' 50th wedding anniversary in Bali at the Ritz Carlton in Jimbaran, and more recently in 2017 we celebrated their 60th at the Bali Oberoi in Seminyak. At both events relatives and families gathered to celebrate our parents' love. I like to call them the '*loro blonyo*' after the inseparable couple depicted by the iconic pair of traditional Javanese sculptures typically given as a wedding gift to newlyweds. My parents always held hands from day one and they still do today. My father always carries my mom's purse and I have taken many candid pictures of them to capture their sweet and tender moments.

On each of their anniversaries relatives came from all

over the world and from distant parts of Indonesia, and we were joined by a number of devoted employees who have become part of our family over the years. Again, during each of these celebrations I so wished your mother had been with us, although I knew she was present in all of our hearts and memories. On the 60th anniversary Stephen and I made a video presentation of images captured during my parents' life together, starting from their wedding and progressing right up to the moments before their anniversary. The images consisted of pictures and letters I have gathered all these years. I made sure your Mom's pictures were part of the video, as I knew it would mean a lot to our parents and family. To say that we were emotional was an understatement. Besides celebrating their love and accomplishments as a couple, it was also a reminder of those loved ones who were no longer with us, their parents and grandparents, their siblings, aunts and uncles, cousins and their daughters, friends and even a number of strangers who became part of our family life. I think Anniversaries are always a bittersweet event in older couples' lives.

It was during this last anniversary trip that we gathered again as a family at one of our favorite resorts in Bali: The Oberoi in Seminyak. This hotel has become yet another home-away-from-home for Stephen and I. We have had so many holidays there, just the two of us, as well as with our extended family. This time we arrived a few days early to prepare for the anniversary party—we were hosting about sixty people. It was a week of memorable moments in the resort as well as around Bali, visiting some of our favorite places with our loved ones—and yes, you guessed it, food spots were a main feature!

Our favorite moments are always the meal times, and usually during breakfast and dinner at the hotel we lingered for hours just to be able to enjoy our time together, appreciating the beautifully designed resort. Australian architect Peter Muller designed The Oberoi. Peter also designed the Amandari in Ubud and he admitted to having been inspired by the Tanjung Sari. We found these hotels all have similar qualities that we love, especially their atmosphere that captures the feeling of a Balinese village. They are naturally beautiful, and feel unmistakably Balinese. We enjoyed the sunset cocktails and spent idyllic moments looking out over the gorgeous pool and villas to the ocean as the sun went down. That week we took turns visiting each other in our thatched-roof villas, hosting cocktails at ours and at the open air bar facing the ocean. Once more I felt as if this was heaven and I had found my utopia. I was so excited to be able to visit all my loved ones in-house whenever I wanted during that week while we all were neighbors.

Apart from telling us the stories about how they had met and their courtship and their engagement story, as well as other parts of our family history and romances together, my parents talked about each one of us and their past memories of our childhood. It was very touching. Inevitably, as I had expected, Wewe played an integral part in their stories. Yes, they told us about the happy, good and fun times they had shared with her, but one evening when we had all gathered in a smaller group they also spoke about the sad time when Wewe was dying, and the funeral—at that time I believe it was just my parents, David, his wife Rina, and a few nephews along with Stephen and I, listening to their story.

It wasn't until after dinner, at the end of one of those lingering candlelit evenings that we heard the melancholy tale. My Mom has been known to repeat things all throughout her life. We used to either make fun of this habit, or roll our eyes when she started retelling a story, and sometimes we would find it really annoying, but we knew she couldn't help herself. That evening for once we simply listened and let her be.

She started by reminding us and retelling the story about her dearest wish. Of course she had always thought Wewe would survive her. All throughout our lives our mother used to say that when it was their time to retire, as they grew older that they wanted to stay with Wewe or perhaps even Wewe would want to move back in with them.

"Of course, we don't expect anyone to take care of us and we would not want to burden any of our children," she told us.

Over the years she had made it clear to us that out of all their children it was your mother that they would both prefer to stay with in their elderly days. Well, for them the days of old age, those imaginary far-distant days, had already arrived, and sadly for them and for all of us, your Mom was no longer with us. We all understood of course, without ever discussing it, that it would be ideal for your Mom to take care of our parents, not only because of her professional and formal education in the medical field would come in handy, but also because of her personality—she had the sweet and kind, compassionate and loving nature that made her the ideal caregiver for our elderly parents. None of us had the patience or ability to put up with our parents the way your Mom could. Without ever discussing it with my siblings or my parents of course, I knew that only your Mom had the skills and character this would demand, and she was also the one daughter, the only child of theirs with this most generous attitude and kind manner towards my parents. She was the perfect daughter.

I feel more than confident in saying that no one had ever witnessed your Mother talk back at my parents. Neither had I heard nor seen her complain about our parents or family, ever. She had never been unpleasant in the slightest to anyone— not to the maids, not to the staff, not to our neighbors, not to the people in the market, let alone strangers, and certainly not ever to us, nor to our parents. She was the perfect, true lady, a genuinely good human. While we, the biological children of our parents, as teenagers and later in our twenties and thirties continued to give our parents misery by talking back or telling them how to live their lives.

As we were growing up, we other children could have written a handbook for pure rudeness. It wasn't just our anger that we expressed by yelling and screaming, or the combative ways that all of us had; we all had more subtle but clear ways of expressing our indignation by muttering under our breath or complaining loudly to and about our parents, showing them our bad attitude and giving them heartaches in various ungrateful ways. Your Mom, to the contrary, did all the opposite. She never subscribed to what we considered the norm. She always complied with my parents' wishes and obliged their needs, while thanking my parents for their advice and support. It was like night and day, dark and light. In total contrast to us, she was always sweet to them, asking them what she could do for them and letting them know how appreciative and grateful she was.

To say that she was the best child my parents had ever had is an understatement. Not only was she their best-behaved daughter, she was also an exemplary child for many other reasons. I suspect, besides being the amazing human and daughter that your mother was to both my parents and her biological parents, she was a lot wiser than us all. I used to fear that she behaved that way because she always knew her 'place' as an adopted child, and this thought always made me sad. How I wished I could liberate her from that place in her life so she would not have to feel that she should be the perfect daughter to our parents. I didn't want her to feel indebted at all. Yet she happily and graciously accepted her role, simply by giving love to us all and being that special person in our parents' lives.

*　　*　　*

My Mom continued that evening's conversation by recounting the story of the wake at your Mom's funeral. Neither Stephen nor I were at her funeral. While my Mother directed this story toward Stephen and I, it was also her way of sharing her emotions about your Mom with everyone present that evening. She told us the story of what happened when our parents were at the wake. They were sitting with your biological grandpa, Empek Edo, in the closest place they could to be near Wewe in the casket. To start with, this already sounded to me like a setting that did not make sense. It felt so wrong for those three parents to even be at their daughter's wake—or for any parents, for that matter—it was a most terrible moment in our parents' lives, and in my sister's biological father's life too Thankfully, your grandmother had already passed away by then, and she didn't have to share this terrible moment of burying her child.

Together they were facing the last time they would have the chance to see the face of their beloved daughter, one last time to bid her farewell. There they were, in this tragic and heartbreaking situation, the three of them, sitting right in front of her coffin, as her earthly remains were being viewed and visited by those who wanted to pay their last respects. All his life, Empek Edo had told his daughter to be good to our family. I had witnessed this many times in the car or in the rare moments when they chatted with me present, perhaps thinking I wouldn't hear or would not care or understand as I was very young. Well, not only did she keep her promise to her father to be a good daughter to our parents, she had exceeded all his wishes in her short lifetime. If there has ever been any angel in our family, it was she.

At this time, according to our Mom, Empek Edo was crying while telling my Mother how sorry he was and then the next minute she heard him addressing your Mom in the coffin, as if she was still alive, saying as he sobbed that Wewe had not yet paid my parents back for everything they had done for her. This made my Mom cry even harder, and she told him their daughter never had to pay them back anything as she was their daughter they loved with all their heart and soul.

Once my Mom finished telling that sorrowful story as we gathered around her in our beautiful villa at The Oberoi, I added my own words of defense for my sister.

"Wewe was not only your daughter, but she was the best child among all of us." There was a silence, and I looked up to see my Mom's eyes wet with tears, as were others in the room.

Your mother not only was an ideal daughter and child of our parents, she was the perfect sister to me, and the sweetest aunt to so many, not just my own nephews and nieces. She was the most amazing woman and unusual human being in a sense that she was not only a kind and compassionate person; she was also always pleasant and amicable. As well as being gracious, lovely and humble, she had a dry sense of humor that always hit the high note among us, and her willingness to help earned her an expression in our culture as *ringan tangan* that describes her hands as being always nimble and ready to help. I always describe my sister as a 'saint', as she had not a drop of hate in her blood. To the contrary she was so filled with love, she had no room for anything else.

It was that love—her love—that made me believe we could heal our family in so many ways. The love she shared with me as a child, as you have read, was so abundant it seemed to be limitless. The same could be said about her love for our parents and family. She showed her gratefulness and gratitude in all her actions, including her selfless lack of demands upon others, in total contrast to the rest of us.

You have also now learned how our family was not necessarily an ideal or perfect family. We fought amongst ourselves, and at times this exploded to a level beyond what was normal. The verbal, mental and physical abuse was at times unbearable for me as a child. David's actions resulted in me disowning him for twelve years. My aversion to my eldest sibling Edwin for his difficult personality and laziness has been compounded by my resentment of him for being unkind to my sister Edna and his taking advantage of my parents financially during their hard times, then later using my financial support as well. This has become a constant issue in our rapport as siblings. The four of us always had some kind of issues with each other, with the exception of Edna and I; we stick together and even though we have an emotional relationship, it is understood that we love each other no matter what happens between us.

Animosity generally arose between Edna and Edwin, or Edwin and I, or David and Edwin, or David and I constantly as we were growing up. There were times where Edna and I would be on the same team and just not talk to Edwin for a length of time. Whereas I have an amazing relationship with Edna's husband Ko Ise as I have mentioned, as well as David's wife who has always been lovely and easy to get along with, I have never had a decent relationship with Edwin's wife. The same thing can be said about Edna and her. We have both always found her hard to get along with and it added to our animosity towards Edwin.

*   *   *

It was your Mom's death that I believe brought us together and healed some of our family anger and bitterness towards each other. During her last month of life, as you will find out in the next letter, my dears, my sweet husband Stephen who also has the biggest, most generous heart, suggested we throw Wewe a surprise birthday party, knowing very well that it might be her last one. For your Mom's sake, I put aside all my personal aversion to my sibling Edwin and his wife and I also asked Edna and David to do the same, so we could come together as a family for your Mom to give her a happy memory and a special time, in the short time she had left to share with everyone she loved. It was not about us, but about her. You will learn later what happened that evening and I am happy to say that we pulled it together as a family to show our love and respect for our beloved sister, Wewe. We managed to put our differences aside prior to that evening as well as during the few last days we had a chance to spend with her.

We had no idea how much time we would have with your Mom after that, but that evening made us realize more than ever that time was growing short for her. We all knew she wasn't going to last much longer. The way she looked on that day, the last time we gathered to be with her, removed any doubts we may have had. She was forty-six years old and it was exactly one month after her birthday when she passed away, a very young age by any standard for anyone to die. Zef, you were four, and Grace, you were six years old. Her death was not only a wake up call for us all, but also a realization for our family that any of us including our parents could die at anytime. It wasn't that we didn't think about it before your Mom became sick. Of course we did, however, her death made it real, and much more vivid in our minds. Time became more valuable. Suddenly life was getting shorter for all of us. Beyond that, we also realized that our family had become smaller.

What happened next as I observed it was that our family slowly and steadily became less intense, softer and gentler with each other. We all seemed to be a little kinder—it was as if your mother's death took the cancer away from our family and we started to heal, slowly yet steadily. I am not sure that I could even say that in fear that I may make you upset or sad, making it sound that your Mother was sacrificed so our family could heal. There is another way of looking at it that I think could be more uplifting and healing for us all. Your mother was a saint during her lifetime, as I have tried to convey as sincerely as I could in this letter of love to you. She had nothing but generosity, love, kindness and compassion to share with us. Her selflessness was extremely apparent and powerful. I prefer to think that even in her dying process and death, she gave us yet another gift, yet another act of love. It was her generosity to our family that healed us. It was this thought that made me realize that I must share this story of her healing love—not just with you, the children I know she loved so very much—but I want to share this love with others who it might heal.

I do this not only to respect and honor her memory, but also in order to perpetuate, share and spread the love your Mother had for you, for me, for us, and for all the children whose lives she touched. Those people so blessed to have her in their lives include both her biological family and ours. Had Wewe continued to live, I believe she would have gone on spreading her kindness and love, and now it is up to us to do so. I believe her life actions, her love and her story are extremely powerful, and as I see it in retrospect, she had the power to turn anger, bitterness and conflict into patience, respect, understanding and peace.

Now, almost fourteen years since she died, our family is more peaceful than ever. This is not to say that we don't fight, or everything is perfect and lovely. We still fight, we still have disagreements and we have bumps along the way, but one thing is clear to me, it is obvious that our family has become closer, and we understand as a family we have been given a second chance to be better. The irony that continues to haunt me is that the one person who could heal us, who deserved to enjoy the fruits of her love is no longer with us.

I turned forty in 2010, exactly four years and seven months after your Mother turned forty-six, and exactly four years and six months after she passed away. We share the same birthday date, and as I am a rather sentimental and melancholy person, every month on our birthdate I light a special candle for us as a way to tell myself and your Mom: "Dear Wewe, I am thinking about you, I am thinking about what we shared and what I will always do, and I will never forget our love for each other."

I planned my fortieth birthday about a year in advance, starting in 2009 with the help of my best friend, my sister-in-law Reny. I knew from the start I wanted to do it in Bali, as you know it is a very dear place to me, with a place in my heart and life for so many reasons. Reny used to live in Bali where she worked as a tour guide and graduated in hospitality management. She has always been kind and sweet to me, and she is another woman in my life who has lifted me up since my childhood. Having her involved in planning the party was also a gesture from me to show my support for her and to let her know how important she still is to me.

I decided to invite about sixty people from around sixteen countries: the list consisted of family, friends and a number of special people who had once been strangers and yet over the years have became family to us. It was a celebration in which I hoped to return a little of the love they had shown for me over the years. I would turn forty in 2010, and I decided that I wanted them all to meet each other and also to be able to share them with my family.

As I mentioned before, I call the strangers who have become my family my *ohana*. My parents, all my siblings, aunts, uncles, best friends and their family and partners as well as Bob my savior in San Francisco, my husband and I flew in from all over the world. Childhood friends I hadn't seen in decades joined us, along with more recently acquired friends. Stephen and I decided to invite our aunts whom I never met from my father's side—the fruits of my grandfather's affair. They had been turned down by my uncle's family at his funeral, but I insisted that they come and join us so our family could meet them, as I believe it was not their fault, and I felt it was time to spread the healing to our big extended family. People came to join us for this event from the Americas, Europe and all over Asia and Australia.

That was one of the longest years of my life, as I couldn't contain my excitement to be reunited with those sixty people who loved me enough to make such a big effort to be in Bali with me for that entire week. When the day finally came for us to leave our home to take the thirty-hour journey to Bali your mother was on my mind—my heart ached and I wished she could have joined us there. I made a decision to pack her pictures and memorabilia carefully, including your picture, Grace and Zef, and the candle I had next to her picture. Your Mom and you both came with us to Bali, even if it's only in a form of pictures and memories, but you were with us. Sadly we could not invite you, as we knew your father would not allow us to bring you to Bali. You were in our hearts.

We arrived in Bali a bit early so we could prepare for the arrival of our guests that had confirmed they would make the journey. I was super excited to embrace each one of them as they arrived at the hotel we had booked for everyone to stay with us. Reny and I planned to show them Bali's places of interest and to share with them some of the island's cultural wealth, so each day was filled with a balance of activities and relaxation time to allow us to have a chance to re-connect with old friends, and for them to meet new friends through Stephen and me. One of my joys in life is connecting people and I think we created quite a few new friendships that week.

The days went by fast as we shared our time, and our meals and drinks daily. We ate breakfast, lunch and dinner together, invading the pool and tourist attractions en masse, and we laughed and cried many times that week for various reasons, as we reminisced upon old times and remembered friends and family who were no longer with us. Sadly of course, those absences were a reminder for all of us that this week might be not only be the last time, but it was probably also the only time all of us could be together. While we never know what will happen to any of us, we acknowledged that some of us in the group had already reached their eighties and the sun was setting.

A week of this blissful life was my version of heaven on earth. To be in close proximity with those people that I care and love, as I mentioned before, is my ideal in life, what I think heaven would be like. Well, that week was just that, I lived my slice of heavenly life then and there. This was what life was designed for. To be able to wake up and kiss one's loved ones, then share coffee and an abundant breakfast prepared by the most solicitous people on earth in a Balinese setting like no other. To watch the sun set every day, hanging out together simply to enjoy each other's company and still be around to kiss one's loved ones goodnight, or hug and hold hands. To laugh and to cry, and build memories, what more could there be?

From the moment I arrived I dreaded the day we would have to say goodbye. I knew myself too well. Yes, I was elated, ecstatic and happy beyond anything else I had ever done. It was wonderful to be surrounded by my loved ones and those I considered to be part of our extended *ohana* family at the same time. I also knew it would be the only time ever in my lifetime that something like this would happen. It was an event of a lifetime. My elderly uncle, his wife and my cousins were the first to say goodbye to fly back to Australia, and our mood was somber but I still had to be a good host for the rest who stayed on a few days longer.

The day we all had to leave to go back to our respective homes, thousands of miles away—while some stayed on a bit longer in Bali—was a day that felt to me like the end of all days. I knew I was alive but I felt as if I was at my own funeral. The sadness I felt—and I knew some of us did feel the same—was so profound that it cut deeply into my heart. I wondered if these people would be the same ones who would make the effort to come to my funeral in the future—assuming they survived me, of course. I recognized the feeling that I had when I couldn't make it for your Mom's funeral. A sinking feeling of loss that I experienced when I couldn't be there; in a way, this felt like it was my funeral for her.

On my 40th birthday, instead of gifts—for me their presence and the effort to get there were the biggest gift they could possibly give anyway—I asked my friends and family to donate to our favorite cause in Bali, in honor of your mother and her love for all children. We donated to an orphanage as well as to some schools that needed supplies and furniture. And since that year, my husband Stephen and I have continued to contribute to orphanages and send funds for the children who otherwise could not go to school, in honor of your mother, her love and her life.

On a cool sunny day that week, before starting on our first set of goodbyes, we hosted a tea party on the lawn at Amandari, one of the most beautiful spots in the hills of Ubud. I wanted to thank everyone for their love—not just for coming to Bali, but for showing their love over the four decades of my life to someone, anyone like me—someone who is different, needy, and comes from such a dissimilar background to their own.

Each individual there came from all sorts of different socio economic backgrounds, cultures, religions and varied demographics. At the end of our get-together I made a

plea for each one of us to go back to where we came from
and continue to spread the love we shared. I asked them to
continue to show love to everyone the way they have loved
and supported me, and to continue to support humanity,
to uphold equality and to treat those who have a different
upbringing and background to our own with kindness,
love and compassion, the way they have treated me. I also
promised them that I would continue to do the same. I told
them to do this in memory of my sister and her love for me
and for all children.

As the sun was setting, I read the following poem, as
it resonated with my state of mind at that time, and I saw a
number of tears fall during that brief time that we shared. I
know the memories of that day will always be imprinted in
our hearts.

In My Good Death, by Dalia Shevin[8]

I will find myself waist deep in high summer grass. The
humming shock of the golden light. And I will hear them
before I see them and know right away who is bounding
across the field to meet me. All my good dogs will come then,
their wet noses bumping against my palms, their hot panting,
their rough faithful tongues. Their eyes young and shiny
again. The wiry scruff of their fur, the unspeakable softness of

8. Dalia Shevin has self-published two books: *The Mystery of the Missing
Puzzle Piece* (a limited edition of one) and, coauthored with Sophie Bady-
Kaye, *The Best Comics You Have Ever Read In Your Entire Life, Seriously* (a
limited edition of two).

their bellies, their velvet ears
against my cheeks. I will bend to them, my face covered with
their kisses, my hands full of them. In the grass I will let them
knock me down.

* * *

On the days that led up to your Mom's funeral the
pain from my sadness was exponentially made worse by
not being able to be there in Indonesia with our family. I
drowned my sorrows in my work and listened to music all
day and night. There was one particular song by a band called
Snow Patrol that was constantly playing at the time on the
radio. The song is called "*Run*"[9] and it spoke to me of my
emotional state over the past year, after learning about Wewe's
illness, feeling hopeless and unable to alleviate her misery; for
me this was a period of feeling helpless, it lasted until the end
of her life and the song seemed to capture it perfectly:

I'll sing it one last time for you
Then we really have to go
You've been the only thing that's right
In all I've done.
And I can barely look at you
But every single time I do

9. "Run" is a song by Northern Irish alternative rock band Snow Patrol
from their third studio album, Final Straw (2003). Conceived in 2000
by frontman Gary Lightbody, it was released in the U.K. on 26 February
2004.

I know we'll make it anywhere
Away from here
Light up, light up
As if you have a choice
Even if you cannot hear my voice
I'll be right beside you dear

I felt as if I was whispering that song and that's what
I imagined I could do, to sooth her soul and heart even if I
could not take away her pain as she was slowly dying.

That moment I had to say goodbye to the very special
group of people in my life who came to Bali for my birthday,
it felt like a repeat of saying goodbye to my sister, and that
song played over and over again in my head till I could hear
it unceasingly, without being able to shut it down. It felt like
I was essentially playing some kind of funeral music for her
in my head. All of us were in a similar mood at our farewell,
even those who never met my sister but knew me well and
had heard about your Mom and her death. Especially after
having seen her picture in Bali, on the evening of my 40th
birthday when I kept it with me. I carried her picture with me
everywhere I went, even at the dinner table, so they could tell
how sad I felt.

Although we never spoke about our emotions in detail,
we seemed to understand each other perfectly as a group. The
evening before we had to say our farewell we had our 'last
supper' and they handed me a marionette of a local Balinese-
made Mickey Mouse—my favorite Disney character—and

a beautiful little notebook. In it there were love notes hand-written by dear friends and family, the most appropriate gift for my birthday celebration of my heaven-on-earth week. Needless to say, more tears were wiped away, marking an unforgettable week in all our lives.

Although our emotions were heartfelt, few words were exchanged. At times, those are the kind of moments in life that leave the strongest impressions. Your mother and I had so much of that kind of wordless communication going on in our lives, as we connected at a deep level emotionally, a level where we didn't need to say a word or explain anything to each other as we understood and felt for each other profoundly. I felt so lucky to have that relationship in my lifetime.

* * *

Something happened to me not long after Wewe passed away. A few weeks, or perhaps it was a month after her passing, Stephen and I decided to get away for a long weekend to do some R&R and also to reflect on what had happened to our family and to us that year. Losing someone so close to me, to both of us, had taken a toll on us both. When we could not travel, but needed time to regroup and relax, we always tried to take the time to get away locally.

This time I had just received a very nice gift from our client. Her name is Ann Ferrel Millham, a client who has always been kind and generous. I met her parents and was always touched by how they treated me. In my industry at that time I was a florist—people sometimes treated me as their servant or even worse—with disrespect and rudeness. Ann Ferrel and her husband Steve had always been kind and humble and treated me not only respectfully but I felt how kindhearted they were. They not only trusted me to do their flowers at home, but I had also designed party settings for them. As a thank you gift they gave me a gift certificate for us to stay in a resort that we happened to love to visit but had never stayed at. Usually we stayed down further in the Carmel area where later we had a cottage. This resort peaked my interest when I had prepared flowers for a wedding there. It turned out to be where Ann Ferrel and Steve had their wedding too.

We checked in, and as usual, as soon as we had scouted the property and explored their amenities, we unpacked and settled in. As we had decided to use this time to reflect on your Mom's passing, I brought her framed photograph and placed it next to my bedside with my journal and a few other items that reminded me of her, such as the last letter she wrote to me. While walking around the property we had been to the spa to make an appointment for our massage. We both have always been addicted to massage—it's become a part of our lives. There was a gift shop beside the spa and I was drawn to the candle display. I always liked to have a candle in our hotel room, so I bought some, but I wanted to explore further and looked at some more. I picked up another candle that was labeled 'Egyptian Jasmine' and smelled the exact same scent that we grew up with in the front yard of our rental home when I was a child. It reminded me of the jasmine buds that were scattered throughout the hotel where I saw your Mom for the last time ever in my life.

The sense of smell is one of my strongest and most powerful senses, as it can be for some people. In that instant I was reminded of our childhood and I felt her presence envelop me. My heart was touched with the surprise and happiness of the sudden memories, yet simultaneously it felt heavy with sadness. I shared my reaction to the scented candle with my husband, and he insisted on purchasing it for me for our room.

We had a wonderful light lunch outdoors, enjoying the beauty of California's hills in the springtime. We didn't talk much as we both were in a rather somber mood. Stephen has always been a staunch champion of my emotions, ever since we met. We sat outside for a while and then went to our room and relaxed before our massage appointment later that afternoon. I think we must have dozed off, falling in and out of sleep, and this was a perfect opening to our long weekend, but I was still restless in some ways, not knowing exactly how to deal with my feelings.

As it happened, we decided to go to the massage earlier so we could enjoy the steam and have a sauna after our bath, as we really enjoyed relaxing in the cozy, well-heated lounge room with its fireplace, candles and extra blankets. As well as reading materials they provide fruit and healthy snacks.

Usually we booked a couple massage in the same room, but this time they didn't have a slot or a room for us, so we agreed to have separate rooms and therapists.

I was chosen first by an older lady who introduced herself as Igreja. Her build was small, but her presence struck me as being calming, grounding and strong. I made small talk with her about how her name reminded me of a word in Indonesian, where *gereja* means church. She explained to me her name did actually mean church in Portuguese. It was a name that she had chosen for herself later in life, and she had always gone by that name ever since.

Igreja set me up in the treatment room and stepped out for me to get comfortable on the massage table, face down. She knocked and I made a sound to signal her that it was fine for her to re-enter. The room was cozy and airy and felt like a cocoon. The temperature was just perfect; soothing music always had a calming effect and helped me relax. The scent in the room was spa-like. Lavender was in the air, like the flowers I had seen growing all around the property. I am lucky to have enjoyed massage and spa treatments almost all of my life. At home in Indonesia we had a regular traditional Javanese massage therapist who we called Mbok Pijet—'Big Sister the Masseuse'. Both Stephen and I love massage as a treatment to help our bodies deal with muscle pain and to enable relaxation. He prefers a deeper massage, and I like it firm but relaxing, which was what I had informed Igreja on my intake form. I was ready.

She uncovered me half way, tucking the blanket and

cover around my hips, and proceeded to do her opening treatment making a long movement with her palms along my back and stretching them diagonally, a familiar move that I fully anticipated. Then she touched my shoulder firmly with one hand on each side, and put some pressure so that I would take a deep breath, and without any warning as I breathed in deeply I let out a great bawl and then continued crying uncontrollably.

This crying of mine went on for the entire session and she did not say a word throughout the massage, simply offering me tissues from time to time, and continuing to massage me as she saw fit. I sobbed and sobbed, and I could hardly breathe. As I became congested she simply rubbed me with a mixture that smelt like Eucalyptus oil, which helped me to breathe easier, and brought back memories of a favorite remedy from my childhood in Indonesia, *minyak kayu putih*, which we used a lot in our family. Your mother used to put it on me to relieve insect bites, or to reduce congestion when I had a cold. While it helped relieve my nasal passages, the memory of that particular Eucalyptus aroma triggered something in me that made my sobs even more heart wrenching. I don't think it was so very loud, but I was unable to control the awful sound and I felt overwhelmed by emotion.

It was not until just near the end of the massage that I finally managed to say I was sorry that I had cried throughout the session.

"Don't be sorry," she told me. "It's OK. I sensed you

needed to cry. I felt your pain, and I am with you."

Still sobbing, at times even harder, I told her about my sister who had just passed away. I kept my explanation as simple as I could, about how Wewe was like my mother and how close we were, and that she had left two little children behind—the two of you. She responded by sharing that she lost her son when he was very young, in an accident, and this was near the time of the anniversary of his death.

The power of our connection made me think not only about your Mom and me, but the possibility of her presence in that instant or her energy connecting Igreja and me in that moment, both of us mourning the loss of our loved ones, that one person in our lives who we were so close to had left this earth forever, and we were left behind to feel the sorrow.

My feelings of sadness and loss were also felt by Igreja, and then somehow reflected back to me. From what I gathered, it had been over twenty years or more since she lost her son. I had lost my sister only a few weeks before. She was sensitive to my strong emotions even though she was still mourning after all those years. While she remained very professional, she was such a warm human and powerful being. I think this was what enabled us to connect in such a special and powerful way.

We embraced before we said goodbye, connected by our sorrow for the loss of our loved ones. While I was fully aware she was not my sister, during those intimate moments we shared for the last two hours, I felt my sister's presence in her. This presence, and that of her son, both felt so vivid and strong, although in a different, intangible form. I will always be grateful to Igreja, another woman, practically a stranger, who was there for me when I needed her, who helped me to start my journey in mourning the loss of your Mom, my dear sister, Wewe.

Stephen came out of his own massage session to find me embracing this woman, with my face and eyes still wet and red. Fortunately he understood that the moment was a special one for both Igreja and I. Later in the evening I was able to share with him what had happened. Stephen, as a psychologist who was educated in a formal school that embraced knowledge from both the East and West, believes in the complexity of energies and how they affect us as humans, especially in how we relate to each other. Of course he believed that it was only natural that such a connection could happen. He saw it as a positive event in my life. We walked back to our room in silence, as we struggled to absorb the magnitude of what had just happened.

That night we had a romantic dinner at the resort where we were staying. We toasted in honor of your Mom, her life and the love she had given to me, and her contribution in shaping me as a human. She was responsible for me becoming the person that I am, and she played such a big role in my life. We went back to our suite which had a nice fireplace, and lit our candles, and I brought out the one Stephen had purchased earlier that day, the one that reminded me of my childhood and spending time with your

Mom outside on the veranda. We curled up together and held hands, looking out at a majestic California oak tree that had been up-lit. It looked gorgeous. The night was clear, the stars were shining bright and we were content to be together. We put on our music and we shared a nightcap, my husband's favorite neat bourbon.

I started to reminisce about your Mom and the music that came on the background was that of Dixie Chicks' *Not Ready to Make Nice*[10]. While I knew perfectly that song was not about me or my sister—it was about American politics—but that song hit just the right notes in my heart in expressing my anger and frustration and emotion about how cruel it was for my sister to die the way she did and how unfair it was for everyone: unfair for her to die so young and in such misery, unfair for you both to lose your Mom at a very young age, and unfair for me to lose my dear sister. This time I let out a wail and gave in to the uncontrollable sobs that I had not allowed before. My sadness and crying in the massage room was the beginning of my mourning in a true sense, something I had not allowed myself to do since she had passed away, and tonight I knew I finally had permission to feel the way I did.

Listening to the music I tried to understand how the lyrics truly speak to me and as she belted out her chorus, I too joined in with her with my wail:

---

10. Dixie Chicks' *"Not Ready to Make Nice"* - Songwriters: Martha Maguire / Natalie Maines / Emily Robison / Dan Wilson

Forgive, sounds good
Forget, I'm not sure I could
They say time heals everything
But I'm still waiting

I am still waiting as I write this, for time to heal my loss. It is May 22, 2020 and in two days time my sister would have died exactly fourteen years ago, and I am still mourning for her.

- tigabelas -

"Forever birthdays…"

Today is April 23, 2020 in San Francisco and it is about 6.19 pm, which is April 24, 2020 at 8.19 am in Lampung, where she was born. Today is the day your Mom, my dear sister Wewe would have turned sixty.

When I wrote the sentence above I had just been desperately searching for the soap, shampoo, conditioner and body lotion that we were provided in our hotel room at the Dharmawangsa, where we had gathered before we threw her a surprise birthday party, exactly a month before she passed away. I have a collection of hotel amenities that I keep from all over the world. Some I like to use, others I simply keep for the memories. Stephen thinks I am a hoarder and there is some truth to that—I like to keep things that I have a special emotional connection to.

As I write this last letter to you, I have been frantically trying to find the lotion I had carefully put aside since April 24, 2006, the last day I spent with Wewe on her 46th birthday. It was the last time I actually touched my sister in the flesh. In fact, it was the very same bottle of body lotion that I had spread on her arms and shoulders that day of her birthday, after her shower. I remember that her body was so frail and her parched skin clung to her bones like shrink-wrap. I gently smoothed the lotion into her skin to ease the dryness I could see, and felt just how fragile she was.

Today when I finally found the bottle along with the

soap, shampoo and conditioner we had from that same hotel, I pulled it from the toiletry bag which holds all the bottles and soap, opened it and brought it to my face, searching for a hint of familiar scent. The bag I had found it in was from Singapore Airlines, that flight we took to see her for the last time. I held the bottle reverently, as if it contained the last drop of my memory of her on that trip.

I desperately wanted to honor her on the day she was born, to make it special, to pay some kind of homage to her and to make up to her for the times when I did not pay attention to her after I left Indonesia. I wanted her to know how special she has been and always will be to me, and to say that I am sorry, I am sorry—not only for the pain she had to go through—but for the fact that I wasn't able to be there for her. I also want to let her know that I will always love her and how much I miss her...

Every year since she passed away I make sure that I text or call our parents and family to remind them that today is her birthday. I want them to remember that we love her on this day, and that we will think of her always. It is almost as if it is my responsibility to make sure that everyone whose life has been touched by my sister will know and remember that it is the day she was born, the day for us to honor her.

As an active participant in this world of social media we live in now, I also feel the need to post something about her on this day, and tell the world about her birthday, to make sure my online friends know how important she still is and will always be to me. I go through my pictures of her and decide which one is most meaningful to me today, choosing a new one each year.

I go through the box that I keep with all of her pictures. It is a very special keepsake and I open it periodically and remember her picture by picture. Today I decided to crop a picture of her saying goodbye to me at the airport when I had to fly back to the U.S. It was with our cousin, Ci Tian. I was in the middle, and my sister was next to me, my arms holding both women who had loved and raised me and gave me so much goodness in my life. I chose this picture as to me it was not only symbolic that I was in the middle of those two amazing women; it was also a moment of farewell. Every goodbye to me at the airport is always heart wrenching. I hate that feeling that that it might be the last time I would ever see my loved ones. While this photo was most probably taken in the late '80s or early '90s, and it was not the last time I saw her, it was, in a way, as it always is the last time for a while. The ritual of saying goodbye at the airport to her and other family members is always a teary one for me. Typically on occasions like this the female members of our family and I always sob as if it was someone's funeral. The tears typically started to flow around forty-eight hours before I had to leave Indonesia, regardless whether I was leaving from Sumatra, Java or Bali.

I always found the drive to the airport painful; in the car I usually hugged whoever was next to me, or held my sister's or my Mom's hand. The stress of pre-departure logistics distracted me, but the moment I had to go into the departure area where well-wishers could not join me was usually the moment I started bawling, and so did they. From then on I'd put on my sunglasses, as my tears would constantly stream, like a spring river in the Grand Teton National Park gushing out with freshly melted snow water.

My crying sometimes got louder and harder as the plane taxied and the flight attendant would hand me a box of tissues. They didn't ask, they simply anticipated my need. During our takeoff it felt so painful physically that I literally felt as if someone had stabbed my heart with a *keris* or squeezed it in their hand, and with every mile or sunset I saw through the window, I always felt so much more alone, even if my husband was holding my hand. It is the price I pay as an immigrant, for the life I chose to live.

But one of the biggest reasons I chose that picture was how wonderful your Mom looked in it; she looked absolutely vibrant, her hair looked so healthy, and that was her signature hairstyle, just slightly touching her shoulder, perfectly cut in a bob style, with bangs touching her brows and tucked behind her ears on both sides. Her round glasses always framed her face perfectly and her smile and eyes spark with joy. She was sad to say goodbye to me but I can still see her vivaciousness and the brightness of her soul, the purity of her love and the humility that always enveloped her. Her cute smile always made her look as if she was biting part of her lower lip and that signature mole on her chin was perfectly placed halfway between her lower lip and chin. In

French she would be referred to as 'gamine': a girl with mischievous boyish charm. I also love the fact that in the photo my hand was resting lightly on her shoulder and I can still feel the touch of her skin.

So today I bought some French tulips, as I couldn't find jasmine or tuberose for her, the fragrance that reminds me of her and home. French tulips always symbolize underrated beauty and elegance to me, and the variety I chose is called *La Plus Belle du monde*—'the most beautiful in the world'. To me, that is what she truly was, still is and will always be. My husband Stephen baked her a birthday cake, and I got the number candles for six and zero. We toasted her with our favorite cocktails and lit our dinner candles plus one extra jasmine candle that I got when she passed away, the candle I also put next to her picture with the dried jasmine, along with the pottery vase that says 'forever' from beside my bed.

I also posted an excerpt of this book about the time when we would walk together to visit her biological parents' house, about how she always held my hand and would carry me no matter how tired she was. It is important to me to share with the world, with anyone and everyone who is willing to pay attention to my declaration, that she is the person who is responsible in making me the way I am, the good part of me came from her and her love. I want the world to know that it is possible for someone so understated, so petite in her appearance and humble in her demeanor, to be so powerful and have such an impact in influencing another human being. When I say this I am talking about myself, but beyond me I know she has left her mark on others in this world as she is loved by many, even after almost fourteen years of her passing.

I texted family members to remind them as I always do on a yearly basis that today is her birthday but not just any ordinary birthday it would have also been her 60th. Our cousin in the picture sent back hearts and tears, emojis, our nephew sent notes remembering what a kind person she was, my father sent a lot of heart emojis and flowers. Emojis have taken the place of words for some people, it seems, but I understand their meaning and I can grasp the intention of the senders.

I also texted you, Zefanya. I wanted to let you know that I had posted her picture and a caption on my social media. You said how sweet I was to let you know. It's not so easy to tell you, not in so many words, especially not on social media, how important she was to me, not just a sister, but also a mother to me and my protector and angel. I sent you a few pictures of her and you responded that finally you realized how much you resemble her. To which I agreed and added that you also look like Empek Edo, your grandfather, and your uncles Afat and Nyen Nyen. I asked you what you remember about her most. You said that you were so young you have very little memory of her, but you always remember how patient and kind she was, and of course I confirmed that was true and it was what everyone says about her. This corroborated what I wrote to you in the beginning of these letters...that you may not remember everything about her, and that is perfectly normal and understandable. You were very young when she left.

I was worried I was making you sad by talking about her, but you convinced me that you didn't get sad that much and I tried to let you know it's ok to feel however you feel now... or in the future... that someday, you may feel more sad or remember her more than ever, as one never knows how or what will trigger memories or emotions. Certain things may trigger some memories, as we bury memories, either consciously or not. I also asked if you dream about her a lot, as I do, but you haven't and you said you didn't usually dream much. In my mind I wonder if this is a natural defense mechanism as someone who lost his mother at such a young age.

One thing I am happy about is that we chatted, and I know that would have made your Mom happy. I also am pleasantly surprised at how good your English is, and I am absolutely thrilled that you sent me your picture. You do look like her a lot and your grandpa too, and how cute you look in your singlet, just like him and me as a child. We chatted a bit more about your sister and how often you see her and I hope we will all see each other soon. I feel that in a way it was a gesture of keeping my promise to my sister that I'd keep an eye on her children, to know that you both are well and it's hard to believe that you are in college already. It made me think about how smart your Mom was, as she navigated her school and career; from junior high school, she decided to go to nursing school, worked as a nurse then carried on to be a midwife. Later she decided to be an anesthesiologist.

I know your Mom would have been so proud of you and I know from a psychological point of view she too has left the biggest marks in your hearts and minds even if you don't remember her much. They say the first five years of a child's life are the most important phases in a human life; how a person is raised in those five years will determine how they go on throughout their life. I can't help but wonder, had she still been with us, what we would be doing for her sixtieth birthday. But for now, this is sufficient for me: to celebrate her life text messaging with her son over the phone.

Today I also will go through my ritual of looking at her framed picture next to my bed and pick up the dried jasmine flowers from the birthday party at the hotel in Jakarta, and I will smell the faint yet powerful fragrance which will transport me to the evening of her last birthday on earth…

When we learned about her cancer and what stage it was at, we knew we didn't have much time. My husband Stephen had met your Mom a few times and while they could not communicate with each other, their conversation was made up of smiles, hugs and gestures as well as body language. My husband has heard my stories about my childhood and always knew how important your Mom was, is and will always be to me. When we received her last letter, in December 2005, it was Stephen who suggested that we should visit her on her birthday, hopefully she would still be alive and we could throw her a surprise party.

We got in touch with our parents and siblings from California, and arranged for them to start inviting all the cousins and their children as well as my sister's biological family, her dad Empek Edo and all her brothers and sisters and their kids. By this time Wewe's Mom had already passed away. Essentially we wanted to invite everyone whose life had been touched by her, all those people we knew we could get hold of. Stephen suggested we should hold the party at our favorite hotel in Jakarta and give her the fanciest birthday party of her life, the kind of party she had never had, to let her know not only that she deserved it, as a message from me to her and to our family that she was the most important person in my life. We wanted to show our gratitude in a way that had never been shown before in our family.

It was also to let her know that it was the right thing for people to be nice to her, and that this time it was our turn to pamper her and to take care of her and make her feel deserving. I coordinated things with the help of Reny again, asking her to arrange all the necessary logistics for this special and important event. Rooms were booked for the out-of-towners, a restaurant in the hotel was booked privately just for us, and a cake was made by our sister Edna as her way of showing her own support and love.

Stephen and I made the 30-hour flight journey with a heavy heart and some butterflies. In my heart, I knew, this would be the last time I would see her. I was sure of it. We arrived a day earlier in Jakarta and checked in to the Dharmawangsa to make sure all was in order. My parents did what they needed to do to have your parents come with no suspicion of our arrival. The next day, it was agreed that the family would greet Wewe at the hotel entrance as she arrived.

When the moment arrived, Stephen and I were hiding behind the lobby door so she could get out of the car without seeing us. My heart was pounding, not knowing what to expect and how she would look, I could barely breathe with the anticipation of seeing her after such a long time.

The moment I saw her I could not hold my tears at the sight of her, looking like a walking corpse was beyond anything I could handle, but I knew I had to be strong for her, yet, tears were simply pouring uncontrollably. Your Mom was visibly shocked at the sight of Stephen and me, but what was even more alarming was her wail. When she saw me she instantly cried out like a wounded animal and clung to me like a baby koala to its mother. I never expected such a reversal of roles to happen. We embraced as we always had, but this time it was stronger, longer and more intense than ever. We hugged and we sobbed and cried for what seemed a lifetime, and I became aware that we were creating a spectacle in front of everyone at the hotel lobby entrance, but we were not completely aware of our surroundings and unwilling to untangle.

My father who had recently become an amateur photographer was hovering around us and constantly clicking his camera, which angered me and I scolded him.

"Dad!!! Stop it! Stop taking our pictures! Not everything has to be captured on camera..." I shouted at my father as I continued to stroke my sister's hair, face and hug her as hard as I could without fear of breaking her bones, as she was so frail and weak. Not until years later would I be grateful to have those pictures my father had captured, and I felt sorry that I had yelled at him at the time, as now I understand his intention was good, and I have become like him. Now I am the one who snaps every moment of our lives, clinging on to the memories we capture in photographs.

Not until later, when both your Mom and I finally had a chance to gather ourselves together, overcome our emotions and calm ourselves down did I realize that everyone in the hotel lobby who had witnessed what just happened was whispering, and wiping their eyes. Few words were exchanged by anyone, and a somber mood hung over us like a dark cloud before a storm, a cloud that lingered for what felt like an eternity.

That moment was permanently imprinted in my heart and soul and I shall remember and carry it till my own last breath. I also know that moment would stay in my husband's heart as well as others who witnessed us being reunited at the lobby. We were all shocked by the appearance of your Mom. She was already petite in her build to start with, even during her healthy life. But this time, she had literally become just skin and bones, and looked as emaciated as an anorexic patient or those African starvation victims I had seen all my life on TV and in magazines. This time it was not a stranger, nor something I had watched on TV. It was my sister, the person who had raised me and showered me with love all my entire life. The spark in her eyes had dimmed and I could only see what an effort that she made for me, as she tried to show me that she was so happy to see me. She did her best to smile for me, yet she knew, and I knew, it was only a matter of time before she would slip away. Her skin was dried up and cracked. We had to hold her to help her walk and she dragged her steps like Kas our dog had when he was shot and bleeding. Every step was a painful labor, and how I wished I could carry her the way she did me when we climbed those steep stairs to her parents' house. How I wished I could take all her misery and pain away in an instant. How I wished I could turn back the clock.

That day we stayed in the hotel, simply to be together. We booked her the nice suite near our room and I visited her as often as I could, at times just lying next to her on the bed and cradling her; no words were exchanged and tears streamed down our faces. Our parents and your dad and my husband gave us our space and privacy, knowing how much we loved each other and allowing us our special time. It was during this time that I asked her if she knew she was dying, as everyone in our family believed she would be healed in Jesus' name, something which still angers me until today. Instead of being realistic and supportive of her leaving this earth in a way that was humane, everyone had false hopes and expectations.

It was during this time we spent privately together, when I asked her to be honest, to be real and to acknowledge the truth, that she nodded, and acknowledged that she was aware that she was dying. We embraced, acknowledging the inevitable. This was the time she asked me to promise that I would look after both of you. I promised her I would do my best.

Stephen and I had brought her some gifts, mostly clothing for her to wear for the party, as she didn't know about it in advance. All of these items of clothing were too big of course, even in the extra small size, but she obliged us by trying them and showered us with gratitude and kisses. To see her changing her clothes, as I always had all my life, was normal and it never bothered me. But this time, it was like witnessing a concentration camp victim, and I had to look away to cry as I was helping her, but she grabbed my face and wiped my tears and kissed me. Another profound moment passed between us, that I know I will carry with me for the rest of my life. It was after this that I helped her to moisturize her skin with the fancy body lotion from the hotel. She thanked me for putting her up in a very nice hotel. I told her it was nothing, and we were just happy to be with her. She understood our intention.

That night I gathered our family, my parents, my sister and your uncle David the monster—by this time I had forgiven him for what he did to me—and I also asked their children to gather around your Mom and just to be together as a family again for the evening. I also asked my brother David to ask for forgiveness from your mother, for his behavior in our younger days, for hurting her physically even though it was intended for me.

We all had dinner together, we told jokes and reminisced about the past, and for a precious moment, it was a pleasant and peaceful time in our family, something that had rarely happened in our past, or before she got sick.

The next day we went to her room and we repeated our gathering, and then we rested together, just the two of us. Then we all took turns to visit, or as she lay down weakly small groups of us would gather around her. She managed to smile and stroke my hair, and that of our nephews and nieces. Dad took our pictures and by this time he was more careful, only taking those pictures I gave permission for.

That afternoon after lunch we let her rest while we were getting ready for the party, and I met with the staff and Reny to go over the timing, and hatched our plan to usher all relatives who attended directly to the restaurant, which was still being prepared. This was the most fancy restaurant in the hotel, possibly one of the nicest restaurants in Jakarta. It was decorated with wood paneling and elegant crystal chandeliers, with a touch of colonial decor to go with the rest of the hotel, designed by the most famous Indonesian designer, Jaya Ibrahim. It was one of our favorite hotels in the world as it evokes the romance of Batavia, old Jakarta, during the Dutch colonial times. It speaks of hushed luxury, elegance and traditions and it is located in the most posh neighborhoods of Jakarta where expats and politicians live.

I wanted everything to be just perfect for my sister for many reasons. Mainly I wished to reveal to her how important she was to our family and to me. I knew it was her send-off to the next phase of her life and it had to be perfect. It was the only time I spent my own money for her in an elaborate way and that was important to me. Flowers were placed everywhere and candles, ready to be lit.

We took a little time to rest and to gather ourselves and finally the time had arrived to pick her up. Earlier on we had told her that we would pick her up to have dinner, although she barely ate the day before, so I didn't know how she would manage. I assumed her loss of appetite was part of her being sick, and it killed me to watch her struggle with her food. Because I had told her of our plans to leave the next day for my business trip, and this was the evening before her actually birthday, she did not suspect we were plotting anything. I helped her put on a chic black dress with a light blue cardigan that we had chosen for her, and she gave me another kiss to say thank you for our gift. By this time everyone was already in the restaurant waiting for our arrival.

Stephen and I walked with her and your dad. Wewe was leaning on my arm, and we took our time to walk slowly from her room to the restaurant. Again, all eyes were on us. I recognized some of the staff and some guests from yesterday and it seemed everyone was watching us, not sure where to look, but it felt like they were giving us warm and empathetic support. One only could guess what they were thinking by then, but I didn't care, all I cared for was to show my sister my love, gratitude and all the appreciation I had for her in the only way that I knew how.

The restaurant was located near the entrance of the hotel so we walked together all the way from her suite to the lobby. What I didn't know would happen was the surprise the hotel's Director of Food and Beverages had planned for us. He had lined up all his staff on either side of our path, from the lobby all the way to the restaurant, creating a guard of honor, as a way of showing their respect to Wewe, in a very sincere and compassionate way. As soon as I saw the avenue of lovely smiling faces stretching all the way to the restaurant, I could not help but to shed more tears, while holding her as best as I could. My husband sensed that I needed support. First he held my shoulder then he moved to help hold your Mom, so by this time we were walking on either side of her. As we got closer to the restaurant, she started to weep, but when she realized our entire family, her Dad and everyone were waiting there for her, she started to wail and sob and by this time everyone in that space, including the staff of the hotel, was wiping tears.

I let her go and handed her to her father, Empek Edo. I had never witnessed him cry until that night. As soon as we got her comfortable everyone came to kiss and hug her, one by one. I believe there were close to seventy people in attendance, and I am not sure why you were not with us, as we invited you both.

The evening went on and later we sang happy birthday to her with the cake made by our sister Edna, more tears and some laughter. I made sure dinner was served perfectly and everyone had enough to drink and to eat. Periodically I would hug her and kiss her. The evening ended with everyone saying goodbye to her and for some it would have been their last time to see her. Children of all ages lined up to give her a kiss, one by one, struggling to hold back their tears. We all knew it would be our last chance to pay our respects to our very special angel on earth.

Later as Stephen and I took care of the logistics of the evening with the hotel, the Manager, who was French and didn't understand much Indonesian, said something to me about what a wonderful son I was to my mother. It took me a few seconds to realize that he thought your mother was mine. I explained briefly that she was my sister but practically she was my mother.

"It was very clear that she was your mother," he told me. "I watched you both and I could see, it was a mother and son..."

*   *   *

Today as we lit the candles to commemorate, honor, remember and love Wewe in our hearts and mind, these memories came back to me. I thanked my husband for treating her with such deference and for helping me create a memory of a lifetime. Her last birthday in the Dharmawangsa Hotel in Jakarta was more than just a birthday party for us all, it was the best we could do at the time as we wanted to give her the gift of reflecting upon her life, recognizing the love she had shared with us all. It was our medal of honor for her, in recognition of her being not only a true sister, but also a wonderful Mom, caregiver, and protector to so many of us, but especially me.

It was a gesture I like to believe she understood and appreciated. For selfish reasons I'd like to believe that she was touched to be recognized, and I know in my heart she was. I wanted to give her an appropriate send-off for her next journey, a farewell that would give her courage and confidence in herself, being surrounded by her loved ones, those of our family that she had helped to grow so much, physically, emotionally and mentally. We all learned so much from her. I do believe I was only able to survive my difficult times because of Wewe's touch, her strong influence and limitless love. She influenced so many people in her lifetime and we were lucky to be her intimate family. We are the way we are because of her influence.

The following day was the day we had to leave, and my dear friend Paige had written a letter for Wewe that I read and translated for her. Paige had never met Wewe, but she felt that she knew her, through me. Through all my ordeals in San Francisco, Paige was sweet enough to listen and be there for me. There were days I would simply burst into tears and she would hug and hold me or listen to me in her kitchen, and serve me her homemade cookies and milk. So when it was time to say goodbye on Wewe's birthday, I read Paige's love note to my sister. It was so poetic and moving. The only thing we could do was cling to each other, knowing this was the last minute of our lives that we would ever be together. I wish I had kept that note, but I know it was not mine to keep.

We returned to California after my business trip and we heard that Wewe's condition had worsened, so I tried to call her a few times in the first week but breathing was by then such a difficult challenge for her, I didn't want to add to her misery. I called my cousin frantically hoping to hear more news about her daily, my biggest concern being her comfort and relief from pain. I kept hoping that someone would find morphine to help her ease the pain. I called my cousin Ci Tian, the doctor who lived just three or four hours away from her to see if she could help. She promised she would do her best. But later I learned that your father did not allow her to take any western medication because of his faith, and until now I still have a lot of anger and pain thinking about her last year of suffering on this earth, but these letters to you are not about my anger for anyone, they are about the love I have for your Mom. The next week I called her and she could hardly talk or hear but the last thing she said to Stephen and me was: "Yoyo... Stephen, I am sorry..."

Those last words have been haunting me all these years not understanding what it was for. Why was she sorry? If anything, it was we who should be sorry, sorry for her pain and misery that we could only imagine. Tonight I finally understand her: she was sorry for the sadness she would burden us with, she was sorry that we would be sad, you, me and so many other people who loved her. She was sorry that she could no longer hang on, that the pain was too much, she was sorry she could no longer care for us.

"There is nothing to be sorry about, my dear sister, Wewe…

Instead, thank YOU dear sister for all you have done for me, for us, thank YOU for all the unconditional love you have bestowed upon me, thank YOU for taking care of me, thank YOU for protecting me and for taking the beatings for me, thank YOU for making me dolls, thank YOU for loving me as I am, thank YOU for defending me from those who bullied me, thank YOU for the laughter, thank you for teaching me handicrafts, and how to be resourceful, thank YOU for putting my needs ahead of your own, thank YOU for carrying me when I was tired, for comforting me while I was sad, thank YOU for bathing me, making my cold sweet condensed milk, thank YOU for teaching me to be patient, thank YOU for being so patient, thank YOU for picking me up from school, thank YOU for never leaving me behind, thank YOU for this story, thank YOU for being a good mentor, role model, someone I look up to, thank YOU for the life lessons you taught me, thank YOU for being my inspiration, thank YOU for fighting as long as you did, thank YOU for coming to the party, thank YOU for being a nurse, a midwife and anesthesiologist, thank YOU for being so helpful, selfless, so generous, so humble, so sweet, so kind…thank YOU for making me the person that I am today, thank YOU for giving me a solid foundation in my life, thank YOU for teaching me what truly is important in life, thank YOU for the memory, but most of all thank YOU for being the amazing human, person and woman that you were, thank YOU for having so much love that you shared every single second of your life, and thank YOU for teaching me to spread that love, thank YOU for being my sister, my Mother, my Protector, my Angel… and Wewe, my Dear Sister, thank YOU for the garlic peanuts you always brought home from school."

Epilogue

My sister died on May 24, 2006, exactly a month after her forty-sixth birthday. It has been fourteen years since she left my nephew Zefanya and my niece Grace. They are now young adults of eighteen and twenty. Although I have not seen them since the last time in Lampung when they were young children, I have kept in touch with them via phone and texting. This book was originally intended for them so they might learn and know about their Mom from my point of view and experience. I am grateful that this book is to be published for anyone to learn about my sister and the love she shared with me, and all children.

My sister's unconditional love to me and for all children has not only influenced me in how I lived my life but also shaped my view of the world and humanity, especially of those who are less fortunate. Her work in the medical profession as a nurse and midwife and later as anesthesiologist not only inspired me, it also sharpened my attention to those who need help. I know for a fact that she refused to take payments from patients who had no means, or could afford very little. She not only donated her time and service, she also helped them with their necessities and money. Her soft heart and compassion made her an angel on earth during her lifetime; she was always helping the needy without any expectation. When she gave, she gave without even thinking that she was giving, it was an act of pure love. My sister never lived lavishly and when she gave, she gave all she could.

In honor of my sister, my husband Stephen and I always do our best to continue her work and spread her love in any way we are able to. While we don't have a formal non-profit foundation, we do our best to help those who are in need, especially in places that we spend a lot of time such as Bali. The Balinese people are one of the warmest, most hospitable and loving people we have ever encountered during our travels all over the world. The last time we spent quality times with my sister when she was in good health was in Bali. We always have the fondest memories of her when we spend time there, and we go to Bali twice a year on average. Accordingly, over the years we have developed such a lot of affection for the people of Bali, as well as a feeling of indebtedness. It is definitely because of them we have had such amazing times on the island, and this has become such an important part of our lives. We call this our 'island life' and someday we plan to move there when it is possible, to make it our home.

For these reasons, annually we donate to various organizations such as Kesayan Ikang Papa Orphanage in Gianyar, and a number of children from poor public schools in Jimbaran, as well contributing to other trustworthy and legitimate institutions. We also help various individuals and families in Bali that have become our *ohana* throughout the years, and support small, family run businesses the way my sister did when she owned her little stationery store.

I feel extremely blessed and fortunate I have been given

a life in a part of the world where I can be self-sufficient and also help others. Inspired by my sister's love for humanity, I vowed to help those who are less fortunate, especially with education. My husband and I have dedicated our lives to helping a number of children with their tuition so they may have a better future.

Due to our personal experience, we have a great concern for those who are affected by cancer, especially breast cancer as that was the terrible disease that took my sister's life. Whenever possible, we donate funds to breast cancer or directly to individuals who need the money for their treatment and support.

Regretfully we were not able to be with my sister in her final days, but we were blessed to have been able to help Stephen's parents, my parent's-in-law, during their final weeks on this earth by directly caring for them with the help of hospice staff. In my sister's honor, we also try to help various hospices as we believe they are doing tremendous loving work for those who need their help the most during their final days on this earth.

During the Covid-19 global crisis in 2020, we also organized some fundraising for a number of Balinese hospitality staff who had lost their jobs and found themselves desperate for basic needs such as food and daily supplies. Our *ohana* and friends rose to the occasion with their contributions, so we were able to send funds to the needy on our favorite island.

I encourage everyone who reads this book to do the

same, to continue my sister's work and what she did best during her lifetime: spreading the love and sharing your blessings the way she did with everyone she encountered.

All our actions have been deeply influenced by my sister's kind heart and generous lifestyle. I vow as long as I live to continue her passion in helping others, especially children. I am tempted to start a formal foundation called "The Garlic Peanut Story", inspired by, dedicated to and for the love of my dear sister, Wewe.

For now, you may follow me on my website and social media:

www.thegarlicpeanutstory.com

instagram: @thegarlicpeanutstory

Acknowledgements

While this book was written for, inspired by and dedicated to my Angel sister, Wewe, and her children, I must also acknowledge other angels who have contributed in so many ways to enable me not only to realize my dream, but also to keep my promise to my sister. In many ways I owe my life to them.

To Mom and Dad, my perfect *loro blonyo* parents, the inseparable couple: while you are imperfect, I would never trade you for anyone else. Thank you for loving me the way you do, for being a true moral compass and role models. Not only do I forgive your absences, I am more than grateful for the life you have bestowed upon me and for your saying sorry. Thank you for loving me for who I am and accepting and loving my husband as you do all your other children-in-law. I feel your love every day and I miss you every day I am away from Indonesia.

To Bob, my angel on earth: your patience, kindness and generosity is immeasurable—I know Wewe loves you for loving me and I love you always. Thank you for supporting all my dreams in my life. I am so glad you met Wewe and you were there at her last birthday party. We are family, forever! I will keep my promise to you, always...

To Stephen: *Aku cinta kamu* - Eternity is too short; Eternity is not long enough. No words can express my love for you, "*Kipper, Ku'uipo, I love you today more than yesterday, but less than I will tomorrow"*. Thank you for showing and teaching me what love means... thank you for encouraging me to start, to carry on, and to finish this book. Thank you for planning the final birthday party for Wewe and for coming along. Your love to me not only made her happy, it completes me.

To Ibu Janice: thank you for inspiring me to continue with my book and for introducing me to Sarita. I am so proud to call you my Balinese family. Your big heart, kindness and beauty remind me of Wewe. Bali is blessed to call you her daughter. *Suksma*!

To Sarita: I am grateful for your patience, guidance and style. No one else can edit or publish this book the way you can: your knowledge of both worlds, the East and the West, makes you the perfect editor who understands all the nuances only we expats can relate to and understand. I am so glad we met and more importantly, your heart and compassion make you the best editor and publisher. Your family and I are lucky and blessed to have you as our angel on earth. Terima kasih!

To Judith: I have gained a sister and family in Spain - because of you. I love you mi hermana, Wewe would be so happy knowing you are in my life.

To all my ohana and angels: di sini or di sana: Empek Edo, Bang Kasan, Ada, Jacquie, Mak Welahan, Wak Ie Surabaya, Wak Ie Jakarta, Ie Lie, Ci Magda in Australia, Kirsten, Prof. Hansen, Prof. Bright, Karen H, Lili, Deven, Court, Denise H., John, Suroto, Rusmini, Pinky, Tjun Mei, Ferliana, Mbak Ti, Mary Frances, Grace my twin from another mother, Eliza, Penny, Anna, Mbak Tini, Reny, Donut, Keke, Astrid, Juliana, Denny, Harsono, Engkus, Uwan, Alex, Mami Engkus, Ibu Susilowati, Pak Trisno, Pak Man, Ibu Kelas Tiga, Suster Diones, Laurent, Fanny, Emma, Simon, Max, Manuel, Sunsui, David H, Basri, Oom Ong, Tante Vonny, Benny, Michiel, Keith, Marie, Tomblos, Dharmi, Oprah, Kathy, Ninive, Marc J, SJP, MB, JH, M, GPP, Mary Jo, Paige, Eugene, Linda T, Mona, Pete, Nancy, Veronique, Vincent, Mrs. Murphy, Mrs. Nakashima, Pak Reggeng, Acai, Wahyudi, Afa, Dhermawan, Wowo, Ci Peck, Ci Leli, Ci Siong, Ci Tian, Ko Tie, Ko Khing, Suparni, Andi, Kris, Maria Luisa, Monica, Erik, Jeffreeee, Monique, Haerul, the three Chris, Yuni, Kristen, Andi, Dhara, Nerryl, Claire, Clare, Ko Ise, Rina, Ci Wawa, Mami and Papi Teluk, Mami and Papi Pluit, Mbak Tini Jakarta, Ci Na, Aunt Patty, Uncle John, Aunt Marty, Michelle E, Elliot Hoffman, Gail Horvath, John Grubb, Cie Lien and Ko Wie & family, Oom and Tante Giok & family, Ko Tusin and Noni, Ruth Levy, Dada Jack, Kriiiis, Mama Darcel, Diva Margot my number one, Hannah my gorgeous, Daddy Claud, Jemma, Mary, Dean, Elijah, Elliot, Eddie, Jake, Rachel, Doretta, Dada Jack, Jenny, Nia, Budinah, Jim, Barbara, Jeff, Marcia, Siska, Jenna and Denise my Empress: while I can't possibly name you one by one, you know who you are... I am indebted to all of you. Thank you for your support and love and for believing in me. I wouldn't be here without you... My sister Wewe would be so happy to know that you have taken care of and loved her little brother. To my ohana and angels I failed to mention, you are in my heart, and I never intended to forget you, but my half-century mind is showing its age.

Lastly, to our fairy godchildren and grandchildren: we love you more than you know and thank you for allowing us to be your ohana, we hope you won't turn us into hidden figures and don't forget to spread the love even when we are no longer around and help us spread *The Garlic Peanut Story*'s message of love and forgiveness.